# STUDYING SHAKESPEARE

This book is dedicated to our own teachers of Shakespeare, Paul Kent and Raymond Salter.

# STUDYING SHAKESPEARE
## A Practical Guide

Katherine Armstrong and Graham Atkin

 PRENTICE HALL EUROPE

LONDON  NEW YORK  TORONTO  SYDNEY  TOKYO  SINGAPORE
MADRID  MEXICO CITY  MUNICH  PARIS

First published 1998 by
Prentice Hall Europe
Campus 400, Maylands Avenue
Hemel Hempstead
Hertfordshire, HP2 7EZ
A division of
Simon & Schuster International Group

© Prentice Hall Europe 1998

Typeset in 10/12pt Times
by Dorwyn Limited, Rowlands Castle, Hants

Printed and bound in Great Britain by
T.J. Press (Padstow) Ltd, Padstow, Cornwall.

Library of Congress Cataloging-in-Publication Data

Armstrong, Katherine.
    Studying Shakespeare: a practical guide/Katherine Armstrong and
Graham Atkin.
        p.    cm.
    Includes bibliographical references (p. ) and index.
    ISBN 0-13-486788-2 (alk. paper)
        1. Shakespeare, William, 1564–1616—Outlines, syllabi, etc.
    2. Shakespeare, William, 1564–1616—Study and teaching.   I. Atkin,
Graham.   II. Title.
    PR2987.A76 1997
    822.3'3—dc21                                                            97–41126
                                                                                  CIP

British Library Cataloguing in Publication Data

A catalogue record for this book is available from
the British Library

ISBN 0-13-486788-2

1  2  3  4  5    02  01  00  99  98

# Contents

# A note on texts

After some thought, we decided to use the New Arden (Arden 2) texts of Shakespeare throughout this book, since to date only a few titles have appeared in the Arden 3 series.

# Preface

As our title suggests, the aim of this book is to provide students with an introductory guide to the practicalities of studying Shakespeare's plays at degree level. It is not a reference book of facts about Shakespeare's life, works or critical heritage, but a 'how to' book, which gives clear and concrete advice to those embarking on advanced study of Shakespearean drama. Wherever possible, we use worked examples in order to help our readers bridge the gap that may exist between knowing what to do and how actually to do it, though this should not be taken to imply that we are dogmatic about the reading and critical practices we recommend. We have tried throughout to be suggestive rather than prescriptive, and to emphasize that there are many valid ways of approaching Shakespeare.

We have assumed that most of our readers will be aged sixteen or above and studying literature or cultural studies at college or university, but we have not assumed that they will have a knowledge of critical theory, and so we have tried to explain all the specialist terms we use as they occur. We are, however, convinced that the student/tutor dichotomy is largely a false one, and whenever we talk of 'students' of Shakespeare we are including ourselves in that category. The extent to which we draw upon the experiences of those we have taught should confirm that we have been their students quite as much as they have been ours.

Since a number of introductory books on Shakespeare are already available, we ought to explain at the outset our decision to produce yet another. For all that the traditional canon of English literature has been critiqued, expanded or revised in recent years,

Shakespeare has remained a central figure in school and college curricula, and most students of literature or cultural studies will have to study him in one way or another, either as a 'Special Author', considered in isolation, or as a major element in a course or module on early modern literature. (And a significant number will focus on Shakespeare's language as part of the linguistic component of their English degree.) Although this has created a healthy demand for guides and handbooks of various kinds, it would not in itself justify our adding yet another book to the international mountain of text-book material on Shakespeare, were it not for the changes currently taking place in the way Shakespeare is studied and taught at college and university. Some of these are attributable to the ever-widening gap between Shakespeare's world and ours, illustrated, for example, by the peculiar problems of studying a play such as *The Merchant of Venice* in the shadow of the Holocaust, as we are bound to do. Some result from the general shift in education to more student-centred methods of learning. Some arise as a result of the electronic revolution and its transformation of the ways we can store and use information.

This book examines the implications of all these changes and suggests ways in which students might exploit the opportunities they have created. In Part I, Chapters 1–3 deal with what might be termed the 'basic' issues: why we study Shakespeare and how we do so in the first instance, through discussion and writing. Part II, Chapters 4–9, is subdivided into three and considers how to study Shakespeare in more depth. First, we examine the *text*, in chapters on Shakespeare's language and the context(s) of his plays. Second, we explore the *media* through which we encounter Shakespeare, in performance and in electronic forms such as audio- and video-recordings and multimedia. Third, we discuss Shakespeare's *reception* by critics and theorists.

To expand a little on this summary, in *Chapter 1* we reflect on the continuing controversy over Shakespeare's place in the literary canon. It has become commonplace for critics to state their theoretical and ideological positions explicitly at the outset of any project. That Shakespeare should and will remain central to literary and cultural studies in the future is a conviction we hold un-equivocally, and Chapter 1 seeks to explain why this is so. Yet a willingness to acknowledge – and delight in – the diverse possibilities of the critical enterprise will be one of our central themes in this book, and Chapter 1 will also, therefore, advocate the need for self-consciousness and provisionality with regard to one's critical assumptions.

Chapters 2 and 3 focus on the skills needed for studying Shakespeare effectively at undergraduate level. *Chapter 2* stresses the importance of discussion as a practical tool for engaging with Shakespeare's work, and suggests that talking about Shakespeare in a variety of contexts, both formal and informal, is a way of developing and testing one's ideas without some of the constraints attendant on writing them down. A willingness to discuss is seen as part of the openness of mind so vital to critical analysis, as is a willingness to listen to, and engage with, the ideas of others.

*Chapter 3* takes a pragmatic approach to writing about Shakespeare, beginning with the hidden but crucial matter of note-taking, and proceeding to consider a range of modes from formal essays, to reviews, to close commentaries, to dissertations, to exam answers – all of which the student may be asked to produce in the course of studying Shakespeare. The emphasis is on the need for meticulousness, both in the use and acknowledgement of sources and in the planning of the final product; but being prepared to take intellectual risks and write imaginatively are also seen as vital.

*Chapter 4* begins by acknowledging that for many students in further and higher education Shakespeare's language presents certain difficulties, but goes on to argue that this should be seen as challenging rather than intimidating. The chapter points out that Shakespeare's own style was highly idiosyncratic and experimental, and then shows how an increased knowledge and understanding of his lexical range, syntax, rhetoric and other stylistic features can enhance our enjoyment of his work.

*Chapter 5* deals with the questions raised by attempting to contextualize Shakespeare. The traditional advice to students might have been to read one or two 'background' books in addition to works of criticism. However, such an approach has certain limitations. Even if we acquire some knowledge of the political and social conditions of Shakespeare's age, we may have little experience of interdisciplinary thinking and be at a loss to bring our historical knowledge to bear on Shakespeare's plays without either reducing them to mere products of wider cultural forces or implying that history is somehow less significant because it fails to match the 'transcendence' of the literary text. In Chapter 5 we also discuss some of the theories of cultural production which have informed Shakespeare studies in recent times, and which have helped to problematize the conventional boundaries between literature, history and politics. As with other chapters, we give a range of specific examples to show how the student might tackle contextualization at a practical level, notwithstanding the potential difficulties of relating literature and history with due subtlety and care.

*Chapter 6* responds to the general shift within the discipline of English to a more performance-centred, less 'literary' approach to dramatic texts. Nowadays students may and, some would say, should wish to refer to productions of a play in a range of media – televisual, cinematic, theatrical, perhaps – rather than confining themselves to the text on the page. Attention to the text-as-performance can prompt us to take the realities of the Elizabethan/Jacobean stage into consideration, or it can lead us to reflect on the extraordinarily diverse interpretations which Shakespeare's plays have inspired up to our own time.

*Chapter 7* considers the impact of new media on the study of Shakespeare, technological developments having led to an exponential rise in the information available, in forms other than the printed word, to students of literature and of Shakespeare in particular. The widespread availability of film, audio, televisual and video versions of his plays has had a significant impact on the way Shakespeare is studied; even more significant, perhaps, have been CD-ROM (Compact Disk-Read Only Memory), the Internet and multimedia. In addition to the general indices and bibliographies available via the Internet or on CD-ROM, there are now a number of databases dedicated solely to Shakespeare. They include several CD-ROM versions of Shakespeare's works, some of which incorporate substantial archives of primary and secondary source material, and at least one is a bibliography of recent Shakespeare criticism. In the last couple of years creative multimedia packages have appeared which allow students freedom to role-play and devise their own theatrical interpretations of Shakespeare. The consequences of such innovations are far-reaching; the already blurred distinction between undergraduate 'study' and postgraduate 'research' is likely to erode still more rapidly now that almost anyone can produce an accurate statistical breakdown of linguistic features in a text or texts, undertake a search to compile an instant bibliography of secondary literature on the most obscure aspect of Shakespeare's work, or experiment, using virtual reality, with camera angles, close-ups, voice-overs and even casting.

The information revolution can, of course, be paralyzing rather than enabling, as many commentators have suggested. *Chapter 8* confronts the irony that, while the historical distance between Shakespeare and his audience inevitably widens with each year, the industry devoted to interpreting him is such that students may feel they are faced with unmanageable volumes of material from which to select their secondary reading. In the least well-stocked academic library there is almost certain to be an embarrassment of riches for any reader looking for criticism on Shakespeare, and on-line catalogues and other databases can seem to exacerbate, rather than alleviate, the problems this raises. In this chapter we have therefore suggested ways of managing this vast critical heritage – through selective assimilation – so that it can inform your own discussions of Shakespeare without swamping them.

Building on the insights into the uses of Shakespeare criticism outlined in Chapter 8, in *Chapter 9* we look more specifically at the theoretical dimensions of recent critical approaches. Rather than attempting a schematic summary of the best-known theoretical schools, it illustrates a number of ways in which students might apply the insights of two perspectives, cultural materialism and feminism, to their own readings of particular Shakespearean texts.

It is the guiding assumption of this book that all these developments, within literary studies and beyond, represent opportunities rather than problems for the student of Shakespeare. In our opinion Shakespeare has never been more exciting, provocative and demanding than he is today, when on the one hand innovative research resources and tools are continually being made available, and on the other controversy rages ever more fiercely over how his work should be edited, interpreted, read and taught. At most institutions of higher education, studying for a degree used to be based in large part on the ability to pin back one's ears in a large, impersonal lecture hall and make notes which could be accurately reproduced under examination conditions. Of course, degree-level English has always depended to a certain extent on dialogue, but nowadays students are expected to do far more than simply participate in class discussions, defend their essays in tutorials and produce polished exam answers. They may find themselves work-ing in small groups on tasks which require them to report back to the larger class, either then and there or at some future date. They may have to give regular seminar presentations as part of their assessment, and these may be prepared individually or collab-oratively. They may need to identify and research a dissertation topic on Shakespeare with only minimal guidance from their tutor. Arguably, they will have greater responsibility for their own learn-ing than students generally did in the past: classes grow ever larger, staff–student contact time diminishes, and aside from these econ-omic factors, independent study skills are now an explicit aim of many undergraduate courses.

The overwhelming majority of those students quoted in this book were finalists or recent graduates who had taken a year-long compulsory course of Shakespeare as part of the English literature component of a combined subjects degree. We are very grateful to all of them, but particularly to those who allowed us to describe or quote from their written work (Sarah Hornsby, Susan Lee and Haydn Smith), or who responded to the letter we sent them (see Appendix), especially Sadie Bentall, Louise Burnett-Wells, Norma Casement, Samantha Clark, Agatha Dunlop, Kathy Dyson, Edward Cooper, Elisabeth Eastwood, Alan Ewing, Alex Figgis, Alison Foster, Christopher Goodwin, Tracy Goulding, Rebecca Green, Richard Hulse, Danielle Marks, Anita Reid and Ilse Von Brandis. Thanks are also due to Andrew Dethick and Ann Mackay, who told us about their experiences of studying Shakespeare on a part-time single honours degree programme in English literature.

In addition we would like to thank those who read and commented on earlier drafts of the book: the readers at Prentice Hall, Marion Wynne-Davies, Sally Atkin and Lucy Armstrong. For advice on multimedia we are very grateful to Peter Williams, Deputy Librarian at University College Chester. For a helpful suggestion about *The Tempest* thanks are due to Michelle Haslem.

We would like to take this opportunity to thank University Col-lege Chester for a grant which gave one of us study leave to make substantial progress with the preparation of this book.

Our greatest debt is to our dedicatees.

**PART I**

*Basic skills for the Shakespeare student*

# CHAPTER 1

# Why study Shakespeare?

## Introduction

To ask why we study Shakespeare is a conventional enough way to open an introductory guide of this kind, but it is a provocative question none the less. A cynical answer might be that we study Shakespeare because we have to: he is compulsory for the majority of students at school in Britain and the United States, and anyone who pursues literature in English at a higher education level will probably find, on graduating, that they have been watching, reading, talking and writing about Shakespeare more or less annually for eight years or longer.

Yet if this explains, it certainly does not justify why we study Shakespeare, and over recent years many commentators have argued that Shakespeare's pre-eminence in the canon of English literature (the body of classic authors commonly studied at school and college) has more to do with tradition, issues of national identity and ideological coercion than it has to do with his intrinsic literary merit.

It is the chief purpose of this chapter, and indeed this book, to argue that Shakespeare richly deserves his unrivalled place in the curriculum, since to us the most compelling answer to the question, 'Why study Shakespeare?' is that we benefit immeasurably from doing so. Pleasure is one such benefit – the majority of students like studying Shakespeare and are enriched by the experience – and instruction another – through studying Shakespeare we learn about society, the ways individuals behave, language, and so on, and also develop our skills of critical analysis and expression.

But before exploring in greater depth these reasons we ought to consider the argument, frequently proposed in recent years, that we study Shakespeare merely because students have always done so, at least since the birth of English as an academic discipline. No book on Shakespeare published today can afford to ignore the fierce, if sporadic, debate about his canonical status which academics, critics and directors have been conducting since the 1980s. Numerous critical books and articles have dealt with the issues arising from this controversy, and it received a wider airing in the 1994 Shakespeare season ('Bard on the Box') on television. Though the canon of English literature has been much discussed and attacked in recent years, Shakespeare's place in it has provoked particularly intense discussion amongst those responsible for the teaching of English in schools and universities in Britain and, to a lesser extent, North America. The first part of this section will try to explain why so much energy has been expended on this issue.

**The Shakespeare debate**

The issue boils down to politics: for every traditionalist who insists that all fourteen-year-olds should study at least one Shakespeare play, there are scores of educationalists and critics who argue that the teaching of Shakespeare has more to do with ideology than literature. To these commentators, Shakespeare has been foisted on us by a reactionary educational and political establishment determined to safeguard its values and traditions.

This may sound extreme, yet it is undoubtedly true that politicians and other public figures have at times used Shakespeare for dubious ends, and professional teachers of English have naturally resented their doing so. To take one example, John Redwood, formerly Minister for Wales, used Shakespeare's history plays to defend Anglo-Welsh unity following the pit closures in South Wales, on the obscure grounds that 'Glyndwr in *Henry IV* [Part 1] bridged the two cultures by speaking both Welsh and English'.[1] More notoriously, Nigel Lawson, formerly Chancellor of the Exchequer, quoted from *Troilus and Cressida* in his autobiography, using Ulysses' disquisition on the need for social hierarchies to defend the economic policy of the Thatcher government.[2] And the tendency to use Shakespeare rhetorically has not been confined to

politicians: the Prince of Wales, for instance, has repeatedly promoted Shakespeare as a key element in the shaping of British
national identity.[3]

These are instances of overt ideological appropriation, and are
ultimately, perhaps, of limited significance, but some have argued
that Shakespeare's very place in the curriculum is a question of
politics. As the American critic John Bender observes, for certain
left-wing British academics:

> the stress on Shakespeare goes beyond any question of residual aes-
> thetic admiration to become a contest with established ideology (and
> especially with Thatcherism) over the significance of a playwright at
> once deeply embedded in the British system of education and central to
> an outworn and delusionary nationalism.[4]

It is easy to take for granted the terms of a debate which has
been continuing for some years, and it is as well to remind ourselves of the reasons for the deadlock between the political left and
right over Shakespeare. In brief, those who defend Shakespeare's
unique status in the literary canon are driven by the conviction that
studying Shakespeare is vital to the moral and spiritual development of the student, and they subscribe implicitly to the view that a
universal knowledge of his work will be conducive to social
cohesiveness and a common pride in Britain's national heritage.
Their opponents, however, feel that this agenda is politically inde-
fensible and misguided, if not indeed disingenuous, in its underlying claim that Shakespeare's appeal is universal, transcendent
and ahistorical. In a pluralistic, multicultural society it can seem
inappropriate to insist that all students study the work of a long-
dead, white male playwright, even if room is made for other
writers who speak more obviously to the concerns of our times.

Most famously, Jonathan Dollimore and Alan Sinfield prefaced
their influential volume *Political Shakespeare*, first published in
1985, with a trenchant discussion of the institutional uses to which
Shakespeare has been put in the last four hundred years, concluding that the plays can only be understood in relation to the socio-
political contexts of their production. According to Dollimore and
Sinfield, who describe themselves as cultural materialist critics,
we should be seeking not to uncover an intrinsic meaning in
Shakespeare, but to understand the conditions which have

determined his interpretation by successive generations. They conclude their preface with the following declaration:

> cultural materialism does not pretend to neutrality. It knows that no cultural practice is ever without political significance – not the production of *King Lear* at the Globe, or at the Barbican, or as a text in a school, popular or learned edition, or in literary criticism, or in the present volume. Cultural materialism does not, like much established literary criticism, attempt to mystify its perspective as the natural, obvious or right interpretation of an allegedly given textual fact. On the contrary, it registers its commitment to the transformation of a social order which exploits people on grounds of race, gender and class.[5]

To the dismay of one traditional critic, M. C. Bradbrook, who asked if Shakespeare himself had been completely lost sight of in *Political Shakespeare*, another materialist critic, Graham Holderness, pointed out that there is no immanent, inviolable Shakespeare, only a series of readings of him.

In the eyes of many left-wing participants in the controversy, Shakespeare has been particularly susceptible to co-option by the forces of reaction. As Holderness puts it, he 'functions in contemporary culture as an ideological framework for containing consensus and for sustaining myths of unity, integration and harmony in the cultural superstructures of a divided and fractured society'.[6] This argument is a tendentious one, and we can only determine its validity by exploring in specific terms how such ideological functions might be carried out.

An obvious starting-point might be to scrutinize the ways in which examination papers implicitly encourage students to think and write about Shakespeare. Alan Sinfield has written eloquently on the uses and abuses of Shakespeare by GCSE and A-level examination boards, arguing that the overwhelming majority of exam questions require the candidate to respond to Shakespeare in a spirit of humanistic celebration: 'Almost invariably it is assumed that the plays reveal universal "human" values and qualities and that they are self-contained and coherent entities; and the activity of criticism in producing these assumptions is effaced.'[7] Through a multitude of examples Sinfield demonstrates that the teaching of Shakespeare in post-war British schools has been subtly coercive. His argument may seem initially unpalatable to those readers, myself included, who were trained to think of Shakespeare as 'not of an age but for all time',[8] and innocent of any bias, least of all political. Yet it was confirmed for me only recently by the candid responses of a class of mature women students to whom I was explaining the cultural materialist critique of Shakespeare's place in the literary canon. A number of the students admitted that they had never liked Shakespeare at school and had deeply resented his attitude to women; they also said that they had never articulated these feelings on the assumption that any attempt to criticize 'the Bard' would be penalized.

Once such responses are voiced and discussed, the class becomes theorized in the sense that the Shakespeare text is being approached not as an autonomous, historically transcendent artefact, but as a product of cultural forces, past and present. Cultural materialists and feminists are not necessarily opposed to studying Shakespeare *per se*, but they wish to question the ways in which he is typically taught and studied. As well as critiquing his patriarchal bias, they have, for example, pointed to his patriotic representations of the Plantaganet, Tudor and Stuart kings in the history plays, and argued that his popularity continues to rest, in part, on his appeal to English nationalism. Plays about Agincourt and Bosworth Field still have emotional power in a country increasingly devoted to its past. We hanker after 'Tudorbethan' homes for our families; county councils continue to use the red and white roses to symbolize Lancashire and Yorkshire; and *Henry V* was being used for nationalistic purposes as recently as 1975, according to those who have suggested that its performance by the Royal Shakespeare Company at the time of the first oil crisis was suspiciously opportunistic.[9] And Shakespeare did more than appear to paint a flattering portrait of Tudor and Stuart power; many of his plays evoke a lost world of folklore and festivals, and have contributed greatly to the sentimental idea of a 'Merrie England' which is supposed to have existed prior to industrialization.

Whereas traditional critics try to divorce literature and education from ideology, the materialists regard them as inextricably intertwined. For the traditional critic Shakespeare is vital as a means of testing the ability of students to respond sensitively and intelligently to literature. Cultural materialists would object first, that other authors could serve the same purpose, and second, that what constitutes a sensitive and intelligent response to literature is not a given; rather, it is defined in particular ways by particular cultures and historical periods.

Of course, to say that some of Shakespeare's advocates admire him for elitist, or politically questionable, reasons, or for no good reason at all, is not necessarily to imply that he should be removed from the syllabus or relegated to a lower league in the literary tables. He may still be worth studying, even if we recognize that he has sometimes been studied for the wrong reasons. Having said this, I would agree that unacknowledged factors have been far too influential in creating an institutional culture of 'Bardolatry'. For some, Shakespeare is almost a cultural icon, a figurehead of Britain's national identity. Shakespeare remains compulsory in the Key Stage 3 'SATs' examination, and each summer for the past several years the broadsheet newspapers have run articles discussing the advantages and limitations of studying Shakespeare for all secondary school pupils irrespective of their ability. For some his difficulty for the modern reader is perversely what makes his study seem essential for fourteen-year-olds.

The 'Shakespeare Debate' looks set to continue, given that Shakespeare retains much of his former importance in the syllabus, even as educators, critics and students become increasingly sophisticated in their understanding of how his mythological status has been created and maintained. Given the nature of degree study, students are increasingly likely to participate in the Shakespeare debate themselves: many will find themselves taking a course in Shakespearean drama alongside theory courses which question the basis of the traditional literary canon. Shakespeare remains one of the 'Top Ten' authors studied in the English departments of colleges and universities in Britain even as the number of books which query the value of 'Dead White European Male' authors proliferate and as applications from finalists to undertake postgraduate research on early modern literature slow to the barest trickle.

And, of course, new critical approaches to the study of Shakespeare such as feminism and cultural materialism reflect a wider cultural shift; there is less interest in other canonical authors amongst students now than there was fifteen or even five years ago. In 1992 the *Guardian* reported the findings of the Consortium for College and University English (CCUE), whose survey showed that some twentieth-century authors are now more popular than Shakespeare on degree courses in new and old universities. The *Guardian* expressed surprise and disquiet, but the gap between the National Curriculum (which has enshrined Shakespeare from the very beginning) and the typical college or university English syllabus (which increasingly favours the likes of Sylvia Plath, Angela Carter and Emily Brontë) will probably widen in the future with potentially controversial results.

None the less, the anxieties of the lecturer or tutor about Shakespeare's appropriation by individual politicians or indeed the state can look misguided when it is placed alongside the optimism and interest of many students, few of whom come to Shakespeare weighed down by a knowledge of his abuses at the hands of the British establishment. It can be salutory, if disconcerting, for lecturers to find themselves more chary of Shakespeare than are their classes: their initial assumption may have been that teaching Shakespeare would require them to devise ingenious strategies for 'sugaring the pill'. When I began teaching Shakespeare, I looked for all kinds of ways of engendering enthusiasm in my students. With *Richard II*, for example, I discussed an exhibition on the Wilton Diptych (which Richard is thought to have owned) at the National Gallery in London, brought in pictures of a nearby National Trust house in order to illuminate references in the play to windows bearing the family coat of arms (III.i.24–5), and handed out a family tree of the descendants of Edward the Confessor. Rightly, the students were polite but tepid in their responses, explaining that they wanted to analyze the text itself, and saw no obvious advantage in contextualizing it, at least in the early stages of their course.

'I'm looking forward to *Antony and Cleopatra*'; '*Twelfth Night* was amazing'; 'Why on earth cut Shakespeare?' These were the unselfconscious reactions of some third-year students (graduating in 1995) to whom the news that next year's cohort would be studying only half as much Shakespeare as was currently offered. The new module was pedagogically sound – we would be reading three Shakespeare plays rather than ten, plus three plays by some of his contemporaries. We would, therefore, be focusing not so much on the isolated achievement of one dramatist as on the milieu which produced many outstanding authors and many less-known ones who are equally deserving of close study. Yet my explanation did not convince the students, even though they admitted they would have liked the chance to read Christopher Marlowe, Ben Jonson and John Webster. And in the end, a course exclusively on Shakespeare was restored by popular demand, though not without misgivings. Were the students justified in asserting their right to study Shakespeare, or were they guided by a conservative instinct of the kind which the educator has a responsibility to counter? Having for the most part read no other sixteenth- or seventeenth-century authors, were they in a position to make an informed choice? In the end, these issues remained unresolved: it was accepted that the restored course, like its successor, had its strengths and weaknesses.

For the students I quoted, Shakespeare's greatest attractions were, they declared, his range and profundity, exactly the qualities which professional critics and scholars have admired in him. 'How could any course be more varied?' asked one student – exactly the point put by one of Shakespeare's most extravagant admirers in the nineteenth century, Professor Edward Dowden, who wrote of Shakespeare's 'enormous receptivity' and the 'vast and varied mass of information' contained in his plays.[10] More recently, the director of the newly opened Globe Theatre in London has said he could spend the rest of his career working on Shakespeare, and not get to the bottom of him.

Of course, the same could be said of any number of prolific and excellent writers, but Shakespeare's diversity is certainly astonishing. For a start, he wrote tragedies, comedies and history plays, and even these widely different genres can be further subdivided, Polonius-fashion (*Hamlet* II.ii.392–6), into revenge tragedy, Roman tragedy, the chronicle play, the problem play, tragi-comedy, romance, contemporary comedy, historical comedy, the Venetian play and pastoral comedy. His characters range in social terms from royalty to beggars, and he deals with every conceivable emotion from passion to horror, as well as with a vast range of moral, political and philosophical issues.

Of Shakespeare's achievements with form there is similarly no doubt. Though some more recent critics have asked why coherence, complexity and ambiguity have been traditionally valued so highly in Western culture, there has been no attempt to reject such qualities in absolute terms, merely to re-estimate the worth of others (informality, for example). Additionally, in many colleges and universities the trend has been towards expanding the numbers of authors read and studied, rather than replacing traditional figures with less familiar ones: the course in seventeenth-century drama mentioned above is an example of this practice. Although Shakespeare has ceased to be unquestioningly regarded as the last word in literary excellence, he remains at the core of English studies. In the second half of this chapter, then, I will discuss why, notwithstanding the debate just considered, Shakespeare deserves to retain his privileged status in the literary canon.

## Why we should study Shakespeare

To appreciate the pleasures and fascinations of studying Shakespeare we need look no further than the opening exchange of *Hamlet*:

*Enter* BARNARDO *and* FRANCISCO, *two Sentinels.*
*Bar.*  Who's there?
*Fran.*  Nay, answer me. Stand and unfold yourself.
*Bar.*  Long live the King!
*Fran.*  Barnardo?
*Bar.*  He.
*Fran.*  You come most carefully upon your hour.
*Bar.*  'Tis now struck twelve. Get thee to bed, Francisco.
*Fran.*  For this relief much thanks. 'Tis bitter cold,
          And I am sick at heart.
*Bar.*  Have you had quiet guard?
*Fran.*  Not a mouse stirring.
*Bar.*  Well, good night.
          If you do meet Horatio and Marcellus,
          The rivals of my watch, bid them make haste.
*Fran.*  I think I hear them.[11]

(I.i.1–15)

There are three times as many words in the Arden edition notes and longer notes to this passage as there are in the passage itself (249 as compared with 82), which testifies to the wealth of meaning in even the simplest dialogue by Shakespeare, as well as to the acumen and scholarship of the Arden editor, Harold Jenkin. The first line is a question, which seems an apt beginning for a play much concerned with perplexity and doubt. It is a martial greeting, reminding us that Denmark is at war, vulnerable – like Hamlet himself – to alien enemies. Francisco's reply is even more wary; he will not give his name until he is sure his questioner is friendly. He asks Barnardo to 'unfold' himself – that is to say, to disclose his identity. But the form of words is interesting, implying a discrepancy between outward appearance and inner reality which will prove a key theme in the play itself: 'one may smile, and smile, and be a villain' (I.v.108), as Hamlet puts it.

Barnardo's reply is extraordinarily resonant: 'Long live the King!' Is this an expression of loyalty to the old king, or a tribute to the usurping Claudius, Hamlet's detested stepfather – 'the King is dead, long live the King'? In other words, are these sentries on the side of Hamlet and his father, or are they merely ciphers, insignificant except in so far as they illustrate the submissiveness of ordinary Danes to the tyrant ruling them? The audience cannot be sure, and it is a question which will plague Hamlet, who is rightly suspicious of his supposed friend, Rosencrantz. Hamlet will finally pronounce him a 'sponge', one 'that soaks up the King's countenance, his rewards, his authorities' (IV.ii.14–15).

Even now, Francisco wants to make absolutely sure of his interlocutor, and will not be satisfied until he knows his name. Once Barnardo has replied, the tension is immediately released, and the two proceed to informalities: Barnardo has been very punctual, says Francisco gratefully, and Barnardo urges him to go to bed after his long vigil. Francisco punningly acknowledges he is glad to do so: 'For this relief much thanks.' Then he confides that he is 'sick at heart', but does not elaborate. The audience or the reader is bound to wonder whether he has no need to spell out his reasons, or whether he is simply afraid of being overheard. Again, the dialogue anticipates Hamlet, who likewise suffers from ennui and nameless forebodings.

The tension increases again with Francisco's answer to Barnardo's asking if he has had a quiet watch. 'Not a mouse stirring' awakens more anxieties than it quells since, according to dramatic convention, such moments of unnatural peace are frequently the prelude to a violent disturbance. Seemingly loath to part with Francisco, Barnardo reluctantly bids him goodnight, and urges him to send his co-sentries as soon as possible. By referring to them as 'rivals' he does not mean to imply enmity, only that the three are sharing the duty. But the word, as so often in Shakespeare, leaves an aftertaste. None of these men seems quite at ease with the others: there is a sense of distance and watchfulness about them, which the opening scene manages to convey both literally and metaphorically. In some ways the entire play could be said to be about waiting and watching, suspicion and dread, and as in so much of Shakespeare the first scene condenses many of the most important themes to be developed and elaborated in subsequent ones.

We might automatically think of tragedy as more subtle and complicated than other genres, but Shakespearean comedy is equally multilayered. In *As You Like It*, for example, we are confronted with a bewildering disparity between the simple, pastoral setting and the intellectual content of the play. Contrary to appearances, *As You Like It* is ultimately about neither love nor youth, but the relationship between nature and art. Duke Senior, exiled in the forest by an ambitious brother, discourses on the virtues of the country life:

*Duke Sen.* Now my co-mates and brothers in exile,
    Hath not old custom made this life more sweet
    Than that of painted pomp? Are not these woods
    More free from peril than the envious court?
    Here feel we not the penalty of Adam,
    The seasons' difference, as the icy fang
    And churlish chiding of the winter's wind,
    Which when it bites and blows upon my body
    Even till I shrink with cold, I smile, and say
    'This is no flattery. These are counsellors
    That feelingly persuade me what I am.'
    Sweet are the uses of adversity,
    Which like the toad, ugly and venomous,
    Wears yet a precious jewel in his head;
    And this our life, exempt from public haunt,
    Finds tongues in trees, books in the running brooks,
    Sermons in stones, and good in everything.
                     (II.i.1–20)

The speech is crammed with paradoxes. The Duke tries to sound spontaneous, but his speech is clearly premeditated and highly mannered, rich in alliteration and other rhetorical devices. It is about the value of simple, earthy things, yet its philosophical underpinnings are enormously sophisticated. Most significantly, the Duke's tribute to pastoral is couched in terms that vindicate the values of civic, courtly life: language, books, sermons.

Even the 'Now' with which the speech begins is suggestive of these contradictions: it attempts familiarity but succeeds only in sounding slightly portentous. The Duke addresses his audience as 'co-mates' and 'brothers', implying his equality with them, but of course he remains their superior, confident of their attention and assent. He is intensely self-conscious, despite his apparent ease, for he is acting a role, that of the brave and resolute exile.

His second sentence is typically equivocal: does he mean that the country is made all the sweeter for its contrast with the court, or does 'old custom' refer to the tradition of preferring rural to urban life in classical literature? The latter is a reminder that, for all their paeans to the country, writers such as Virgil (an important influence on *As You Like It*) were also strongly drawn to the civilized life of the metropolis. Custom may have made the countryside more popular in theory, but history shows that in practice most writers, Shakespeare included, have opted for life in the town. As with the opening of *Hamlet*, then, the passage is clearly deeply implicated in the central themes of the play to which it belongs: even the reference to the distant past ('old custom') reminds us of the play's preoccupation with time, and its sense of an Arcadia where time is sometimes suspended and sometimes hurrying on apace.

Much has been written of Shakespeare's 'meta-theatre', his fascination with drama as artifice and his addiction to the device of the 'play within the play'. Unlike some later playwrights, Shakespeare was not interested solely in creating the illusion of reality but also in the illusory nature of theatrical realism. Duke Senior's speech, therefore, alerts the audience's attention to the physical building in which the play is being performed, for although he refers to the pretensions of court life in general, the setting of the play's performance must have been particularly conspicuous for its 'painted pomp'. The contrast between the supposed woodland setting of *As You Like It* and the appurtenances of the Elizabethan theatre would have been especially meaningful if, as is thought, the play was first performed at Wilton House, the country seat of the Pembrokes. Wilton, like *As You Like It* itself, was remote from the metropolis in geographical terms yet was also a monument to the elaborate tastes of

Renaissance courtly culture. For Shakespeare's original audience, therefore, the invitation to appreciate the virtues of pastoral retreat would have had a particularly ironic resonance in the context of a setting which was in one sense rustic, but in another the very opposite.

Although the Duke addresses his companions as equals they are clearly expected to defer to him – his questions are rhetorical only. Their effect is complex, however, since unanswered questions inevitably raise more questions. Is the forest really more free from peril than the court? The court may be envious, but the country can be dangerous too for those without food and lodging, as Orlando and Adam will shortly remind us. The idea that the country is a place of comfort and peace is a luxury one can afford more easily in the safety of the town or court than in the country itself, and in any case it is easier for a duke to enjoy rustic tranquillity, protected as he is by his knights, than for a weak old man – Adam, for example – to do so.

Adam is also brought to mind by the Duke's allusion to Genesis, the first book in the Bible, and the seasonal cycle which was the consequence ('penalty') of the Fall. There were originally no changes in season in Eden, and indeed no death or decay; the Duke implies that his company enjoys the same conditions in Arden. To a certain extent *As You Like It* does seek to convey the sense of a prelapsarian eternal summer, but of course a world without time carries its own penalties for those who seek to return from exile. In fact, we learn from the Duke's description of his winter privations both that his reference to a world without seasons is symbolic only, and that he has endured at least one long winter since his banishment. There is time and change in Arden, then, and a consequent need for endurance.

The Duke also acknowledges that the forest is no Eden, describing its climate in terms which suggest it harbours wild animals. His imagery anticipates the subsequent appearance off-stage of a savage lioness, and is characteristic of Shakespeare's concern to give his plays an underlying unity of structure through the use of recurrent imagery and allusions. Structural coherence and thematic unity are perhaps less highly prized literary qualities than they once were, but changes in critical fashions do not alter the fact that Shakespeare's ability to interweave related images and ideas is extraordinarily successful in helping his audience and readers to understand his purposes. Thus, while the Duke likens the weather to a savage animal, he also compares it to a rough and honest plain-speaker whose 'churlish chiding' contrasts with the sycophancy of the court: again the speech suggests the antithesis of court and country, and again it is less about the country than the predatory world of the court. For all the Duke's efforts to discover the 'uses of adversity', he can only praise the forest in the terms of his former existence: the elements are 'counsellors', their benefits 'jewels'. Even his vocabulary is learned and latinate: 'persuade', 'adversity', 'exempt'. As Amiens comments, the Duke is blessed in being able to 'translate' his fortune into 'so quiet and so sweet a style', and of course the irony is that he can only prosper in pastoral seclusion by exercising the arts of the court. To theorize about one's life in the country is inevitably to reveal one's social origins; a genuine rustic is capable of no more than Corin's 'natural' philosophy (though this, too, is suspiciously cultivated). Compressed in this single speech are all the complex ironies of Renaissance pastoral, which is rarely, as it might appear, about nature itself, but almost always about ideas, whether of nature, art or society.

These passages from *Hamlet* and *As You Like It* are by no means exhausted by my analyses, for no reader can cover the infinite range of possible interpretations of any text, and Shakespeare's plays have proved more susceptible to exegesis than any others. A close commentary like the above can, however, convey some of the intellectual satisfactions of studying Shakespeare; by analyzing and understanding his language we almost feel we are taking on some of his ingenuity, resourcefulness and subtlety.

Moreover, Shakespeare enables us to reflect on the relationship between the theatre and the 'real' world in a way which many mimetic[12] dramatists do not. In one sense the plays are remarkably realistic – sentries, we imagine, would talk like this, and so would dukes who had fallen on hard times – yet they are also highly stylized and make continual reference to themselves as illusions. *Hamlet* contains an extended discussion of theatrical conventions, and *As You Like It* draws repeated parallels between the role-playing of the actor and the ways in which people in real life act parts. In many of Shakespeare's plays we are encouraged to maintain a dual perspective, on the one hand suspending our disbelief, and on the other recognizing that this is art, which is by definition not 'truth'. The music strikes and the wonderfully painted statue in *The Winter's Tale* steps down from its pedestal (V.iii.103), but as it does so we realize that only in the theatre could a statue credibly appear to come to life. Nature is most of all art when it seems most natural, a contradiction which fascinates Shakespeare and through which he has exerted an enormous influence on experimental modern playwrights such as Bertolt Brecht.

The ramifications of Shakespeare's preoccupation with what Anne Barton has called 'the idea of the play'[13] will be explored further in later chapters, but it deserves mention here because it is so central to our pleasure in studying Shakespeare. The self-conscious theatricality of a drama in which boy actors played young women, who in turn dressed up as men – and in Rosalind's case then played herself, whatever her true self might have been – these complexities interest students at school and college just as much as they do professional critics and actors. Shakespeare's plays are a means of exercising our skills of imagination and intellect whether we are new to his art or long-practised in writing about and discussing him. As we read or watch the plays, we visualize, empathize and analyze, all the time reminded that we are interpreting an illusion of reality, not life itself, and the effect is sometimes intoxicating.

In *King Lear*, for example, the reader is made to feel mentally disoriented and physically giddy alongside the tottering Earl of Gloucester, as Edgar uses a wealth of circumstantial detail to evoke the vast, sheer drop from the cliffs of Dover (IV.vi.11–24). Like Gloucester, we cannot literally see the cliff, yet also like him we are made dizzy by the idea of looking at it. What makes the speech all the more startling is our simultaneous consciousness that its effect is highly contrived. No real cliff could be as high as this one; Edgar offers a surreal vision of impossibly tiny human beings at the mercy of nature. Yet even whilst we distance ourselves from the horror by noting Edgar's hyperbole, his vision strikes us as fundamentally truthful. Nature in this play is not benign as it was in *As You Like It*; instead it is savagely indifferent.

In the theatre, of course, the effect is arguably even more impressive, since the incongruity between Edgar's language and his actual surroundings is unmistakable. And when we see the scene enacted, Edgar's treatment of his father seems disturbingly like cruelty, even though his motives are fundamentally kind.

## Conclusion

So there are extremely good reasons why Shakespeare does and probably will continue to exert considerable influence on the study of literature in English for the foreseeable future, even if we cannot expect him to please all the people all of the time. Some recent commentators have suggested that there is no intrinsic 'Shakespeare', merely the sum of all our previous experiences and preconceptions of his work. I would agree with them that our responses to Shakespeare tell us as much about ourselves as they do about his plays, but I would also assert that there is a body of texts we call 'Shakespeare' which exists independently of its readers, and which offers some resistance to the successive interpretations imposed on it.

The voices of students are less likely to be heard than those of professional teachers and critics in the debate about Shakespeare, which is one reason why this book draws so heavily on the remembered comments of and written feedback from those we have taught. In our experience, students have few doubts about the validity of studying Shakespeare and indeed often produce their best written work on him. A very experienced lecturer once told me that she considered Shakespeare the easiest author of all to teach in terms of enthusing her students; she attributed this to the sense of achievement gained from understanding language so different from our own.

Two students, Heidi and Lorraine (1994 graduates), who candidly found the study of literature hard-going, explained that they used role-play to help them understand Shakespeare, and had read ten of his plays aloud together in the five weeks before their final exams. As joint honours students in English and History they also had to commit vast amounts of primary source material to memory, but it is hard to imagine them reading their historical texts aloud to each other in the evenings. Shakespeare, on the other hand, was a recreation as well as a necessity.

It is perhaps worth remembering that inexperience does not necessarily denote critical insensitivity. Anyone relatively new to Shakespeare has one advantage over the more experienced student: a fresh perspective. I was fifteen when I first read *Macbeth*, and had read no other early literature besides one or two Metaphysical poems. Lady Macbeth's invocation speech intrigued and puzzled me:

> Come, you Spirits
> That tend on mortal thoughts, unsex me here,
> And fill me, from the crown to the toe, top-full
> Of direst cruelty! make thick my blood,
> Stop up th' access and passage to remorse;
> That no compunctious visitings of Nature
> Shake my fell purpose.
>
> (I.v.40–6)

Surely Shakespeare was talking here about the menstrual cycle, I thought; Lady Macbeth is repudiating the badge of female sexuality with its implication of physical and mental weakness. When I hesitantly suggested this in an essay, the teacher explained that Shakespeare merely meant that blood is the vehicle of our emotions: as the Arden editor, Kenneth Muir says, quoting A. C. Bradley, 'She means "so that pity cannot flow along her veins" and reach her heart.' Looking at the play fifteen years later, though, I wish I had trusted my original instinct, for it now seems blindingly obvious that Shakespeare did want us to think about menstrual blood as well as the arterial kind. Catherine Belsey has pointed out that the play is extremely rich in imagery of breasts, milk and babies, and suggests this is because Lady Macbeth is represented as having violated nature when she sublimated her 'normal' female drives, sexual and maternal, for evil ends.[14]

Studying Shakespeare hopefully involves us in developing our understanding of his art without losing our initial ability to respond to him imaginatively. There may be something after all in A. C. Bradley's view of Shakespeare's plays as a unique tribute to the human spirit, in that studying him really does seem to enhance many readers' sense of self. Without any of the embarrassment and self-consciousness which inhibit those versed in debates about the canon, one mature student, Anita, summed up her feelings about *King Lear* when she asked rhetorically how we could possibly hope to study it in two weeks – a year would hardly be sufficient. Her commitment would put many professional Shakespeare critics to shame, but it is shared by many students and indicates that for the most part we do not study Shakespeare in order to pass exams but because we want to. In the chapters that follow we proceed on the assumption that Shakespeare fully deserves the attention he continues to receive from audiences and readers; our aim throughout is to help students maximize the emotional and intellectual satisfactions of studying his plays.

## Notes

1. John Redwood, 'Mother tongues', in the *Liverpool Daily Post*, 10 August 1994, p. 6.
2. Nigel Lawson, *The View From No. 11: Memoirs of a Tory radical* (London: Bantam, 1992), p. 6.
3. See, for example, the Shakespeare Birthday Lecture, delivered by the Prince of Wales at Stratford-upon-Avon in April 1991 and reprinted in edited form in *The Times*, 23 April 1991.
4. John Bender, 'Eighteenth-century literature', in *Redrawing the Boundaries: The transformation of English and American literary studies*, ed. Stephen Greenblatt and Giles Gunn (New York: Modern Language Association), p. 90.
5. Jonathan Dollimore and Alan Sinfield, *Political Shakespeare: New essays in cultural materialism* (Manchester: Manchester University Press, 1985), p. viii.
6. Preface, *The Shakespeare Myth*, ed. Graham Holderness (Manchester: Manchester University Press, 1988), p. xiii.
7. 'Give an account of Shakespeare and Education, showing why you think they are effective and what you have appreciated about them. Support your comments with precise references', in *Political Shakespeare*, ed. Dollimore and Sinfield, pp. 134–57, at p. 138.
8. Ben Jonson, 'To the memory of my beloved, The Author Mr William Shakespeare, And What He Hath Left Us' (line 43), *Ben Jonson: Selected poems* (Oxford: Oxford University Press, 1995), p. 137.
9. Alan Sinfield, 'Royal Shakespeare: Theatre and the making of ideology', in *Political Shakespeare*, pp. 158–81, at p. 172.
10. Edward Dowden, *Shakspere: A critical study of his mind and art*, 11th edn (London: Kegan Paul, Trench, Trubner, 1897), p. 44.
11. All references to Shakespeare in this book are from the New Arden (Arden 2) edition of his plays.
12. 'Mimesis' was Aristotle's term for the realistic imitation of life in literary texts.
13. Anne Barton, *Shakespeare and the Idea of the Play* (1962; repr. Penguin: Harmondsworth, 1967).
14. Catherine Belsey, 'Afterword: A future for feminist criticism?', *The Matter of Difference: Materialist Feminist Criticism of Shakespeare*, ed. Valerie Wayne (Hemel Hempstead: Harvester Wheatsheaf, 1991), pp. 257–70, at pp. 260–1 and 264–5.

# CHAPTER 2

# Discussing Shakespeare

## Internal dialogue

> Sure he that made us with such large discourse,
> Looking before and after, gave us not
> That capability and godlike reason
> To fust in us unus'd.
> (Hamlet IV.iv.36–9)

> I'd sit around and think about the plays, argue with myself over
> the pros and cons. (Richard)

To add words to Shakespeare's words and to the words of the
thousands of others who have commented upon Shakespeare's
words is a daunting thing indeed. The best way to start to understand Shakespeare is to talk about him. Initially this may be a
private, internal dialogue as you question and answer yourself
whilst reading a particular play. The epigraph above, from a student at Chester, makes the point admirably. Argue with yourself as
you think about Shakespeare's plays. We are creatures bound
in discourse and we cannot escape the discursive nature of
human society and experience. Listening to others talking about
Shakespeare might not always be an option, though when we are
in class situations we must pay careful attention to others' words
and not merely wait to make our own point (or not say anything at
all). What we can always do is listen to ourselves. Turn over possibilities in your mind as you are reading Shakespeare, possibilities

of interpretation and meaning. Explore the text rather than seek to solve it.

We can take our cue for discussing Shakespeare from Shakespeare himself. Shakespeare is a poet of conversation, of discussion. Even in soliloquies the character is often engaged in discussion, posing and ruminating on questions such as 'To be or not to be'. Like Hamlet we should be *using* 'that capability and godlike reason'.

In *Henry IV Part One* the incomparable Falstaff ponders the meaning of the much used word 'honour':

> Can honour set to a leg? No. Or an arm? No. Or take away the grief of a wound? No. Honour hath no skill in surgery then? No. What is honour? A word. What is in that word honour? What is that honour? Air. A trim reckoning! Who hath it? He that died a-Wednesday. Doth he feel it? No. Doth he hear it? No. 'Tis insensible, then? Yea, to the dead. But will it not live with the living? No. Why? Detraction will not suffer it. Therefore I'll none of it. Honour is a mere scutcheon – and so ends my catechism.

> (V.i.131–41)

Falstaff speaks aloud, for the benefit of the audience, his inner thoughts. The best way to set up a similar internal private dialogue is first to make the play your own. Read it through to yourself, as much aloud as you dare or wish. Enjoy it. Play the parts, perform the poetry, mouth the metre. Use the many materials that are available to you: cassette recordings and discussions of the plays, videos of film productions, different editions and critical works. I think you will find that the more you can experience the text – and that does involve hearing it – the more confidence you will have in seminars, and the more confidence you will have in essay writing. Students testify to the usefulness of reading aloud: 'When I read Shakespeare I like to read it aloud as if I'm an actor because this helps me overcome the difficulties of language – and I read long speeches over and over to be sure I have understood their mean-ing' (Agatha). Once you do overcome difficulties of language and have understood the meaning, you will be well placed to contrib-ute intelligently in discussions about the plays.

Taking a scene and reading it through can alert you to all sorts of complexities, puns, problems, characterizations, images and rhythms that you might miss with a silent reading. Take the following:

*Romeo.*   I dreamt a dream tonight.
*Mercutio.*   And so did I.
*Romeo.*   Well what was yours?
*Mercutio.*   That dreamers often lie.
*Romeo.*   In bed asleep, while they do dream things true.
*Mercutio.*   O then I see Queen Mab hath been with you.
(I.iv.49–53)

By speaking this, rhyme and pun become clearer. The metre of the shared lines stands out. This is not to say that a silent reading could not produce these insights, but the translation into speech makes access to them easier. Anything which assists you in preparation for classes is valuable, and not just to yourself; your understanding of the play is part of the learning experience for the other students. You are partly responsible for the teaching-and-learning environment in any class of which you are a member. (See the final section in this chapter on the group and the text for further discussion of this point.)

The word 'discuss' does not occur often in Shakespeare and in fact is only used (to mean 'to tell') by minor low-life characters such as Nym, Pistol and Fluellen (see *Henry V* III.ii.65/IV.i.37/ IV.iv.5/30). The word *talk* is far more common in Shakespeare, and is perhaps the word we should use here, except that 'discuss' suggests an investigation or examination by argument, a sifting and debating, an opposition of thesis and antithesis with the aim of arriving at a synthesis. If discussion does not lead to synthesis (that is, building up a whole out of parts), it can lead to fragmentation. Either way, at its best, discussion will leave all those who have truly taken part, either as speakers or only listeners, aware of other points of view, other emphases, other agendas. In short, a good discussion will leave you aware of other readers and their readings.

## Listening and talking

Listening in on others is something we all find difficult to resist. Arguably it is connected with that very part of us that draws us to literature, or more widely, stories of any sort, whether factual or fictional. We want to hear about other people's lives. We have an urge to invade their privacy. In Shakespeare's plays there are plenty of examples of characters overhearing others. In the theatre the walls do indeed have ears. The fourth wall of the audience is full of ears, lent to the actors to fill with their noises, whether words, music or stage sounds.

Say a group of people are discussing *Hamlet*. If you conceal yourself behind the curtain you might hear the following:

A. What is this play about?
B. Young lovers.
A. No, politics surely.
C. Or friendship?
A. At some points it seems to be about the theatre itself.
D. Yes, but really it's about revenge.
E. I'd have said death.

This conversation might surprise you, especially if you do not know the play. How can so many different views be held about the central concern of *Hamlet*? The answer is that in approaching a play through talk with others we are bound to encounter a number of opinions. The exciting thing about discussion is the liberty offered by its free-ranging and unfixed nature. You can say very speculative things and withdraw them, or revise them as you speak. Discussion is a form of team exploration.

Our appreciation of Shakespeare is not simply a personal matter, it is arguably a social matter also. Many of the points that can be made about discussing Shakespeare can and have been made about discussing literature more generally. In his excellent chapter in *Studying Literature*,[1] Bill Hughes identifies two reasons why it is important that students actively participate in discussion:

> The first has to do with the nature of works of literature. Like any work of art, a literary work functions only when it is being experienced by an individual. A novel or play or poem needs the reader to complete the circuit. . . . The process of sharing viewpoints can be an illuminating one.
> The second reason that dialogue and discussion forms a central part of degree-level literature classes is concerned more with the personal development of each student. . . . We can discover what we mean only by listening to what we say. (pp. 25–6)

And 'listening to what we say' means you listening to others – but not being afraid to add your voice to the continuing discussion.

Of all the forms of literature drama is the most suggestive of the social, for as well as the peopled worlds of Illyria, Venice, Rome, Arden, Bohemia and Sicilia we have the peopled theatre, both the acting troupe and the audience. The complex interaction of these worlds truly makes the theatre a semiotic and aesthetic marvel. In the figure of Shakespeare we also have a cultural marvel, one of the modern wonders of the world. But how are we to begin speaking of this marvel?

A few words from the French essayist Michel de Montaigne (1533–92) are helpful. Montaigne is thought to have had no small influence on Shakespeare. Some have claimed that Hamlet owes much to Montaigne's sceptical and stoical philosophy. Certainly Shakespeare possessed a copy of John Florio's English translation of Montaigne's essays (published 1603). In an essay, 'On the Art of Conversation', Montaigne sets forth, in his remarkably modern voice, a whole compendium of advice on the subject of talking with others – advice, I believe, with which Shakespeare would have wholeheartedly concurred.[2]

Montaigne makes various observations concerning the pleasures and benefits of conversation. He claims that 'to my taste the most fruitful and most natural exercise of our minds is conversation. I find the practice of it the most delightful activity of our lives' (*ibid.*, p. 1045). And he goes on to say:

> If I am sparring with a strong and solid opponent he will attack me on the flanks, stick his lance in me right and left; his ideas send mine soaring. Rivalry, competitiveness and glory will drive me and raise me above my own level. In conversation the most painful quality is perfect harmony. . . . Just as our mind is strengthened by contact with vigorous and well-ordered minds, so too it is impossible to overstate how much it loses and deteriorates by the continuous commerce and contact we have with mean and ailing ones. (*ibid.*, p. 1045)

Like Montaigne we should learn to relish 'the duel of words' (*ibid.*, p. 1061) which conversation can be.

To enjoy conversation fully Montaigne suggests that we 'embark upon discussion and argument with great ease and liberty' (*ibid.*, p. 1046). He claims that 'contradictory judgements neither offend me nor irritate me: they merely wake me up and provide me with exercise' (*ibid.*, p. 1046). And he strengthens his argument:

We avoid being corrected: we ought to come forward and accept it, especially when it comes from conversation not a lecture. . . . When I am contradicted it arouses my attention not my wrath. I move towards the man who contradicts me: he is instructing me. (*ibid.*, pp. 1046–7).

To cap his point Montaigne refers to the founding father of Western philosophy and simply states: 'Socrates always laughingly welcomed contradictions made to his arguments' (*ibid.*, p. 1047). If Socrates could stand to be contradicted I dare say we all can. Montaigne also invites us to consider a wider definition of discussion:

Perhaps we may include in the category of conversation and discussion those short pointed exchanges which happiness and intimacy introduce among friends when pleasantly joking together and sharply mocking each other. (*ibid.*, p. 1063)

If taken for what they are (only 'words, words, words' [*Hamlet* II.ii.192]) the comments of friends (and one should endeavour to befriend one's fellow students) can make us question our assumptions and show us the limitations of our approaches and perspectives, however acerbic their remarks might at first seem.

Montaigne is perhaps at his sharpest when undermining the pretensions of the arrogant academic. He points out that 'studying books has a languid feeble motion, whereas conversation provides teaching and exercise all at once' (*ibid.*, p. 1045). Going further, he claims that he 'would prefer a son of mine to learn to talk in the tavern rather than in our university yap-shops' (*ibid.*, p. 1049–50). We should not kowtow to the opinions of others too readily for, as Montaigne warns, 'in discussion the gravity, academic robes and rank of the man who is speaking often lend credence to arguments which are vain and silly' (*ibid.*, p. 1054). We should always listen to what is being said, and not be fooled by the seeming certainty of the speaker. For as Montaigne observes: 'the surest proof of animal-stupidity is ardent obstinacy of opinion. Is there anything more certain, decided, disdainful, contemplative, grave and serious, than a donkey?' (*ibid.*, p. 1063). In the end we must not lose sight of the fact that 'this world is but a school of inquiry. The question is not who will spear the ring but who will make the best charges at it' (*ibid.*, p. 1051).

Montaigne's words should awaken us to a better appreciation of discussion and conversation. His sense of detachment from the statements he makes, his fascination with those who contradict him ('My thought so often contradicts and condemns itself that it is all one to me if someone else does so' [*ibid.*, p. 1047]) and his total lack of close-minded certainty are all traits which the student embarking on the study of Shakespeare, and indeed any topic, would do well to emulate.

As soon as they are spoken aloud comments or questions can become foci for debate and consideration, that is starting and returning points for discussion. Where the discussion will lead and the path it follows will vary with any group, although we may be surprised at the degree of similarity between various discussions of Shakespeare's plays. All the time we should bear in mind the ever-important framing questions: are these the sorts of question we should be posing, and are the points we are making in discussion justified, valid, useful, spurious, frivolous? What is their value? And how do they help us to analyze the texts of William Shakespeare?

## Reflecting

What do students think about discussing Shakespeare? What are the benefits of discussion and the best way of preparing for it? We wrote to a number of students asking them about their experience of studying Shakespeare and we were surprised and pleased by the response.

On the topic of preparing for discussion Elizabeth wrote of the benefits of brainstorming (writing down as many thoughts on a particular subject in a few minutes): 'brainstorming . . . was fascinating – opening up possibilities for all of us which had not hitherto been considered. I found the whole experience extremely stimulating.' However, Elizabeth did have some difficulties, and some suggestions for dealing with these difficulties:

> If there was a problem at all, I think it was, for most of us, the language barrier. I think that this can be a huge source of discouragement for many first-time students. For me, the way to overcome this problem was to read through a play fairly quickly to start with, and not waste time mulling over words and passages that were not clear. Having

grasped the sense of the play I then found it easier to read it for a second time at a more leisurely rate, and try to intrepret the foggy, ambiguous bits. There is, after all, plenty of critical material available to help. Videos are a great help too, although I feel that they can hinder your own, very personal, interpretation of the play.

Sadie found audio-tape resources useful: 'Having got to grips with the text, I find listening to actors read through the play on cassette very helpful. I notice pauses and changes of tone which influence my reading of the play. However, I realise that these tapes are one interpretation and should be taken as such.' The truth of this means that you must make your own interpretation of different plays, and develop these interpretations, or amend them, in discussion. To prepare properly for discussion you must read thoroughly and think deeply. Danielle makes the point admirably: 'Every word should really be understood and enjoyed. I think students tend to read Shakespeare too fast and thus miss the wonderful intricacies of each sentence.'

Many students testify to the benefits of discussing Shakespeare. Anita wrote: 'I particularly enjoyed the debates and student interaction that usually followed. It was always useful hearing the many interpretations of a text. . . . I do believe there is no substitute for seeing the play staged and would consider going to the theatre essential for any student of Shakespeare. . . . I found group discussion rather than group reading, more stimulating and instructive.'

Three other students also stress, with slightly differing emphases, the benefits of talking about Shakespeare:

> Discussing interpretations of plays with other students is 'essential' since everyone is likely to have a slightly different opinion. . . . Reading aloud in a group, or acting scenes is useful for an investigation of language. (Samantha)

> Discussions are important; the observations and opinions of others are always of value. With discussion, whatever has been misunderstood comes out into the open and will be remembered. (Ilse)

> I prefer informal discussion really because it helps students to get to the heart of the issues being explored within the text rather than dwelling too much upon context. (Agatha)

The only negative thing said about discussion in class situations was that there could have been more. Edward felt that 'there should simply be more lessons and more discussion. I found the study in isolation not conducive to overly fulfilling study . . . there was simply not enough time to discuss each play.' Alison called the relatively short time devoted to discussion a 'major problem': 'I enjoy class discussions and find it helpful in formulating my own ideas to hear the feelings and thoughts of others and develop a response to what they have said. . . . The major problem is that in the short time available one has to whip through several meaty plays and sometimes you are left wishing there could have been discussion about one or two more aspects.'

If, like Alison and Edward, you are left feeling the need for more discussion, you should discuss these other aspects with fellow students. Certainly in my experience some of the students who have produced the best work have been those who discuss the plays outside class. If you don't feel you know your fellow students well enough to enter into this sort of discussion then I suggest using Shakespeare as a way into friendship. If you can get into a conversation about some fascinating aspect of a play or plays with someone previously not well known to you, you will be achieving two things at once: broadening your knowledge of other points of view on Shakespeare and making a new friend.

Though a comment passed in discussion may be outrageous, or seem absurd, it may deserve further investigation and produce valuable insights.

I think Regan must have been sexually abused as a small girl by Lear.

Claudius and Gertrude were having an affair before King Hamlet's murder.

The first of these comments surprised me when voiced in class by a perceptive student. I felt the comment could not really be supported by textual evidence, but when we attended an autumn production of the play in Leeds in 1995 and saw Lear grabbing Regan and pulling her to his knee in the opening scene I was impressed by the similarity of the comment to the director's interpretation. The second comment may also seem mistaken, a matter of reading too much into things, but when one examines the speech of the ghost, who talks obsessively of his 'seeming-virtuous queen', we might doubt that Gertrude is quite the helpless, unwitting woman she seems to be.

The point here is: keep an open mind. Don't prejudge the words of others, based on your perception of the speaker. At the same time don't assume your opinion irrelevant. Your perception is as valid as the other person's, and it will benefit others to listen to what you have to say in the same way that it will benefit you to listen to them. The aim of all discussion and study is to enhance our understanding, to make ourselves more aware of difficulties we might have overlooked and meanings we might have missed. Discussion provides us with the most direct access to another person's mind and truly to discuss anything with others we must, in the fullest sense of the phrase, remain open-minded. And remaining receptive to the thoughts and words of others concerning Shakespearean drama necessitates remaining open-minded towards the texts themselves. Combined with enthusiasm, your openness to new ideas and interpretations of Shakespeare's art (new to you at least) will guarantee your enjoyment of him. Boredom should not be on the agenda, though admittedly some students confess to it. Having completed a year-long course in Shakespeare, Danielle wrote that 'It was quite clear that certain students on the course were not willing to drop the notion of Shakespeare being a boring subject. Class discussion should take into consideration the multitude of interesting topics that can be debated.'

**Question and answer**

Discussion, or conversation, often follows a pattern of question and answer. Shakespeare himself uses interrogative discussion in many ways. For example, it serves as exposition in *The Tempest*, when Miranda questions Prospero about their arrival on the island and provides the opportunity for the revelation of essential information to the audience:

> Sir, are not you my father?
> (I.ii.55)

> Wherefore did they not
> That hour destroy us?
> (I.ii.138–9)

> How came we ashore?
> (I.ii.158)

> And now, I pray you, sir,
> For still 'tis beating in my mind, your reason
> For raising this sea-storm?
>
> (I.ii.175–7)

Prospero's pleas for Miranda's attention, as he explains how he and his daughter came to the island, work on two levels: as convincing, revealing dialogue, but also as a request for the audience's attention, so that they don't miss any information necessary to an understanding of the play's action:

> The hour's now come,
> The very minute bids thee ope thine ear,
> Obey and be attentive.
>
> (I.ii.36–8)

> Dost thou attend me?
>
> (I.ii.78)

> Thou attend'st not.
>
> (I.ii.87)

> Dost thou hear?
>
> (I.ii.106)

> Hear a little further,
> And then I'll bring thee to the present business
> Which is now upon's; without the which, this story
> Were most impertinent.
>
> (I.ii.135–8)

At other times Shakespeare uses questions from one character as promptings for the thoughts of another. In *Othello* the devilish Iago questions the Moor, prompting jealous thoughts of Desdemona's infidelity:

> *Iago.* Will you think so?
> *Othello.* Think so, Iago?
> *Iago.* What,
> To kiss in private?
> *Othello.* An unauthoriz'd kiss.
> *Iago.* Or to be naked with her friend abed,
> An hour, or more, not meaning any harm?
> *Othello.* Naked abed, Iago, and not mean harm?
>
> (*Othello* IV.i.1–5)

Conversation here is far from constructive (except from Iago's perspective: it is very successful in prompting Othello's jealousy). In *Othello* Iago's carefully calculated questions poison and infect. Talk, then, is not necessarily a safe and pleasant matter. As Ben Knights says in his fascinating study of group process, 'groups have enormous potential for destruction as well as creation. . . . The learning group can be the site of obstruction, evasion and sullen privacy as well as of mutual support and breathtaking insight.'[3] It is partly up to you to make classes realize their full creative potential by listening attentively and contributing constructively. I am sure Tracy speaks for many less confident students when she writes that 'in seminars some "older" students tended to take over, you know the "read that", "seen this" crew! It really is very intimidating and not in the least encouraging for people like me who are a tad clueless.'

Shakespeare is fundamentally interested in language, and in what happens when two or more people talk together. There is often sparring with words in his plays, and at times this word skirmishing degenerates into physical fighting:

*Enter* Kent *and* Oswald, *severally.*
*Oswald.* Good dawning to thee, friend: art of this house?
*Kent.* Ay.
*Oswald.* Where may we set our horses?
*Kent.* I' th' mire.
*Oswald.* Prithee, if thou lov'st me, tell me.
*Kent.* I love thee not.
*Oswald.* Why then I care not for thee.
*Kent.* If I had thee in Lipsbury pinfold, I would make thee care for me.
*Oswald.* Why dost thou use me thus? I know thee not.
*Kent.* Fellow, I know thee.
*Oswald.* What dost thou know me for?
*Kent.* A knave, a rascal, an eater of broken meats; a base, proud, shallow, beggarly, three-suited, hundred-pound, filthy worsted-stocking knave; a lily-livered, action-taking, whoreson, glass-gazing, super-serviceable, finical rogue; one-trunk-inheriting slave; one that wouldst be a bawd in way of good service, and art nothing but the composition of a knave, beggar, coward, pandar, and the son and heir of a mongrel bitch: one whom I will beat into clamorous whining if thou deni'st the least syllable of thy addition.

*Oswald.* Why, what a monstrous fellow art thou, thus to rail on one that
is neither known of thee nor knows thee!
*Kent.* What a brazen-fac'd varlet art thou, to deny thou knowest me!
Is it two days since I tripp'd up thy heels and beat thee before
the King? Draw, you rogue; for though it be night, yet the
moon shines: I'll make a sop o' th' moonshine of you.
[*Drawing his sword*
You whoreson cullionly barber-monger, draw.
(*King Lear* II.ii.1–31)

As Kent draws his sword, we see his verbal assault moving towards
physical blows. Human discourse has broken down. Language is
replaced by violent action as Kent begins to beat the cowardly and
petrified Oswald. It would be difficult to imagine anything quite
like this happening in a class, but the example should show that
talk can be pointed and aggressive; and when it is, there is seldom a
constructive outcome.

Shakespeare is a potential starting-point for a myriad of other
subjects. Taking a naive approach and simply discussing the question 'what is this play about?' soon raises thematic concerns and
means that we must, like Shakespeare, ponder abstract and per-
plexing concepts. We might find ourselves asking what is nature?
what is justice? what is madness? what is love? And though we will
find plenty of exploration of these and other questions in the plays
we will not find a definitive statement from the author. The very
nature of Shakespeare's chosen medium, the play, means that our
author is always behind the scenes. We may feel moments where
he comes centre stage and talks directly to the audience, but interpreting the words of fictional dramatic characters as Shakespeare
speaking his own mind is dubious if not foolish. Shakespeare has
left us with a number of plays which provide rich material for
debate. In discussing Shakespeare, either alone or with others, we
are continuing the philosophical consideration of fundamental
human questions, which Shakespeare himself participated in four
hundred years ago.

## Seeing and enacting

In practical terms, I think that it is essential to see the plays performed,
either in the theatre or on video. This has to be viewed as dramatic

English, because pace and timing are so vital to the plays. As so many scholars have commented; these plays are meant to be performed. (Alan)

How often we alter our opinions of a play having seen it in production. The play-text is there for us (leaving textual quibbles temporarily aside) as an unsullied source of imaginative re-enactments. But going to the theatre to see Shakespeare performed can lead us into new ways of thinking of the play. Some productions work for us and some don't. Most are a mixture of the two. Even if we disagree with a version, or certain aspects of a version that we see, nevertheless we are forced to test our own imaginative re-enactment against someone else's real enactment. If we are receptive, open to influence and willing to develop our ideas, the impact of a live performance on our understanding and appreciation of a Shakespearean play is unlikely to be negative.

Live performances also offer an ideal opportunity to listen to what others think about Shakespeare. If you are attending a production with friends you will no doubt be talking about the play and the particular interpretation you are attending with them during the interval and after the final curtain. These exchanges, in more relaxed circumstances than even the most pleasant seminar provides, can lead to valuable insights into the play in question. If you are alone, or not involved in a conversation, perhaps you could benefit by eavesdropping in the interval on unsuspecting fellow theatre-goers. Members of the audience at a Shakespeare play often have very firm opinions as to what should, or should not, have been done with the production. Snatched lines from the conversation of others can spark off your own thought-processes, leading you to reconsider aspects of the play in your own internal dialogue. To cite some specific examples drawn from my own attendance of a number of recent productions:

- Though I felt a neurotic, adolescent, hand-wringing Hamlet played at Chester's Gateway Theatre in 1994 was largely unsuccessful, the portrayal of the prince clearly appealed to the large numbers of teenagers in the audience (a school trip no doubt). Their laughter and enjoyment in the theatre and their animated discussions in the interval and afterwards convinced me that the production had indeed been a success in that it conveyed the essential youth of Hamlet.

- Warren Mitchell's King Lear at the West Yorkshire Playhouse in Leeds in 1995 struck a chord with me as he shuffled round the stage as if suffering a nervous breakdown. From his battered cassette-player there issued forth jangly rapid piano music, creating the effect of goonery gone wrong. In the interval a student took issue with the fact that from the outset Lear seemed senile, which meant he could not 'fall' as the conventional tragic hero should. This comment led to a lively discussion amongst those present about the notions of 'fall' and 'tragic hero', a discussion that would have graced any seminar.
- The battle scenes in the potentially chaotic third and fourth acts of *Antony and Cleopatra*, performed by the Northern Broadsides Company in Liverpool in 1995, were enhanced by the imaginative use of noise and colour. Large blue and orange oil drums were brought on stage as Caesar and his men beat their blue rhythm against Cleopatra and Antony's orange funk. Caesar's more steady (policeman) beat, needless to say, won the day. In a subsequent seminar this staging provided a good starting-point for an involved discussion about the differences between Rome and Egypt in the play.
- At Theatr Clwyd in 1995 the Romanian director Purcarete's version of Shakespeare's swansong *The Tempest* left most of the audience cold and confused. I too felt disappointed at the time, but later found that certain touches gave me new ways of appreciating the play. Purcarete chose to begin with Prospero as a mannequin (though the audience, I think, took the model for a live actor for a good few minutes). In retrospect, the startling and rather magical effect of seeing the clothing removed to reveal a wooden frame brought home to me the essence of Prospero as the manipulative wizard/artist/director, whose creations, including his own persona, are nothing more than a dream.

To achieve a clearer view of the roles played by the *dramatis personae* of Shakespeare's drama, students should be encouraged to enact the plays, or parts of them. Obviously there will be a limited amount of seminar time available for such activity, but its usefulness has been defended by many teachers and students of Shakespeare, amongst them Peter Reynolds:

> Walking through [a scene] should . . . help to crystallize the action, it becomes a 'thing done', and if a student has participated in seeing how

meanings can be made and unmade, then she or he is in a strong position to make the critical judgements about the real or imagined page to stage process . . . the objective is not to create individual performances but to explore collectively issues and ideas that only become obvious once questions relevant to performers (and audiences) are raised.[4]

Though there is a continuing debate about the usefulness of performance in teaching Shakespeare, the words of Ralph Cohen in the editorial to *The Shakespeare Quarterly* of Summer 1995 ('the idea that Shakespeare was meant to be performed is no longer a revelation') suggest a general agreement upon the validity of such pedagogic practice. (You will find more discussion of this issue in Chapter 6.)

To my mind our comprehension of Shakespeare must in large part be based on performance. In practice this may be limited to casting and reading through passages. Discussion in class offers opportunities for enactment, however limited, which a lone reading cannot provide. Take a scene, or some lines, and cast and read it. Listen to yourself and the others very carefully. Perhaps you should read it through again. Meanings or possible meanings, or possible subtexts or nuances may only just be dawning on you. If possible you should attempt some sort of enactment of the scene. The insights you gain make it well worth overcoming the embarrassment which such a method might stir in you.

If you are too timid to act for yourself, then find someone else to do it for you. In this connection the series of video workshop tapes offered by the Open University are particularly recommended. These workshops present a group of actors working with a director on speeches or scenes from a variety of plays. Watching these tapes will make clear to you the benefits of group enactment of the plays. The actors and directors involved are constantly discussing the text they seek to act, and in so doing produce valuable insights. For example, in the Royal Shakespeare Company *Twelfth Night* workshop the darkness of the play is foregrounded by the company's interpretative decisions, whilst in the *Antony and Cleopatra* workshop the relatedness of the language of the play and the props used, particularly armour, became apparent. You too will find even a minimal 'performance' of the text an excellent focus for class discussion. But if your tutor chooses not to employ any performance methods it is quite within your ability to assemble with other students and cast and read through passages. You will be surprised how reading aloud forces an engagement with the text which is challenging and rewarding. Hopefully the reading will only be the start and you will go on to talk about the passage, the play, Shakespeare, and literature, culture and life more generally.

## Class presentations

From a relaxed chat amongst friends it may seem a long way to the formality of the class presentation which you may be expected to deliver during your Shakespearean studies. In the Department of English at Chester class presentations form an integral part of the teaching and learning pattern. Presentations account for 30 per cent of assessment on most modules. Though this may not be the case at all institutions, the likelihood is that most students will have to make a presentation to the rest of the class at some point in their literary studies. The exact requirements will no doubt be explained to you by your tutor, but I think it is worth reflecting here upon the sorts of topics students tend to choose, and considering what is and is not effective.

> Presentations were always useful on many levels. Most of the time they are interesting to listen to, while 'performing' a presentation is a good way of retaining information. (Anita)
>
> I enjoyed the various oral presentations which provided invaluable information and learning experiences. Also, on a personal note, I enjoyed the opportunity of experimenting with my own oral presentation with another student. Videoing ourselves trying to act out scenes from *Antony and Cleopatra* provided much amusement! (Alex)

Of course, when you give your class presentation you are temporarily stepping into the role of lecturer, and leading the group. What is it that captures and keeps your attention as a student? You must endeavour to provide a stimulating learning experience for your fellow students. Too many presentations are useful and educational only for those actually giving them. The listening students need to have their interest aroused and then maintained. In order to help them concentrate you must design your preparation thoughtfully. As Alison comments:

To do your own presentation is obviously valuable. You have to do the work and it is good practice. Listening to other presentations I find less helpful. It may be harder to concentrate somehow. I also feel uncertain at times how credible the ideas are.

Make sure your ideas *are* credible. And make sure you pay attention to the delivery of the presentation. Rehearse it. There is obviously a performative aspect which you neglect to your cost. A polished performance will help buoy up your content. It will make good content seem even better. Most of your mark will no doubt be for content – but the presentation is a unique form of assessment with which you are physically involved. In class presentations you are not an absent author as when you write essays or exam scripts. If you are presenting in pairs or threes, you have the chance to discuss Shakespeare with your associates in front of your audience, thus highlighting contrary views. Class presentations can provide the most memorable educational experiences, but only if the presenters work at them.

With presentations on Shakespeare you have the possibility of utilizing the dramatic nature of the texts. The plays were intended to be performed, and drama students in particular often avail themselves of the opportunity of role-playing, making for stimulating and engaging work. Your tutor may limit your choices, but there are bound to be a variety of topics to work with. In my experience the most successful presentations tend to be those which are specific and focused. An argument is presented, developed and concluded in an engaging manner. Criticism is employed, not as a stale judgment, but as part of the lively, continuing debate on Shakespeare's work and our attitude towards it. The least successful presentations, in contrast, are generally loosely focused, read out dully in an obviously unrehearsed manner, and give the impression of having been created and delivered with little thought for the audience's experience. As Richard says, 'watching two people reading from a few sheets of A4 was usually a deadly monotonous way of receiving information'.

In handling questions and responses which might follow your presentation you do not need to be over-defensive. Your attempts to answer will be unlikely to count against you and may indeed provide further evidence of your work, giving you the chance to mention material that you have omitted from the presentation itself. It is highly unlikely that you will have a tutor who is unsympathetic to the difficulties of responding to questions from the class given that he or she faces frequently the stresses of such a situation. The more you have prepared, through rehearsal and discussion with those you are working with, the more confident you will be in the talk which follows your formal presentation. Remember, you will have done a significant amount of research and preparation and will be in a stronger position to comment on the particular questions and issues which you are addressing than your audience. Be confident. Enjoy leading others in their exploration of Shakespeare.

## The group and the text

I would like to focus now on the forum for discussion and turn your attention to an often ignored aspect of literary studies which necessarily dictates the nature of discussions which take place in class situations: group dynamics.

The class, which is the point at which one enters discussion and becomes open to new challenges and new information from others, is potentially the most exciting educational forum. This is the place where meaning is to be negotiated. Of course your tutor is likely to be the most expert in Shakespearean negotiations but that should not dissuade you from participating wholeheartedly in the negotiation. Let me reassure you that seldom in literary studies can you say something wholly worthless, and you may make some truly insightful and thus valuable points which, if you remain silent, will never be shared.

Here is Ben Knights again, reflecting on his wide teaching experience:

> As time has gone by, I have become increasingly aware that neither the group nor the text is simply a repository of meanings. When people talk about books they are not just mining insights, but negotiating a system of metacommunications for the production of meaning. Learning groups construct their own and others' meanings out of the text they study. The more conscious this process can be made, the more liberating it may become. (Knights, 1992, p. x)

> The group itself is an experiment in cultural production. (*ibid.*, p. 10)

Both text and group are sites where meanings are constructed. They import chaos and export order. Both engage with a potentially limitless field of emotions and social actions. Out of this welter of possibilities both group and text select, compose, organise, create patterns in which some features can be foregrounded and seen as important, and others backgrounded and seen as deviant – or else be totally overlooked. (*ibid.*, p. 13)

Knights makes clear the complexity and uncertainty of group exploration:

The story of textual process is better understood in terms of movement – play even – than in terms of final conclusions and unshakeable judgments. A group of people trying to think about the text is attempting to integrate knowledge (about the text, the author, historical context, language) with fantasy and emotion. (*ibid.*, pp. 7–8)

Frequently, it takes the energy generated in a group to inspire us to leap from the safety of achieved synthesis into the bath of fluid meaning. (*ibid.*, p. 11)

Though he uses the word 'play' to describe the process, Knights alerts us to the risk-taking and trust which are necessary for really valuable discussion:

In the privacy of reading you can indulge in identification, and the emotions called up by the book, without anyone else knowing. In the group you are liable to be observed in the act. (*ibid.*, p. 15)

My own educational belief is that the more people are willing to take the risk of exposure the more productive the work of the group and its consequences for individuals are likely to be. (*ibid.*, p. 16)

We should all be able to think of examples which support the truth of Knights' claim that 'groups have enormous potential for destruction as well as creation' (*ibid.*, p. 12). And we should consider it our responsibility as a group member to do all that we can to avert unhelpful or damaging discussion.

So, the importance of maintaining a constructive atmosphere in the group is paramount. To this end you should avoid carping comments and seek to make your own opinion known, whilst at all times remaining courteous.

In my opinion the tutor should attempt to act as a catalyst for the group's educational process. The group keeps having new insights, new learning experiences, new contacts with new perspectives. The tutor should facilitate this and should enhance the process. To do this she or he may employ a number of different devices to provoke discussion:

- make outrageous comments
- be equipped with lists of questions
- suggest approaching a topic from different directions
- provide stimulating handouts
- suddenly switch topics

## Openings

Rather than choosing to conclude this chapter, I should like it to end with a sense of a beginning, of an opening or entrance. The intention throughout this chapter has been not to impose a way of reading, thinking about and discussing Shakespeare, but to suggest various ways of achieving enjoyable and productive discussions of his plays. I give below an indication of some of the personal qualities which I feel the student who wishes to participate in and benefit fully from discussing Shakespeare might cultivate:

- open-mindedness
- attention to detail
- humility
- knowledge (of the text and the context)
- enthusiasm
- a questioning attitude
- love of conversation
- love of language
- willingness to listen to others
- willingness to talk with others
- a desire to understand others' viewpoints
- a desire to communicate, with dreams, with the past (history and myth and one's personal biography) and most importantly, with others.

To end I shall quote from the final words of one of Shakespeare's greatest plays, *King Lear*. Edgar's voice can be heard on a stage strewn with bodies, but his words apply to anyone entering the continuing discussion of Shakespeare's plays. To be true to ourselves, and to do justice to Shakespeare, we must 'speak what we feel, not what we ought to say' (V.iii.324). Or, rephrasing slightly, we must speak what we feel, not what we feel we *ought* to say, remembering always that we cannot have had the last word, and that others will be discussing Shakespeare long after our own voices have faded.

## Notes

1. Atkin, Walsh and Watkins, *Studying Literature: A practical introduction* (Hemel Hempstead: Harvester Wheatsheaf, 1995), pp. 25–47.
2. *The Complete Essays of Michel de Montaigne*, edited and translated by M. A. Screech (Allen Lane: London, 1991).
3. Ben Knights, *From Reader to Reader* (Hemel Hempstead: Harvester Wheatsheaf, 1992), p. 12.
4. Peter Reynolds, *Practical Approaches to Teaching Shakespeare* (Oxford: Oxford University Press, 1991), pp. 96–7.

# CHAPTER 3

# Writing about Shakespeare

## Introduction

As soon as we start to discuss Shakespeare orally, we are likely to find ourselves being asked to write about him as well. Many of the challenges of writing about Shakespeare are those of writing about literature in general; we aim for thoughtful analysis, subtle interpretation and clarity of expression. In this chapter, however, my focus will be on the special opportunities for and difficulties of writing about Shakespeare as distinct from other authors and texts, for Shakespeare is, after all, remote from us both in time and in terms of the towering genius which is invariably attributed to him. In consequence, writing about Shakespeare is a uniquely alarming prospect for some students, especially those who have read very little of him before reaching further or higher education. As Samantha (a third-year student) put it, 'No previous knowledge of Shakespeare (except two plays at A-level) meant that the compulsory year of Shakespeare at college brought on feelings of panic.'

In the course of my discussion I hope to suggest ways of dealing with this challenge, and I will use some examples of students' work in order to show as clearly as possible what might best be achieved or avoided when writing about Shakespeare at degree level. Writing about Shakespeare can be one of the most rewarding, as well as intimidating, aspects of one's literature studies: so often a student will find her best mark turns out to be for the essay she wrote on Shakespeare in her final year. Perhaps this is because of, rather than despite, the sense of risk attached to the task.

In the following sections I shall be discussing the widely varying forms in which we write about Shakespeare, including essays, commentaries, dissertations and examinations, but I propose to start with some observations on the task of writing about Shakespeare made by past and present students. The students I hope are reasonably representative. Some were at university studying English literature for a single honours degree, others were at a college of higher education following a Combined Subjects degree programme (see Appendix).

Lisa, a second-year student, said she wanted to write her final year dissertation on Shakespeare's villains, but was worried she would have nothing original to say. Susan, who had had some time out before returning to study, regarded Shakespeare as the cornerstone of her work in English, and wanted special coaching in order to make her essays as good as they could possibly be. Phil explained that he prepared his essays by looking for links between the plays and by repeatedly re-reading the texts on which he intended to focus. He explained that he spent more of his time thinking about his essay than he did note-taking.

In all these cases, there seemed to be a peculiar intensity in the students' attitudes to their studies, and this was matched by the enthusiasm with which they later described the actual process of writing about Shakespeare (in tutorials they would say their essays had taken ages to write, that they had read far more criticism than they normally did, and that they had found the experience absorbing). For many writing about Shakespeare becomes a memory to cherish: Anita (a mature graduate) felt 'enriched' by it, and for Elisabeth (also a mature student) it had been a 'high spot' of her education.

How far such intensity and commitment are due to Shakespeare's intrinsic qualities and how far they merely reflect our cultural conditioning is a question already explored in the opening chapter, and I shall leave it to one side here. It is a practical reality that most of us end up writing about Shakespeare at some point during our degree, and happily most of us enjoy it. Starting with the premise that general guidelines on writing essays – those which many departments provide for their new intakes, for example, and those which can be found under 'Study Skills' in the bookshop – do not fully equip us for our Shakespeare studies, this chapter aims to deal with the theory and practice of writing about Shakespeare in a form which is digestible, convenient for reference, and as comprehensive as possible.

## Note-taking

Note-taking is an aspect of writing about literature on which few of us are given much advice. Rarely does anyone else look at our notes, and that person is more likely to be another, probably grateful, student than someone – a tutor, perhaps – willing to give us critical feedback. This can lead us to regard notes as ephemeral and unimportant compared to the polished final product which is the weekly essay or formal assignment. Yet of course the opposite is true, for notes are the foundation on which marked and assessed work is based. For every 2,000- or 3,000-word essay, we will have made dozens of pages of notes, perhaps hundreds of annotations. How, then, to ensure that these notes are as useful as they can be?

The first, and almost the only, piece of advice about making notes I ever received was after my first degree, when my postgraduate supervisor warned me to make a note of the source of every idea or suggestion I encountered in my reading. This advice would have had equal relevance to my undergraduate work, and could be applied to every kind of note-taking. Interesting and fruitful ideas can occur to us when we are watching television, walking between lecture theatres or queuing at a supermarket checkout. A friend might say something inconsequential which unexpectedly provides us with a solution to a problem in our academic work: a phrase perhaps, or a new perspective. If we are alert to such connections we need to make a legible and careful note of our thoughts, and their source, so we can look at them again at leisure, and decide whether they really can be utilized. A student starting her PhD, Michelle, told me she carried a notebook at all times, so she could jot down things which struck her as being of relevance to her thesis. There is no reason why undergraduate students should be any less careful to preserve passing ideas for future reference.

Such notes are likely to be among the least structured we make, but some trouble should be taken to keep them in approximate chronological order. If it is a picture in a gallery or a theatre production of a play which has inspired us, it is advisable to keep an accurate reference. It is of little use to remember a painting which seemed vaguely relevant to *As You Like It* if you cannot remember where you saw the painting, who it was by or when it was produced. Similarly, it is not going to sound very impressive if you describe the unusual way in which a director represented the witches in *Macbeth* if you cannot recall the name of the director, his or her company or the date of the production. On the other hand, if you can note in parentheses that you mean *Landscape with Travellers* by Joos de Momper the Younger (1564–1655) in the Whitworth Art Gallery, Manchester, or the English Touring Theatre's *Macbeth* directed by Stephen Unwin, starring Peter Higgins, and performed at the Buxton Opera House in October 1995, you will sound much more precise and authoritative.

The same principle applies to other kinds of note-taking. In reading a play we will probably make pencilled notes on the text itself, assuming the copy is our own. (Writing in library books is inexcusable.) Sometimes we use a copy we first read for GCSE, then for A-level, and now at college or university. Unless one's handwriting has changed dramatically in the meantime, it can be difficult in these instances to tell when particular notes were first made. Putting the initials of a lecturer, or the name of a critic, in parentheses after a note helps to identify sources in our formal written work, and protects us against unwitting plagiarisms.

Additionally, if we are copying out a quotation from an article or book next to a passage in the primary text we need to make sure that we copy accurately, and give a proper, if abbreviated, reference. Noting next to Orlando's entrance with Adam in *As You Like It* (II.vii.166) that 'Aeneas carried Anchises out of Troy' is all very well, but we would do better to give the exact source in Virgil (*Aeneid* II.700–34), and perhaps make an additional note of the fact that Anchises was Aeneas' father. Better still to cite the lecturer who drew the allusion to our attention – in my case, Dennis Kay. There is a temptation to overlook the sources of our ideas, but being scrupulous about them does not imply a shortage of one's own. A year or two later we might be re-reading a text, and suddenly see another parallel: between Orlando and St Christopher, perhaps, or between Adam and Lear's daughter, Cordelia. To signal that these ideas were original, we might put our own initials after them, particularly if we are likely to refer to the idea in essays or exams.

So far I have been describing quite sophisticated annotations, but simple underlinings or blocks of fluorescent highlighter can be just as valuable in orientating our readings of the text. Some students develop a simple code: a single vertical line denotes an important passage, a double line one they wish to quote, an asterisk a passage which will definitely need discussion, a coloured line a passage relating to a particular theme, character or image. Thus we might go through *King Lear* on a second or third reading and pick out all the references to animals in blue, all the references to nature in red, or circle all the speeches by Kent, Albany and Edgar. These may be obvious ways to make one's future use of the text easier and quicker, but no one ever suggested them to me, and I doubt whether I have ever given such seemingly mundane advice to my own students. It sounds rather blunt and unromantic, perhaps, to suggest that reading Shakespeare can be materially aided by a set of felt-tip pens; one feels that degree-level English should be above that.

Even if you would find colour-coding – or indeed any annotations – unhelpfully distracting, preferring to keep your copy clean for future readings, a text full of markers and 'post-it' stickers is a vital study tool. It must, though, be supplemented by separately written notes. For one thing, a text can easily be lost or stolen. For another, margins and inside covers do not provide enough space for all the notes you need to make. These fuller notes are likely to fall into a number of categories.

First, there are notes on the primary text itself. One method is to copy down the lines and passages which seem significant, along with Act, scene and line references, and follow them up with a comment explaining why they are important. Another is to divide your notes up, and allocate a separate piece of paper to each aspect of the text relevant to your interpretation. Notes on *Richard II*, for instance, might consist of one page containing references to kingship, one page on old age and one on images of the state. This method is most useful on a subsequent reading; at first we are unlikely to know what topics will come to seem significant. It can be a good idea to mark each set of notes as 'First reading', 'Second reading', and so on, in the case of texts we are studying intensively. This helps us keep our notes in chronological order and enables us to see our ideas develop. A couple of pieces of paper for jotting down odd thoughts and queries are useful too, especially when we start trying to decide what should go into an essay and what should be left out.

Alongside thematic notes, it is vital to produce handy revision summaries of the plot of each play, paying especial attention to scene settings and the names of characters. A number of students have told me they have more difficulty with learning all the names than with any other aspect of Shakespeare. Even if you won't have to answer questions on Shakespeare in a formal, 'closed text' examination, you will write much more fluent essays if you know the basic storyline of the plays and have sorted out the identity and name of each character.

In addition to notes on the primary texts, notes are needed on our critical reading. As with primary texts, secondary texts should not be read passively, and notes should be organized either sequentially or according to various sub-headings as we read. One final-year student, Margaret, explained that in the course of her second year, she had changed from noting down indiscriminately every interesting if tangential critical idea she came across, to analyzing critical texts and producing summaries of them, interspersed with quotations. Another student found it helpful to write a brief account of each critical book she read, describing and evaluating its approach. Both these students perceived their critical reading in terms of an imagined dialogue between themselves and the published critic. Margaret said that she gradually became so fascinated by a particular perspective on the sonnets that she found herself reading books on other authors, such as John Donne, primarily for their bearing on her ideas about Shakespeare.

There can be an element of displacement in channelling too much of one's energy into presentation, but citing one's critical sources and providing the reader with an accurate and complete bibliography is good scholarly practice, and part of producing high-quality written work. Careful note-taking is, therefore, essential, since eventually you will have to give the author, title, publisher, date and page reference for every quotation, direct and indirect. A few years ago undergraduates were not routinely asked for scholarly notes in their essays, but nowadays most departments place considerable emphasis on this aspect of students' work, and at an early stage in your degree you will probably receive detailed information on how to reference your essays.

The shift to continuous assessment is partly responsible for the pressure on essays to be highly polished pieces of work (rather than stepping-stones on the way to an exam script). In addition the advent of the word processor has made good presentation more attainable and therefore more highly valued. Fewer and fewer students submit handwritten essays; increasing numbers are not only able to type, but have access to software which enables them to insert footnotes, use italics and format quotations in a smaller font than the main text. It is important for you to cultivate these skills if you want your work to be as well presented as that of everyone else in your class. Above all you will be anxious to ensure that your work is invulnerable to the charge of plagiarism, and that whenever you have referred to an idea which originated with someone else, you have acknowledged your source.

However we choose to organize our notes, they need to be paginated and filed in a logical place. It can be amazingly difficult to remember where one put one's notes on a particular text after a year or two has gone by and one has moved rooms twice or even three times in the interim. Notes must, therefore, be stored systematically. If you work in more than one library, it can help to make a note of the one in which you found a particular book. Again, after a couple of years it can be difficult to remember where one came across an especially helpful, now elusive reference book or critical text. It is frustrating to have to do all the work of tracking material down for a second time, and is sometimes out of the question for reasons of time and cost.

Lastly, there are the 'back-up' notes on relevant primary and secondary works: some sketchy references from a brisk reading of one or two plays by Shakespeare's contemporaries, for example, or a glance through a book on an aspect of his social context. Here it is slightly less important to be painstakingly accurate, since we are less likely to draw on these notes directly. One can be better off looking up any such references if and when the time comes to use them. A comprehensive working bibliography of all sources consulted will let us take notes more quickly from less important sources. In other words, you can use an abbreviated reference (just the author's last name and the date of publication, e.g. Dollimore 1984) in your notes, as long as you have a complete bibliographical record of the text in a convenient place, such as a record card:

> Dollimore, Jonathan
> Radical Tragedy: Religion and Power
> in the Drama of Shakespeare and
> His Contemporaries
> (Brighton: Harvester Press, 1984).
> [University College Chester Library, PR822.30916]

Notice that this student keeps a record not just of the book, but where she found it and what the shelfmark was.

As well as making it easier to make rapid notes, it is worth putting time and effort into compiling a proper bibliography for other reasons. With an extended piece of work, for example, we might collate several different reading lists: a handout from a tutor will be joined by a list of works found for ourselves, and we might also produce printouts from library catalogues or CD-ROMs. It is a good idea to amalgamate all these, particularly if you have access to a word processor. (See the section on 'Dissertations' below for a fuller account of compiling a bibliography.) Whether you create your own database or use old-fashioned record cards, remember to keep those texts you ended up reading and using separate from those you didn't read in the end, or couldn't find. Your bibliography is supposed to cover the material you drew on for your essay, not every single article or book you have heard of on the subject.

If you have taken copious, detailed and bibliographically accurate notes, you are halfway to producing good critical writing. This is true of all your literature studies of course, but Shakespeare is a particularly complicated author by virtue of his extensive output and the huge volume of criticism written about him. If you are relatively new to Shakespeare, you might find the requirement to give Act, scene and line numbers for every quotation extremely irksome, and you will almost certainly find that you have read much more criticism than you normally do, simply because so much is generally available. (Losing sight of the requirement to produce your own personal response is a potential problem dealt with later in the chapter, 'Shakespeare and Criticism'.) All these are merely questions of scale, though: you will probably end up with a thicker pile of notes on Shakespeare than on most other authors, and will simply need to be that bit more careful to keep track of everything.

Admittedly, all this has been the counsel of perfection; few of us keep notes which are uniformly meticulous and well organized. The point is to aim for the best we can, and keep carelessness to a minimum. Good notes ultimately save us time, since they make essay-writing so much easier.

By 'essay-writing' a number of things may be meant, of course. In the past students were probably asked to write about Shakespeare in only one or two ways; in a weekly or fortnightly essay, and in an end-of-year or biennial exam. Now they might also be writing a compulsory or optional dissertation on Shakespeare, or devising a class presentation on him, or writing a review of a production they have seen, or producing a substantial assignment which will form the basis of their assessment for one module of their degree programme. Even if you also have to do an exam at the end of your course or module, you may well have only one chance to write a full-length essay on Shakespeare, and so only one chance to receive substantive feedback on the fruits of several months' work.

## Formal essays/assignments

When it comes to producing a formal essay, Shakespeare is one of the easiest – yet most difficult – authors to write about well. His language is so expressive, figurative and poetic that it provides the richest possible resource for exposition and exegesis. His characters can seem so authentic and plausible that it is tempting to psychoanalyze them as if they were people we had met in real life. His use of thematic parallels and recurring motifs and his exploitation of generic conventions offer as much for discussion as his endlessly varied subject-matter. Any text or cultural artefact, however insubstantial or frivolous, can be subjected to critical analysis, but it is often easier to write about a text which offers a wealth of matter on which to comment. The student in Chapter 1 who wished she could spend a whole year on *King Lear* comes to mind, and in school you probably did inch your way through Shakespearean texts page by page, if not line by line.

None the less, as I acknowledged earlier, students do voice apprehensions about Shakespeare, particularly if they have studied him very little before starting their degree. More so than with any other author there is the sense of hopelessness at the thought of writing anything new on the subject. And with the possible exception of Chaucer, no other author studied routinely at degree level is so difficult linguistically. Shakespeare's English sometimes sounds like a foreign language. And then there are the outlandish, half-unpronounceable names he gives his characters, and these are often duplicated most confusingly in more than one play. By the time we have read a third or a half of the canon, we have had to remember three Antonio's, a Rosalind and a Rosaline, two Antony's (though they are based on the same historical figure), and any number of fools, lords, dukes and knights.

The unlikeliness of writing anything new, the nature of the language, the bewildering number of names to be learnt: these are problems students sometimes perceive as insurmountable. Yet there is no reason why an essay on Shakespeare should be any less (or more) original than an essay on any other author. Alexander Pope's 'True wit is Nature to advantage drest, / What oft was Thought, but ne'er so well Exprest',[1] is comforting to bear in mind; in other words, present your ideas well and remember that there is very little work, even at PhD level, which is profoundly original. You are educating yourself, not necessarily pushing forward the frontiers of knowledge on behalf of humanity. Shakespeare's language is indeed difficult, but this very difficulty makes finding things to say about it quite easy. The names of the characters will start to stick in your mind if you read the play more than once or twice. And, lastly, quoting from memory bothers students far more than it does examiners, and you should not consume valuable revision time rote-learning. Quotations can and indeed usually should be short. Anita, who gave a presentation on Cleopatra with generous references to the text, went on to write an exam answer on Cleopatra which used many of the same brief but telling quotations: 'A lass unparallel'd' (V.ii.315), 'Triple-turn'd whore' (IV.xii.13), 'false soul of Egypt' (IV.xii.25), 'tawny front' (I.i.6), and so on. Anita had not learned them consciously, but they had stuck in her mind, which in itself suggested they were worth discussing. Lastly, it is easy to overdo quotations. Your exam answer should be your work; there is nothing to be gained from packing it out with someone else's, even Shakespeare's.

Hopefully, you are confident enough not to worry about any of these issues, in which case you are probably a skilled essayist who can develop and control an argument, use apt illustrations to back it up, and write in an accurate and elegant style. If any of these skills eludes you, seek advice from the many guides to good English and essay-writing which are currently available, or ask to see your tutor about the 'mechanics' of producing an essay. What follows is not a prescriptive guide to essay-writing as such, but a consideration of various ways of writing essays about Shakespeare.

## Coursework essays

There are differences between essays that will count towards one's marks for a module or course, and those that will be marked but not formally assessed. Some tutors give students the option of writing an additional essay which will not contribute to their final grade; some will listen to you read a weekly or fortnightly essay aloud, and only volunteer feedback verbally. At the other extreme, some tutors will require you to submit a single assignment which will constitute the sole means of assessing your performance on the course or module.

If you do get the chance to write extra, non-assessed essays, take it. The more one writes, the easier writing becomes. Knowing that the essay is a practice exercise, not a vital component of one's degree, is liberating. You might want to write about something esoteric or obscure, or reconsider a topic you first encountered at school. You might want to take a daringly idiosyncratic approach, and relate Shakespeare to some aspect of contemporary society. The most breathtakingly original – and profound – student essay I have ever read related John Donne to Arnold Schwarzenegger. An essay by Adrian on *The Merchant of Venice* turned into a broader consideration of English anti-Semitism from the seventeenth century to the present day. One by Emma on *Julius Caesar* drew subtle parallels between Caesar's Rome and modern-day Westminster, an approach which had particular appeal to Emma because she was active in politics on and off campus. Another student, Annette, wrote reviews of plays for the student newspaper in a much more confident and ironic style than she used for her formal essays.

**Formally assessed essays**

This does not imply that we are best off writing pedestrian and unambitious essays when it comes to formal assessment. External examiners often lament the reluctance of candidates to write adventurously or unconventionally, particularly in exams and particularly on Shakespeare. Perhaps the stress of an examination tempts many people to revert to the way they wrote about Shakespeare at school. But in formal coursework essays too we should try to be individualistic and be willing to take intellectual risks. Susan's essay on *Othello* moved from an exploration of key passages from the text to a review of critical material relating to them, and ended up summarizing and then reflecting on a research paper she had heard at a seminar. Her essay was wide in scope, without losing sight of significant details. Above all, it was unusual, and stood out a mile in a batch of essays, most of which were concerned with analyzing Iago as if he were an actual person suffering from a form of psychosis.

Naturally, the kind of essay question or title you have to address influences your response to a considerable degree. Tutors vary in the freedom they allow you to choose a topic. Some will suggest a subject, such as festivity in the comedies. Some, especially when the work forms part of your continuous assessment, will be extremely prescriptive and require students to write on a limited number of specific questions. Here extra ingenuity is needed to make your essay stand out.

This raises a potential problem: what to do if you violently disagree with your tutor's approach to Shakespeare. Criticism on Shakespeare is livelier and excites more controversy than any other kind, and this disputatiousness extends to the classroom and lecture theatre. One tutor may adhere to traditional, 'Bradleyan' ideas about Shakespeare, while another prefers a Marxist-feminist reading of the texts or a radically deconstructive one (see Chapters 8 and 9). Although you are unlikely to be penalized for maintaining your own position, you may feel frustrated by an apparent lack of understanding on the part of your tutor. Yet it is actually exciting to have to define and defend one's position in a controversy, and if part of the job of established critics is to question the way Shakespeare is studied and understood, students are equally entitled to do so.

Make sure, for example, that you think sceptically about your title or question before you start to write. If you feel your views are being subtly moulded by the question before you even begin to try to answer it, pose some questions of the question itself in your opening paragraph. You will get some credit for independence of mind, whether or not the marker is swayed by your arguments. In other words, as well as bearing in mind the cardinal rules of essay-writing – the necessity for a clear structure, for an initial defining of key terms, and for a readable style which avoids excessive informality – and reflecting critically on the primary texts, question the critical assumptions you and the question both bring to Shakespeare. Like one's reading, essay-writing should not be mechanical. The following two extracts are samples from a batch of essays which counted for 40 per cent of the students' overall marks for the module. Typically, students took between a week and a fortnight to write their essays, though in some cases the reading had begun long before.

*Essay 1*

Haydn addressed the question, 'In what ways does Renaissance tragedy illustrate the similarities and contrasts between the medieval and modern view of the individual?' The paragraph I have quoted is from the conclusion of this long and complex essay, which looked at a wide range of texts from Genesis to the York Mystery Cycle to Goethe's *Faust* and Nietzsche's *Thus Spake Zarathustra*:

---

I am suggesting that Shakespeare anticipates our modern view of the individual but he also transcends it and refuses to be categorized. He will always, in my view, point the way forward to new understandings. A mature Shakespeare play such as *King Lear* supports Wilson Knight's argument [in *The Wheel of Fire*[2]]. Lear defies the pigeon-hole of any particular school of thought. He can be seen, I would suggest, on one level as an orthodox medieval hero, destroyed by the duplicity of his 'pelican daughters' (III.iv.74), just as Eve tempted Adam. He can be seen as a Machiavellian tyrant to be feared and ridiculed: 'Come not between the Dragon and his wrath' (I.i.121).

Alternatively, he can be seen as a Faustian transgressor desiring to 'Crack Nature's moulds' (III.ii.8), or as a victim: 'I am a man / More sinn'd against than sinning' (III.ii.59–60). Lear's failings can be seen to transcend all boundaries of time and condition. His 'fall' is undoubtedly Aristotelian, his hubris compounded by the flattery of Goneril and Regan. Regan highlights his lack of self-awareness – 'he hath ever but slenderly known himself' (I.i.292–3) – and the Fool intimates the possibility of psycho-sexual dysfunction (if we wish to impose, retrospectively, an orthodox Freudian interpretation on the text) when he proclaims that the natural relationship between father and daughter has been perverted: 'thou mad'st thy daughters thy mothers' (I.iv.168–9).

It is Lear himself, however, who best defines the immortal struggle of the tragic individual when he states, 'I am bound / Upon a wheel of fire' (IV.vii.46–7). The purgation through suffering which he experiences has Christian echoes, although the wheel itself is an arcane, secular symbol. There is a sense that man and his sufferings are like a wheel, without beginning or end, impenetrable. There is no 'pre-lapsarian' perfectibility, no Eden, no modern Utopia. Only stoicism and unconditional love offer brief moments of respite to a 'very foolish fond old man' (IV.vii.60) whose tragedy is neither medieval nor modern but simply eternal in its conception.

(Haydn, third-year English and Drama student, 1996 graduate)

---

This essay is stylish and well-informed, but it is perhaps most notable for the intensity with which it advocates the view that Shakespeare's tragic vision is distinct from both medieval and modern conceptions of tragedy. Actually, Haydn's argument was deeply orthodox, in the sense that he used his essay to express his growing conviction over the course of the semester that the cultural materialist insistence on Shakespeare's historical contingency was inadequate in equipping us to understand his plays. Haydn's essay reads like a rallying cry to the old guard of Shakespeareans, and it is no surprise therefore that he uses G. Wilson Knight to vindicate his point of view. Yet his essay is also radical in its fierce resistance to current orthodoxy, and it clearly derives its confidence from an impressive knowledge of many literary sources, old and new.

*Essay 2*

Expressing strong convictions about a text to your reader is difficult to do without sounding overly idiosyncratic. Sarah was studying a course in Feminist Drama alongside a course on Renaissance
Tragedy, and had become fascinated by Shakespeare's representations of women. She chose the question, 'Do you agree with
Catherine Belsey that women are, to all intents and purposes,
denied full human agency and identity in Renaissance tragedy?'[3]
She chose to concentrate on Desdemona:

So what good examples of womanhood are we given in the plays, and
does being the perfect Renaissance female actually get the characters
any further in life? Let us look at the character of Desdemona in
*Othello*. She is passive, gentle and romantic, yet courageous, optimistic
and innocent (unfortunately up to such an extreme point so as to drive
the reader to scream through sheer frustration). She accepts the fact
that she must be obedient to the males in her life, and has a 'divided
duty' (I.iii.181) to her father and her husband. But still this gets her
nowhere, Desdemona remains submissive to the end, and with her last
breath she denies that Othello has murdered her.

(Sarah, third-year English and Drama student, 1996 graduate)

The ideas here are interesting, and not derivative. Sarah writes in
clear, direct sentences and makes a convincing point. Her argument,
though, could have been strengthened by comparing and contrasting
Desdemona with other female victims of male violence: Cordelia,
for instance, does resist a patriarchal oppressor, which might have
reminded Sarah that Desdemona, too, defies her father. More importantly, the essay's fairly formal style was interrupted with collo-
quialisms, which slightly undermined its air of authority. As both
Sarah's and Haydn's essays illustrate, the way you present your
ideas in an essay is just as important as the ideas themselves.

**The critical commentary**

So far I have been assuming that an essay of whatever kind consists
of a broad and clearly constructed argument in response to a

question or title, but some of your written work on Shakespeare may fall into the category of 'commentary'. Courses often ask for close critical analyses of isolated passages, a task very different from putting together a neatly turned essay.

In a sense commentaries are easier than conventional essays because you have the words in front of you, and the extract to write about is probably quite short. But it is more difficult to make commentaries coherent, largely because there is a temptation to plod doggedly through the text line by line, ignoring the need for a concise overview in your introduction and conclusion. And it can sometimes seem impossible to say very much about the text, so that your commentary strays into analysis of the play as a whole, or entertains improbable flights of fancy about the significance of this or that word. One method of slowing yourself down is to think about each word, and then each phrase, separately, and try to decide why Shakespeare used that particular word or words and not a synonym. Much of the best published criticism contains a large proportion of such minute observations. Writing on *Othello*, the enormously influential American scholar Stephen Greenblatt notes the contrast between Othello's view of sexual love as 'a supreme form of romantic narrative', and Desdemona's 'vision of unabating increase' implicit in her misleadingly simple reply: 'The heavens forbid / But that our loves and comforts should increase, / Even as our days do grow' (II.i.193–5).[4] This is a good example of how the most straightforward and inconsequential-sounding lines can yield surprising fruit if we take the time to think about them.

Here is a portion of a student's commentary on *Troilus and Cressida* (I.i.1–63). It suggests that this seemingly rather restrictive component of your Shakespeare studies actually requires you to be tenacious and imaginative:

---

G. L. Brook (1976)[5] describes the figure of 'anaphora' as the repetition of a phrase or word at the beginning of successive sentences. The paradoxical intimacy between Troilus and Pandarus, which coexists with their stylistic and philosophical antagonisms, is illustrated by the elaborate anaphora in their extended treatment of the wheat metaphor in lines 17 to 20:

*Troil.* Have I not tarried?
*Pand.* Ay, the grinding; but you must tarry the bolting.

*Troil.* Have I not tarried?
*Pand.* Ay, the boulting; but you must tarry the leav'ing.

(Pandarus' elision of the last two syllables of 'leavening' puns on 'leaving', and is thus a witty allusion to Troilus' refusal to go to war.) Troilus' rhetoric is highlighted by the homely, simple language of his friend, whose imagery of loaves and wheat is both a direct reference to the bucolic and an indication of his relish for the proverbial, a characteristic of uneducated or lower-class characters in Shakespeare, though of course it is not exclusive to them. Pandarus also uses a multiple negative ('Ill not meddle nor make no farther' (ll.13–14); idiomatic constructions ('heeres yet in the word hereafter', presumably meaning approximately 'but there is also'); 'well go too' (a pause filler which is not necessary for the sentence's meaning); 'as they tearme it' (a pedantic aside), for example, and his sentences are long and digressive. Cumulatively these speech habits suggest his relatively low social status.

(Anne, third-year English student, 1995 graduate)

---

Such analysis is the product of a long-established familiarity with Shakespearean dialogue, a wide reading in critical and linguistic material on Shakespeare's English, and an ability to apply this knowledge to a specific passage. The student conveys the fact that she has subjected the passage to the closest scrutiny, and that she is able to combine a thorough investigation of it, line by line, with an overview of Shakespeare's language. Much of what she says about this passage from *Troilus and Cressida* could have been adapted to any extract from Shakespeare's plays.

The student also uses certain techniques characteristic of good essay practice. By referring to an established authority (Brook) she indicates that she has done the requisite reading for the course. When she compares the passage to Brook's definition of the rhetorical device of anaphora she demonstrates an ability to argue from the general to the particular. This is normally a much more convincing strategy than arguing from the particular to the general; it would not have done to try define the anaphora exclusively in terms of this example from *Troilus and Cressida*. Perhaps most striking is the student's willingness to think about the possible meaning of each word and phrase in the passage; she tries to tease out ambiguities rather than gliding over them. Writing a commentary need not be a pedestrian exercise, then, but a chance to display one's learning on one's sleeve. It is also an important skill to acquire. Persuasive and informed close readings are just as vital in discursive essays as they are in commentaries on isolated passages.

## Writing dissertations

Writing a dissertation, whether required or optional, is obviously more demanding than writing a short coursework essay. With all dissertations it is advisable to discuss your progress regularly with your tutor, and also worth consulting one or two general guides on writing dissertations and theses before you start your research. In most respects, certainly, writing a dissertation on Shakespeare is no different from writing one on T. S. Eliot or Norman architecture. In all cases you need to keep the closest possible control of your argument, and organize your text (and your time) properly. One or two issues, however, are peculiar to Shakespeare: the wealth of secondary material facing anyone who wants to write an authoritative dissertation on him, and the breadth of choice within Shakespeare's own canon. Where to start?

Your first task is to compile a bibliography. Decide which primary texts you want to use most extensively, and those to which you are likely to make only passing references. You might wish to include one or two primary texts by contemporary authors, Christopher Marlowe's *The Jew of Malta*, for example, or Francis Bacon's *Essays*. Obtain your own reliable, well-edited copies of these primary works: when it comes to a dissertation it is no good using cut-price editions which lack any annotations or other scholarly apparatus, and which may be abridged or even sanitized.

Now consult any relevant course reading lists and the library catalogue to help you produce a selective bibliography of secondary material – critical books, histories, biographies. Look through the online catalogue using key words as well as authors' names and subject-headings. If your institution's library is small, use the Internet to search the catalogues of neighbouring academic libraries. Access to the Internet is usually via a username and password, both of which you type in to a suitable terminal. You should then be offered a menu which includes access to JANET, the Joint

Academic Network, which in turn enables you to consult the catalogues of more than 85 college and university libraries.

If, for example, you spend vacations near a well-stocked university library, you can make lists of books you plan to track down, having located them through the Internet. Otherwise you can simply arrange to visit the library in term-time. Many larger academic libraries offer reading rights, and even borrowing privileges, to readers from smaller, sister institutions. As a last resort, your head of department might agree to write a letter of recommendation, asking that you be granted special rights at a nearby academic library, though this is sometimes refused, especially, as in London, where the pressure from library-users is great. Don't forget, though, that most college and universities belong to a reciprocal scheme which entitles all undergraduates to use their local university library (for reference, not borrowing) as well as the one nearest to their term-time address.

Aside from library catalogues, you can also consult the Modern Language Association (MLA) Bibliography on CD-ROM. This is annually updated, and consists of a comprehensive database of material related to literature and language study. The MLA Bibliography is also available in a hard copy, but the advantage of the CD-ROM format is that it enables you to search rapidly under all kinds of headings. A tutorial package introduces you to the few, simple techniques for accessing the database. Once you have identified a list of publications relevant to your research, you can print out a list. Here is a typical example of an entry on *King Lear* from a CD-ROM database:

---

TITLE: New Comedy in *King Lear*
AUTHOR: Miola, Robert S.
SOURCE: *Philological Quarterly* 73:3 (1994), 329 ±46
INDEX TERMS: English literature; 1600 ±1699; Shakespeare, William; *King Lear*; relationship to comedy ±

---

Note that this gives a brief indication of the article's contents, as well as where to find it.

In addition to the MLA Bibliography, you can search for material in the various Abstracts and Indices held by your library. They cover almost all published material in a given year, in book, periodical or other form. A useful one for Renaissance literature is included annually in the winter number of the periodical *Studies in English Literature 1500–1900*. This is a more effective way of finding material than simply scanning through back copies of journals and along the library shelves, though serendipity often does turn up interesting material that you might otherwise overlook.

In researching Shakespeare, who is continually revived in the theatre, you may also need or want to read reviews of past and current productions. The best way to find these is to scan the CD-ROMs for the broadsheet newspapers (e.g. the *Guardian* and *The Times*), again available in the library. It is easy to locate such reviews through keywords, and then to print out a hard copy to take away with you. (The cost of this is normally around the same as the price of photocopying.)

As well as theatre, film and television reviews, look in the mainstream press for material relating to Shakespeare more generally. Most major biographies and critical works on Shakespeare are reviewed in the Sunday and weekday papers, and there has been much media controversy recently about his prominence in the National Curriculum.

As soon as you have compiled a bibliography (preferably on computer, as described earlier in this chapter), start tracking down the books, articles and reviews you have identified. It can take time and tenacity to get hold of everything you want, though if you order a book, or article, or chapter on Inter-Library Loan, you will only have to wait a couple of weeks.

The amount you have to find and read will seem overwhelming at first, but gradually you will become quicker at assimilating and evaluating material on your topic. You do not have to read scores and scores of books: it is important to be discriminating as well as conscientious. On the other hand, if your dissertation is supposed to take you two semesters or three terms, you have scope for some thorough research. Your tutor may be willing to lend copies of obscure papers, or books that are out of print, particularly if they are on a course reading list and in heavy demand in the library. Students ahead of you on the course may be able to help too.

Remember, though, that a dissertation, at least at undergraduate level, is not supposed to be what researchers call a 'literature review', i.e. a summary of everything written on a topic. Your own ideas are more important for your degree result than anything you recite from a published source.

It can be difficult to resist the temptation to read just a little more material before you get down to writing. For this reason it is advisable to draw up a proposed timetable in which you set yourself deadlines for the various stages of the project. Here is an example of a timetable for a dissertation which ran the full course of the academic year from October to May. The official dates by which students had to have completed certain tasks are marked with an asterisk*; the deadlines at your own institution will obviously be different, but are likely to be comparable:

---

*Project title: The nature of the masque in Shakespearean comedy*
*Schedule of work*

*Summer vacation*
Identify and read primary texts: *As You Like It, A Midsummer Night's Dream, The Tempest.* Also Jonson's *Masque of Blackness* and Daniel's *Vision of the Twelve Goddesses.*

*October*
Preliminary meeting with supervisor by October 31*. Re-read primary texts. Compile bibliography of secondary material.

*November–January*
Read secondary material. Write compulsory progress report for supervisor and meet before January 31 to discuss it*.

*February*
Refine progress report into a proposal. Write introduction and first section of dissertation.

*March*
Write second and third sections of dissertation. Meet with supervisor.

*April*
Write conclusion. Check departmental format requirements, e.g. presentation of bibliography. Revise the draft MS. Type or print out, and double-check the final draft. Attach signed plagiarism disclaimer.

*April 23**
Departmental deadline for submission.

*May 16****
College/university deadline for submission of all under-graduate dissertations.

---

The nature of this project made the writing of a proposal or outline in February relatively straightforward. The student was able to keep closely to the original conception of a tripartite dissertation, though she slightly modified her title. Here is the proposal itself:

---

*The masque in three Shakespearean comedies*
*Proposal*

*Introduction*
A definition of the masque will be offered, and an account given of its role in seventeenth-century plays for the public theatre, notably Jacobean tragedies. Previous critical analyses of the masque-within-the-play (Cornelia 1978;[6] Sutherland 1983[7]) will be noted, and the need for a corresponding investigation into the function of masques in comedies will be identified.

*Section One*
*A Midsummer Night's Dream*: masque as Rabelaisian carnivalesque.

*Section Two*
*As You Like It*: masque as ritual.

*Section Three*
*The Tempest*: masque as expression of power.

*Conclusion*
The conclusion will summarize the radical differences between the masques in the three texts; this will be related to the analogous differences between masques proper, such as Daniel's highly orthodox *Vision of the Twelve Goddesses* and Jonson's subtly subversive *Masque of Blackness*.

---

Open- or student-centred learning, where the onus is very much on the individual to identify, plan and execute a research project, is potentially very exciting. It can also be isolating, particularly if contact with tutors and other students is infrequent and one is used to working collaboratively in a supportive study group. Most students, though, adjust to the new conditions, and find they can work more rapidly than when their studying is broken up by lectures and tutorials. And a dissertation allows you to 'own' part of Shakespeare; after all, you have as much right to him as anyone else does.

## Exams

If you have completed all your coursework assignments, given the last of your class presentations and handed in your dissertation, all you have to worry about is the exam! As with any literature exam, respond to the question asked, not to a particular keyword which happens to have attracted your eye. Discuss the question critically with yourself, as described in the earlier chapter, 'Discussing Shakespeare', and do not feel that you have to accept the authority of statements made on the exam paper. Once you have decided on your response, write a brief (not detailed) essay plan, and refer back to it frequently when you start to write the essay itself. Aim to spend all but a few minutes writing, with just a minute or two left over for final checking. The more words you have produced, the more the examiner will have to go on. If you feel you let yourself down in exams, practise writing timed essays during the revision period. With Shakespeare such practice is especially valuable, since you will have so much material to organize and remember.

On the whole, then, there is little difference between writing on Shakespeare and any other author in an exam. One piece of advice is worth repeating, though: don't spend a disproportionate amount of revision time on learning quotations by heart. Read the plays instead.

## Notes

1. Alexander Pope, 'An Essay on Criticism', II.297–8.
2. G. Wilson Knight, *The Wheel of Fire* (1930; repr. Oxford: Oxford University Press, 1977).
3. Catherine Belsey, *The Subject of Tragedy: Identity and difference in Renaissance drama* (London: Methuen, 1985).
4. Stephen Greenblatt, *Renaissance Self-Fashioning: From More to Shakespeare* (Chicago: University of Chicago Press, 1980), p. 243.
5. G. L. Brook, *The Language of Shakespeare* (London: André Deutsch, 1976), p. 24.
6. Marie Cornelia, *The Function of the Masque in Jacobean Tragedy and Tragi-Comedy* (Universität Salzburg: Institut für Englische Sprache und Literatur, 1978).
7. Sarah P. Sutherland, *Masques in Jacobean Tragedy* (New York: AMS Press, 1983).

**PART II**

*Studying Shakespeare in depth*

# CHAPTER 4

# Shakespeare's language

## Introduction

Studying Shakespeare in depth and detail requires us, above all, to study his language. The phrase 'Shakespeare's language' brings to mind the class at secondary school who agreed that Shakespeare was okay, but wanted to know why he hadn't written in English. There are many excellent and useful books on early modern English, and Shakespearean English in particular, which, even as they seek to remedy it, bear out this sense of foreignness we sometimes experience in reading and watching plays which were, after all, written four centuries ago. None the less, with the help of such guides we can painstakingly acquire a theoretical knowledge of late sixteenth- and early seventeenth-century lexis (vocabulary), syntax (word-order), orthography (spelling) and punctuation, and try to let such knowledge inform our reading of his plays as literary works.

'Learning' Shakespeare's language is, of course, easier than learning, say, French or Russian; not only are there many similarities between early modern and modern English, but Shakespeare himself has had a profound influence on the way that English speakers use the language, and many of his lines are so familiar to us that we are almost surprised when we come across them in their original source. 'Neither a borrower nor a lender be' (*Hamlet* I.iii.75); 'Love looks not with the eyes, but with the mind' (*Midsummer Night's Dream* I.i.234); 'All the world's a stage, / And all the men and women merely players' (*As You Like It* II.vii.139–40):

the list is endless, and such examples seem more like catchphrases than learned quotations.

Even so, a page from one of the plays can appear remarkably user-unfriendly. The dialogue can switch unpredictably from verse to prose. In modern texts the annotations are frequently longer than the play itself. Most scholarly editions bristle with abbreviations, requiring the reader mentally to insert the full names of the characters as well as those of any critics cited in the gnomic footnotes. Later in this chapter I will be discussing ways of maximizing the benefits of reading Shakespeare in scholarly editions, using a new Arden text as my example, but even if we have fully understood the significance of the scholarly and textual apparatus surrounding the play, it will not help us perform the imaginative leap needed to transform lines of unfamiliar dialogue into mental sounds and pictures: in fact, it may impede the process. And in certain respects the text may seem skeletal in the information it provides, even when it is reasonably clear. The famously laconic stage direction '*Exit, pursued by a bear*' (*Winter's Tale* III.iii.58) gives little help to a reader who has not seen the play performed and is struggling to visualize how such a moment might be represented in the theatre.

There are two possible and complementary solutions to these problems. The first is to practise Shakespeare as you would practise French, reading and re-reading the plays, preferably aloud (which helps one develop an ear for the characteristic ways in which Shakespeare uses the iambic pentameter and other metrical forms). The second is to see the plays performed, either in the theatre, on video, or in a workshop. As was argued in Chapter 6, certain aspects of a play will probably never become apparent if you have been restricted to reading it only. The rapidity of the exchanges between Benedick and Beatrice in *Much Ado About Nothing* is one example which comes to mind; the box tree scene (II.v) in *Twelfth Night* is another, where comedy largely depends on performance.

Such dramatic effects can be reconstructed if the reader works hard enough, but seeing the plays acted is sometimes vital for a proper understanding of them. Northumberland's incitement of Bolingbroke in *Richard II*; Solanio and Salerio's waspishness in *The Merchant of Venice*; Lepidus' vacuousness in *Antony and Cleopatra*: the significance of the minor characters in particular can be obscured unless we see the plays performed.

Nevertheless, I am going to challenge current orthodoxy by suggesting that reading the play is as vital as seeing it performed, at least when it comes to understanding the significance of individual lines and words. After all, actors will always 'read through' before they start to rehearse a play. Reading allows one time to focus on a phrase and contemplate its multifarious possibilities. Even if we are superlatively responsive members of an audience, we do not always have access to brilliantly illuminating productions of Shakespeare. Some performances undoubtedly do reveal new dimensions of a text, but many – perhaps most – do not. Few actors are able to render Shakespearean dialogue with total clarity while doing justice to its full range of meanings. As the famous Shakespearean actor Peggy Ashcroft put it:

> I think actors feel that the great test in playing Shakespeare is that you have to stretch yourself to the limits – that he requires a kind of athleticism, mental and physical. You have to have tremendous control, physically, to carry through the speeches vocally; and you have to have an athleticism of mind, in that you must think the thoughts very quickly. Take five or six lines of Shakespeare; that thought, with all its complications, has to come out as an *immediate* thought. And I think you should use the pause – which actors are very fond of – very sparingly, because otherwise you lose that other thing which you must always bear in mind: the shape – the wonderful shape, of the verse.[1]

This is a counsel of perfection, and it helps to explain why we need to read Shakespeare attentively for ourselves, and not rely on actors to do so for us. Moreover, a production must inevitably choose between interpretations of a play, whereas a reader's interpretation can be fluid and provisional.

Before I embark on my own detailed analyses of Shakespeare's language it may be worth offering a brief defence of the practice of close reading, since many commentators have asserted that literary critics are prone to absurdly ingenious interpretations, and describe effects which could never be conveyed to an audience. This ignores the fact that, just as we can never prove an interpretation beyond doubt, so we can never prove that one is invalid. It also overlooks the impossibility of knowing what an audience thinks and feels when a play is performed. Who can determine how much we absorb intuitively and unconsciously when we see a play? We know that Julius Caesar is pompous and egocentric even if we are unable to pinpoint the source of our hunch in his tendency to speak in the third person. And it seems likely that Shakespeare's original audiences would have picked up far more than we do from an initial viewing. In any case, the unlikelihood of a nuance being comprehended when a speech is delivered aloud does not mean that the dramatist did not intend his or her words to include that nuance. Lastly and most importantly, a nuance may be present whether or not it was consciously intended.

This chapter is predicated on the belief that even the subtlest reading of Shakespeare is unable to comprehend every aspect of his meaning; it also assumes that the best way to study Shakespeare's language is to focus on specific words, lines, sentences and speeches. In the following sections I shall, therefore, follow the practice adopted elsewhere in this book, and offer one, two or at most three 'worked examples' of close readings for each of the important elements of Shakespeare's linguistic practice. Many studies of his language quite properly aim to be comprehensive, following their detailed accounts of such matters as semantic change and archaic syntax with numerous and varied illustrations. Whilst I will use some of the subheadings common to such studies, my discussion will necessarily be more limited than theirs, and aims to be suggestive rather than exhaustive. The examples given below should be regarded as rough guides rather than as restrictive or prescriptive models; hopefully, you will be able to extrapolate from them in developing your own readings of Shakespeare's language.

**Lexis:** *Henry IV Part 1* I.ii.2–12

Shakespeare's lexical variety – the size of his vocabulary – is astonishing. Concordances and statistical breakdowns of the kind made possible by computer technology bear out this claim, but they cannot really explain the sense of being overwhelmed by language which we experience in reading or seeing a Shakespeare play. Developmental linguists talk of the 'rich soup of language' which is offered to the child by its parents, and the phrase seems equally appropriate to the study of Shakespeare. Shakespearean language is like one of those Italian soups, stiff with pasta, meat, beans, herbs and unidentifiable vegetables. Speaking Shakespeare is the closest one can come to eating, short of food itself. Here is Hal, crunching on words as he hurls affectionate abuse at Falstaff:

> Thou art so fat-witted with drinking of old sack, and unbuttoning thee after supper, and sleeping upon benches after noon, that thou hast forgotten to demand that truly which thou wouldst truly know. What a devil hast thou to do with the time of day? Unless hours were cups of sack, and minutes capons, and clocks the tongues of bawds, and dials the signs of leaping-houses, and the blessed sun himself a fair hot wench in flame-coloured taffeta, I see no reason why thou shouldst be so superfluous to demand the time of day.
>
> (*Henry IV, Part I* I.ii.2–12)

The facility of this speech is arresting. Interestingly, its vocabulary is relatively simple, with few words of more than two syllables and only one of more than three. But its syntactical control is perfect, transforming a crude attack into sophisticated rhetoric. '[A]nd . . . and . . . and . . . and . . . I see no reason': the final sentence mounts to an indignant climax. And the vocabulary, for all its simplicity, is typically Shakespearean in its virtuoso blending of the familiar and the inventive. In sketching Falstaff's decadent lifestyle Hal offers, among other things, a list evocative of tavern and brothel ('drinking', 'old sack', 'cups of sack', 'capons', 'bawds', 'leaping-houses'). Yet as well as drawing on the direct power of these ordinary words (even today we catch the drift of 'leaping', with its farmyard connotations), he coins a compound of his own, 'fat-witted', and thereby makes two ordinary words unfamiliar and intriguing. Falstaff is 'fat-witted' not only because he indulges to the point of stupefaction – though his appetite certainly has made him literally fat – but because he is mentally torpid as well. It is a devastating criticism, but it bears a secondary meaning which almost contradicts the first, that Falstaff's wit, or sense of humour, actually prospers from his idle, feckless way of life. '[F]at-witted' is close to the idea of a 'pregnant [fertile, productive] wit', and Falstaff is, of course, full of cheer and good humour, embodying the popular association of fatness with happiness.

Hal's insult catches the reader's eye and strikes the audience's ear: an actor would have to pronounce it with gusto. The student of literature, straining for the nuances of every line, needs to pause, consider and try to determine why an expression such as 'fat-

witted' is itself so pregnant of meaning. Even less obviously significant words and phrases can be subjected to similarly tenacious
analysis. Re-reading the first sentence of Hal's speech we realize
that he offers three pictures of Falstaff, taken at intervals over the
course of an evening. Falstaff drinks, then unbuttons, then passes
out on the tavern bench. On other occasions, judging by Hal's
concluding sentence, drink 'sets him on' (*Macbeth* II.iii.32), and he
moves from tavern to brothel. Hal's outrage finally inspires him to
draw a comparison between Falstaff's flamboyantly dressed companion and the sun. Compressed in this image are many of the
geocentric ironies of John Donne's defiant poem 'The Sunne
Rising' (pub. 1633), which likewise contrasts the order and preci-
sion of the sun with the disruptive pleasures of sex and love.

Such comparisons with other texts from the period can be helpful,
but should not distract us from the specific effects of the passage in
front of us which, for all its appeal to a universal worldliness (everyone, Hal supposes, knows men who are lazy, greedy and sensual), is
highly individual. The conjunction of 'fair' and 'hot', for instance, is
far from clichéd, and Hal's reference to the capon as a symbol
of Falstaff's relish for good food is especially apt given that the
capon is fattened for human consumption and therefore rather like
Falstaff himself.

At the end of Hal's bluntly monosyllabic catalogue of fleshly
pleasures comes a word which places a haughty distance between
accuser and accused: 'superfluous'. Unlike the words preceding it
this one is Latinate, recondite and deliberately disconcerting.
Though it refers primarily to Falstaff's inconsistency (or disingenuousness) in suddenly enquiring the time of day, it also insinu-
ates that Falstaff is himself superfluous in Hal's opinion.

Studies of Shakespeare's lexical range are typically organized
into sections on words which are archaic (no longer in use), words
which entered the language at around the time Shakespeare was
writing (loanwords and coinages), and words which, though still
current, have altered their meanings since the early seventeenth
century. Identifying words from these categories in a given passage
might seem to require a vast knowledge, but Hal's speech suggests
that this is not the case. Archaic words are perhaps the easiest to
spot: we no longer drink 'sack' or describe brothels as 'leaping-
houses'. As regards loanwords we might make a shrewd guess that
'superfluous' was a relatively new word in the late sixteenth

century simply because Hal places it so conspicuously at the end of his outburst. And reference to the *Oxford English Dictionary* confirms that 'superfluous' entered English no earlier than the mid-fifteenth century, while it was apparently used in the transferred sense, of a person, only rarely; indeed, this very occurrence in *Henry IV Part 1* is the earliest example cited by the *Oxford English Dictionary*.

Words which have changed their meanings since Shakespeare's period are only difficult to recognize when they allow an alternative reading which would not have been understood by his contemporaries. Randolph Quirk gives an excellent example in his essay 'Shakespeare and the English Language', in which he makes the ironic point that we admire Shakespeare in part because we misunderstand him:

> When Iago pretends to relieve Othello's feelings with the assurance that Cassio had spoken his passionate words to Desdemona only in his sleep, Othello says 'But this denoted a foregone conclusion' (III.iii.432) and however carefully we have studied Elizabethan English, it is very hard for us to remember in the theatre that this does not mean what we have since taken the phrase *foregone conclusion* to mean. . . . The extent to which we love Shakespeare . . . for the familiar but exalted language is a measure of our inability to respond to Shakespeare as his contemporaries did.[2]

(As the Arden editor, M. R. Ridley, confirms, Shakespeare's use of 'foregone' is more 'logical' than ours: Othello means that Cassio and Desdemona's adultery must have happened already.)

One (admittedly only partly satisfactory) method for identifying and dealing with semantic change is to examine a word which seems somewhat obscure and try to deduce from its context what its original meaning must have been. 'Hot', for example, is no longer used to describe lust, though we can guess that that is what Hal means from the overall theme of his speech (it also helps to recall the modern phrase 'to have the hots for someone'). 'Flame[-coloured]' we might guess to be a rather different kind of word, one which was perhaps as poetic in Shakespeare's day as it seems to us. Consulting the New Arden editor's notes supports this hunch: all the parallel examples given suggest that Elizabethan prostitutes were commonly associated with gaudy, crimson clothes, but that the particular words Hal uses are unique to Shakespeare (the effectiveness of 'flame' rests, of course, on its echo of 'hot'). As this analysis shows, producing insights into Shakespeare's choice of a word or words is much more about the application of certain principles than it is about deploying an encyclopaedic knowledge of early modern English. Attentiveness to the sheer variety of words Shakespeare uses is perhaps the most essential quality of the good reader, and attainable by all of us. On its own, of course, such attentiveness may encourage a rather impressionistic response to the text, which is why it needs to be accompanied by an awareness of semantic change. A reading of Hal's speech which took 'sack' to mean a hessian bag might be 'valid' in strictly philosophical terms, but it would not take us very far in reconstructing how Shakespeare's contemporaries would have interpreted the line, or in understanding the power his language contains for us today.

**Syntax:** *The Tempest* I.ii.152–8; *Twelfth Night* I.v.272–80; *King Lear* II.iv.262–8

Syntax, or word-order, is arguably the most challenging aspect of Shakespeare's language. This is because we are often no more conscious of a syntactical effect than we are of the structure underpinning a tall building. Whereas words themselves are tangible, syntax is concealed beneath the surface of a sentence, and generally speaking we only notice it when it is difficult or confusing. A complex sentence which none the less conforms to the word-order characteristic of modern English (subject, verb, object) will seem readily intelligible. 'I have no spur / To prick the sides of my intent', declares Macbeth (I.vii.25–6), and despite the metaphor we immediately understand that the sentence is about dilatoriness and lack. But when Macbeth tells Banquo 'So foul and fair a day I have not seen' (I.iii.38), which is altogether less subtle and abstract, his words have a distinctly old-fashioned note and we hesitate before we take in his meaning. A mental translation into modern syntax would probably run along the lines of 'I have never seen a day of such extremes', which would, of course, sacrifice the tone of surprise conveyed by Shakespeare's syntactical inversion.

Like his lexis, Shakespeare's syntax is discussed at length by most books on his language. Yet a theoretical grasp of its characteristic features can only help us to approach particular lines taxonomically, allowing us to describe, not analyze them. Conversely, insights into particular lines can be reached without an extensive technical knowledge of Shakespeare's syntax, as the following examples illustrate.

At the beginning of *The Tempest* Prospero explains to Miranda (and thus the audience) the reason for their island existence in a series of speeches which contrive to be remarkably animated despite their expository function. Some of the animation is directly attributable to the unusual syntax Prospero deploys in telling his story, which is thereby transformed from pedestrian narrative into poetry:

> O, a cherubin
> Thou wast that did preserve me. Thou didst smile,
> Infused with a fortitude from heaven,
> When I have deck'd the sea with drops full salt,
> Under my burthen groan'd; which rais'd in me
> An undergoing stomach, to bear up
> Against what should ensue.
>
> (I.ii.152–8)

Of course, some of the speech's power lies in Prospero's diction: he uses the informal 'thou', for example, which suggests both his authority over and his affection for Miranda. And a daring metaphor is contained in line 155, in which his tears not only decorated ('deck'd') the sea, but seemed to fall from him as he stood weeping *on deck*, in the midst of the storm. Yet the emotion which the speech conveys is mainly attributable to its syntax. In the first sentence Prospero's inversion of conventional word-order throws his emphasis onto the word 'cherubin', which strikes the keynote of the speech and suggests a whole train of ideas, many of which will be developed in succeeding lines and, indeed, in the rest of the play: Miranda as symbol of innocence and grace; Miranda as object of admiration; and the redemptive, baptismal effects of love and suffering.

Emphasis is also placed, appropriately, on 'preserve', both by its position at the end of the sentence and Prospero's use of the auxiliary 'did', which helps to highlight the contrast between the beatific image of the infant and the grief of the father. The idea of preservation is reiterated and developed in the long second sentence, in which images of anguish and endurance are juxtaposed in successive subordinate clauses. Miranda is passive ('infused'), a repository of faith, whereas Prospero is active both in expressing his sorrow and in deriving inspiration from the child 'to bear up / Against what should ensue'. What close attention to the verbs in the speech reveals is that Prospero survived his ordeal by learning the passivity instinctive to the child: at first he wept and 'groan'd'; finally, he learned merely to 'bear up', an altogether less active response to his circumstances.

What is most striking about the passage in terms of syntax is its willingness to switch between tenses (which makes it more immediate, and also suggests that the episode continues to influence Prospero's attitude to his daughter) and its elliptical, almost parenthetical 'Under my burden groan'd'. The inclusion of this amplificatory clause is highly naturalistic, conveying Prospero's eagerness to impress Miranda with the depth of his despair and also his confused recollection of a profoundly stressful experience. It is as though recalling his pain delays him from reaching the end of his sentence where he will return to the idea of Miranda as his saviour.

As all this suggests, understanding Shakespeare is frequently dependent on the reader's ability, not so much to dissect his syntax and identify the parts of speech which make up each sentence, as to tolerate a degree of illogicality. To take a famous example: Othello, addressing the Duke and Senators, seconds Desdemona's plea that she be allowed to go with him to the wars:

> I therefore beg it not
> To please the palate of my appetite;
> Nor to comply with heat – the young affects
> In me defunt – and proper satisfaction;
> But to be free and bounteous to her mind.
> (I.iii.259–63)

The unconventional grammar of lines 261–2 renders paraphrase very difficult and, since the supposed crux is not resolved by comparing variant editions of the text, has prompted many editors to emend the lines. Yet Othello's meaning is plain: he wants Desdemona with him for the purest of motives, being past the first flush of youth with its appetite for sexual 'satisfaction'. His syntax is disjointed and awkward, to be sure, but then he might be expected to feel pressured and uncomfortable about speaking on so personal a matter in public.

Othello's speech suggests that syntax, and syntactical disruption, can convey meaning in itself. Another example of syntax as the vehicle of meaning occurs in *Twelfth Night*, where the lovelorn and disguised Viola explains how she would behave if she were in love with Olivia:

> Make me a willow cabin at your gate,
> And call upon my soul within the house;
> Write loyal cantons of contemned love,
> And sing them loud even in the dead of night;
> Halloo your name to the reverberate hills,
> And make the babbling gossip of the air
> Cry out 'Olivia!' O, you should not rest
> Between the elements of air and earth,
> But you should pity me.
>
> (*Twelfth Night* I.v.272–80)

This speech is a coded expression of personal agony: the ideal lover Viola describes is Orsino, the very man with whom she is herself secretly in love. It is a speech about rejection, loneliness and self-abnegation, and it does what it describes: it communicates feeling in a way which is unignorable. 'You might do much,' Olivia comments drily.

There is nothing to perplex in Viola's speech, but its syntax is unusual. She omits both subject and subjunctive from her opening sentence, which therefore begins as if in mid-thought: 'Make me a willow cabin at your gate'. The incompleteness of the sentence suggests that she is speaking her innermost thoughts; it also suggests impetuousness, as though Olivia's question has allowed her to articulate a feeling which she was longing to voice. The rest of the speech confirms this impression: Viola produces three different ways in which she would communicate her love, and they trip off her tongue as though rehearsed.

Her speech is also helpful for an understanding of two related features of Shakespeare's syntax, cruxes and ellipsis. When we look closely at it, we can see that Viola's last sentence admits two readings simultaneously. According to the first she claims that Olivia would have no rest unless ('But') she were able to pity her anguished lover. This is close to a threat, and emphasizes both the force of Viola's feelings and the strength of character which makes her so attractive to others. The lines amount to a self-fulfilling prophecy; they virtually make Olivia fall in love with Orsino's passionate representative – as indeed she does. Yet according to the second reading Olivia's capitulation has already happened: she would have no rest from the torments of being in love; none the less ('But') she would find it in her to pity Viola's suffering too. The two readings are, however, not so much alternatives as complementary, and it is this ability of Shakespeare's syntax to suggest mutually compatible meanings which is one of its most distinctive characteristics; it also has parallels, as we shall see later, with the way he uses devices such as metaphor and imagery.

In Viola's speech the word 'But' constitutes a crux or ambiguity in the sense that it can be glossed in two ways, but syntax can also produce ambiguity by being elliptical, that is, by omitting words which are supposedly required for a sentence to make grammatical sense. As with Prospero's speech to Miranda, Viola's speech condenses meaning to the point at which, paradoxically, meaning becomes dual. By missing out the initial subjunctive 'I would', 'Make me a willow cabin at your gate' sounds like an injunction as well as a statement of hypothetical intent. Although we soon realize that Viola is not, in fact, issuing an order, something in the urgency of her subsequent lines bears out our initial instinct that this is a speech of self-revelation as well as exhortation.

One of Shakespeare's most elliptical speakers is Lear, whose solipsism produces a style so direct and personal that many logical connections are assumed rather than stated in his speeches. It is one consequence of Lear's egotism that he never feels the need to explain himself; he simply takes for granted that those around him will share exactly his perceptions, even when this is manifestly not the case. When Regan asks him why he cannot do without a retinue, his response is characteristically terse:

> O! reason not the need; our basest beggars
> Are in the poorest thing superfluous:
> Allow not nature more than nature needs,

Man's life is cheap as beast's. Thou art a lady;
If only to go warm were gorgeous,
Why, nature needs not what thou gorgeous wear'st,
Which scarcely keeps thee warm.

(II.iv.262–8)

We understand Lear instantly – clothes are not merely about keeping us warm, but also about social status – but the lines are very resistant to paraphrase. Lear expects Regan to fill in the gaps of his argument and recognize the parallel between her desire for costly but impractical clothes and Lear's need for retainers, which stems not from their practical but their symbolic value. The most elliptical line in the passage is the satirical 'If only to go warm were gorgeous', which contains the implication both that clothes are about vanity, however much we try to rationalize our feelings about them, and that Regan denies this fact, even as her own appearance bears it out. Lear is voicing aloud what he imagines Regan must be wishing inwardly: that all the conventions by which social distinctions are maintained could be abandoned – which is, of course, precisely what Regan would like, provided she does not have to relinquish her own tokens of wealth and power. Lear's speech mercilessly exposes the disingenuousness of Regan's question, but it also effectively disrobes her. Though she is clad in gorgeous apparel, we suddenly see her shivering from cold like any other mortal too vain to sacrifice appearance for comfort.

Lear's speech could be read, as I have suggested, both as an attack on the vanity of the court, and, conversely, as an indirect plea to maintain the appearances on which its authority depends. The duality stems from the elliptical nature of its syntax and, like the other syntactical features I have discussed, it suggests that ambiguity in Shakespeare is more likely to generate meaning than to obscure it.

**Rhetoric:** *Richard II* II.i.40–4; III.iii.147–53

In classical times the term 'rhetoric' referred to the stylistic embellishments thought essential to oratory or the art of persuasion, but the Elizabethans broadened 'persuasion' to include all literary writing. As a result rhetoric became less functional and more concerned with aesthetics. At the same time early modern writers, Shakespeare included, were profoundly influenced by the prescriptive accounts of rhetorical writing bequeathed to them by the Greeks and Romans – Aristotle, Cicero and Quintilian in particular. At grammar schools, such as the one Shakespeare attended in Stratford, pupils were not only taught the classics through the study of language and literary texts (particularly those of Virgil and Horace); they were also taught how to use rhetorical tropes and figures – stylistic devices – in their own prose and verse compositions.

Nowadays critics stress the rhetoric or artifice of literary texts in terms of more than just these tropes and figures, suggesting that rhetoric is involved in all the many ways an author seeks to interpret or to construct 'reality'. None the less, modern scholarship has revealed the extent to which such devices permeated sixteenth- and seventeenth-century writing, and there are a number of excellent introductions to the subject which explain and illustrate all the important rhetorical tools, from tropes such as allegory, metaphor, metonymy, hyperbole, litotes and synecdoche (all of which appear in standard glossaries of literary terms), to figures such as anaphora (repetition), antithesis (balancing of clauses), ploce (emphasis), and so on. Because of its importance, I will deal with metaphor under a separate heading below. There is no space here to list all the other rhetorical figures which Shakespeare used – several hundred have been identified in his work – but I will take one example to illustrate how a knowledge of early modern rhetoric can inform our understanding of his language.

Anaphora, one of the commonest rhetorical devices, involves the repetition of a word or words in successive clauses, lines or sentences. Spotting anaphora is, as one might expect, a simple, even mechanical exercise. In *Richard II* John of Gaunt delivers an emotive speech on his country which takes the form of a series of exclamatory, anaphoric tributes:

> This royal throne of kings, this scept'red isle,
> This earth of majesty, this seat of Mars,
> This other Eden, demi-paradise,
> This fortress built by Nature for herself
> Against infection and the hand of war.
> (*Richard II* II.i.40–4)

Not only does the speech exploit a specific rhetorical device; it is also influenced by a whole tradition of literary and patriotic pan-egyric. Yet, as the Arden editor points out, 'The speech is shaped by its dramatic context, and none [of its precedents] is a complete analogue.' In order to comment usefully on the speech, its anaph-ora included, it is necessary to explain how it uses and adapts literary conventions, for literary influence is rarely a question of straightforward, unmediated imitation.

In this instance anaphora is being used rather more loosely than it is elsewhere in the play. A more straightforward example is provided by Richard in a speech which comes close to self-deposition:

> I'll give my jewels for a set of beads;
> My gorgeous palace for a hermitage;
> My gay apparel for an almsman's gown;
> My figur'd goblets for a dish of wood;
> My sceptre for a palmer's walking staff;
> My subjects for a pair of carved saints,
> And my large kingdom for a little grave.
>
> (III.iii.147–53)

The comparison is instructive, for while Richard's speech is a catalogue of woes, listed one after the other with a monotony born of self-obsession, Gaunt's speech is unlaboured and effu-sive, and consequently less regular metrically. The repetition of 'This' drives home the point that England's virtues are seemingly endless, while the omission of one 'this' in line 42 (apart from satisfying metrical requirements) suggests sincerity, as if Gaunt is less interested in rhetorical symmetry than in the content of his speech.

A commentary on a passage from Shakespeare which merely listed various rhetorical devices without showing why they occur and how they function would be as bland and uninteresting as a commentary which identified assonance, alliteration and rhymes without explaining the author's reasons for using them. As Brian Vickers argues, rhetorical figures have too often been regarded as 'sterile patterns with no imaginative function', and it is the task of the critic to recognize and understand the 'definite emotional and intellectual effects' they were designed to produce.[3]

**Metaphor:** *Richard II* III.ii.47–53; *Macbeth* III.ii.46–50

Arguably, the most important aspect of Shakespeare's rhetoric is the way he uses metaphor. A metaphor is a non-literal way of describing something, and normally implies comparison between two things. Thus a commonplace Renaissance metaphor described the king as the father of his people and the people as his family. It is important to avoid confusing metaphors with other figures such as similes (in which the comparison is spelled out: 'As flies to wanton boys, are we to th' Gods; / They kill us for their sport' [*King Lear* IV.i.36–7]). It is even more important to use the term precisely, and specify whether you are concerned with a particular metaphor's figurative meaning(s) or its possible pictorial effects. Similarly, the term 'metaphor' is not synonymous with 'symbol', though most metaphors are symbolic in the sense that they involve a substitution: the crown as a symbol of the king, for example. But symbolism is more helpful when it is used to describe a dominant motif in a text: the repeated association of Richard II with the sun, for example, as in this quotation:

> So when this thief, this traitor, Bolingbroke,
> Who all this while hath revell'd in the night,
> Whilst we were wand'ring with the Antipodes,
> Shall see us rising in our throne the east,
> His treasons will sit blushing in his face,
> Not able to endure the sight of day,
> But self-affrighted tremble at his sin.
> 				(*Richard II* III.ii.47–53)

The speech involves a metaphor: Richard's regal presence is implicitly likened to the bright, searching rays of the morning sun. But the sun is only a symbol of the king because of the numerous other comparisons between the two in the rest of the play.

Similarly, though Richard's metaphor depends on a visual image, we should not be tempted to describe his speech as merely evoking a mental picture. An image may be a picture created in the mind's eye (or conveyed by an actor's gestures and movements), but 'imagery' is often used of metaphors which require us to recognize a conceptual similarity (and difference) between two things. The grandeur and colour of Richard's speech lend force to the metaphorical likeness he is asserting, but his imagery is not strictly necessary for his meaning to be conveyed. I shall consider Shakespeare's imagery separately in due course, but I will here suggest some ways of commenting on his metaphors which do more than merely describe the often visual content of the suggested comparison.

One of Shakespeare's most resonant metaphors occurs when Macbeth summons the resolve to have his friend, Banquo, ambushed and murdered:

> Come, seeling Night,
> Scarf up the tender eye of pitiful Day,
> And, with thy bloody and invisible hand,
> Cancel, and tear to pieces, that great bond
> Which keeps me pale!
>
> (III.ii.46–50)

Numerous metaphors are suggested here. First, the day is compared with a falcon, and night with the falconer who sews up his bird's eyes to make it a more efficient hunter. Second, Macbeth's human sympathies are likened to daylight, which is 'tender', while night-time is associated with the evil he now embraces. Third, night is a hand capable of brutal violence. Fourth, Macbeth himself is reduced to a disembodied hand, drenched in blood and poised to stamp its terrible imprint on the document of his friendship with Banquo. And there are many more metaphorical ideas in the speech: for instance, the sewing up of the falcon's eye is like an act of disguise or treachery; and Macbeth himself is like the falconer, who has no pity for the animal he mutilates.

Having teased out these various strands of meaning, we are able to surmise what this extended metaphor conveys about Macbeth. That he draws on the language of falconry is significant, since aside from its appropriate associations with hunting it evokes the feudal world of the aristocracy and hence, obliquely, the code of loyalty which Macbeth is in the process of transgressing. Elsewhere in the play the contrast between night and day is a metaphor for the moral extremes of innocence and evil: when, for example, Macbeth was steeling himself to murder Duncan he was disposed to favour darkness and to imagine himself one of its evil offspring: 'Now o'er the one half-world / Nature seems dead, and wicked dreams abuse

/ The curtain'd sleep' (II.i.49–51). Lastly, the metaphorical links suggested between night, evil, darkness, blood and the remorseless hand of a murderer have, like so many Shakespearean metaphors, a literal quality which counterpoints the difficulty of grasping how things as disparate as a falconer's needle and nightfall can be compared. In one sense the metaphor is extraordinary, and strains credulity; in another it has overwhelming visual logic.

Though I have by no means exhausted the metaphorical meanings of this speech, my last point has led us back to the question of imagery, and in the next section I will discuss how images function, singly or in 'clusters', in Shakespeare's plays.

### Imagery: *Macbeth* I.vii.25–34; I.vii.54–9

In performance the memorable images in a Shakespeare play can be gestural, facial and spatial as well as verbal. Frequently the two kinds, visual and spoken, are interdependent, as we see when Lear contemplates the gulf between actual and deserved status:

> There thou might'st behold
> The great image of Authority:
> A dog's obey'd in office.
>                    (IV.vi.155–7)

The vividness of the image is reinforced by the physical circumstances of its delivery. Lear himself is an 'image of Authority', he is also the outcast cur who has lost almost everything of his former identity. (Gloucester anticipated the speech when he accused Regan of monstrous cruelty in sending her father out into the storm: 'If wolves had at thy gate howl'd that dearn time, / Thou should'st have said "Good porter, turn the key"' [III.vii.62–3].)

In performance the parallel between the visual and the verbal dimensions of Lear's speech would be obvious, but anyone reading the play might have to take care not to overlook such an effect, a point made below in Chapter 6. Similarly, the recurrent images of fluidity and disintegration in *Antony and Cleopatra* acquire a further dimension in the galley scene (II.vii), in which the Romans' drunkenness and indiscipline are echoed by the shifting, unstable vessel on which they hold their revels. In production the movements of the galley can seem to symbolize Antony's vacillations between Egypt and Rome.

By the same token, some images, especially those which are dense or difficult, can be appreciated most easily on the page, and will certainly appear differently there than they would in performance. Once again Macbeth's highly developed visual sense (which ultimately has him hallucinating objects and people) provides an apt example of Shakespeare's ability to evoke startling and unforgettable images:

> this Duncan
> Hath borne his faculties so meek, hath been
> So clear in his great office, that his virtues
> Will plead like angels, trumpet-tongu'd, against
> The deep damnation of his taking-off;
> And Pity, like a naked new-born babe,
> Striding the blast, or heaven's Cherubins, hors'd
> Upon the sightless couriers of the air,
> Shall blow the horrid deed in every eye,
> That tears shall drown the wind.
>
> (I.vii.16–25)

This is a terrifying moment of revelation which occurs at exactly the point when Macbeth begins his descent into evil; its apocalyptic intensity conveys his horror as he faces the consequences of what he is to do. The lines seem to owe something to Marlowe's Faustus who, as he apprehends his dissolution for the first time, cries 'See, see where Christ's blood streams in the firmament' (Dr Faustus V.ii.144). For both Macbeth and Faustus self-knowledge permits sudden access to a vision of terrible beauty.

As with so many of Shakespeare's images, Macbeth's personification of pity is both naturalistic and emblematic; we see a bloody, screaming infant, but we also gain a metaphysical insight into the nature of evil. It is only partly tautologous to describe this image as pictorial, since its inspiration seems to lie not just in the sublimity of Marlowe's Dr Faustus but also in the baroque paintings of the Italian Renaissance. The lines conjure up a vast canvas by Michelangelo in which dimpled putti are simultaneously real children and conduits of ecstasy. The difficulties the lines have presented to editors – as the New Arden editor, Kenneth Muir, puts it, 'I do not understand how Pity – and still less how a naked new-born babe – can stride the blast, i.e. the sound, of a trumpet' – would, therefore, seem to be deliberate, for we are glimpsing the imaginative power which underlies Macbeth's ambition and which will subsequently undermine it; the image is intended to convey a tension so great that logical thought and expression have become impossible.

Writing about Shakespeare's imagery requires rather more than abandoning oneself to its visual dimensions, as this example shows. Images are not designed simply to create pictures for the audience or reader; they have a function, that is, beyond the merely decorative. The key is to explore images in relation to their context; in the example above we needed to consider what was being implied about Macbeth as his language shifted from literalism to allegory.

'Context' also includes the 'network' or 'cluster' of images to which a particular example belongs. Not all Shakespeare's images are thematically linked to others in a particular play, but from the early twentieth century onwards critics have been concerned to demonstrate the degree to which Shakespeare's imagery is designed to articulate and emphasize the thematic preoccupations of the individual texts. The technique is especially evident in the tragedies: *King Lear*, for example, is punctuated with images of predatory animals, *Hamlet* with images of rot, corruption and poison. Macbeth's image of Pity as a 'naked new-born babe' anticipates and perhaps even suggests Lady Macbeth's terrifying asseveration:

> I have given suck, and know
> How tender 'tis to love the babe that milks me:
> I would, while it was smiling in my face,
> Have pluck'd my nipple from his boneless gums,
> And dash'd the brains out, had I so sworn
> As you have done to this.
>
> (I.vii.54–9)

And there are other images of babies in the text, all connected with ideas of blood and violated innocence: 'tis the eye of childhood / That fears a painted devil' (II.ii.53–4); 'Finger of birth-strangled babe' (IV.i.30); 'What is this, / That rises like the issue of a king; / And wears upon his baby brow the round / And top of sovereignty' (IV.i.86–9); Macduff's 'babes' (IV.ii.6); and Macduff himself, who 'was from his mother's womb / Untimely ripp'd' (V.viii.15–16). Such 'echoes' and parallels might seem too obvious to be worth noting, but they suggest the kind of attentive reading which produces the best criticism, and as previous chapters have stressed, detailed analysis backed up with plenty of examples is always more successful than a series of unsupported generalizations. As this list from *Macbeth* implies, you should aim to discriminate between the various examples in an image cluster: some will be more elaborate than others; not all will produce identical associations; most importantly, some will seem much more significant than others.

## Textual issues

So far I have taken a literary rather than a technical approach to Shakespeare's language; I have not, for example, dealt with linguistic matters such as Elizabethan accidence (inflection), word-formation and pronunciation. But one technical dimension of Shakespeare's language which the student of literature cannot ignore is the question of textual transmission. Where do the texts we attribute to Shakespeare come from, and how reliable a representation of the author's intentions are they? What has happened to Shakespeare's words in the interval since they were first performed and published?

Shakespeare's plays did not appear in print until after they had been performed, and we cannot be certain that any are based directly on the author's own manuscripts. So-called 'Quarto' texts (the term refers to the size of the original volume) of some of the plays appeared in Shakespeare's lifetime, but seem either to be pirate versions or versions based on texts which had been modified (usually shortened) for performance. The 1623 Folio edition of the plays, which was published by Shakespeare's first editors, Heminges and Condell, just after his death, drew on a number of sources, all of which had the potential for introducing errors. Heminges and Condell used scribal copies of manuscripts (which might or might not have been the author's), actor's reconstructions from memory (which were almost certainly inaccurate), and theatrical prompt-books (which are likely to have been emended by the companies in the course of rehearsal). A Folio text might well have derived from a Quarto which was itself based on the unreliable recollections of an actor some time – even years – after his performance in a play.

In the past, editors have tended to be distrustful of the Quartos, which appear to contain many inaccuracies attributable either to errors of memory on the part of the actors and copyright pirates who apparently first wrote them down, or misreadings and unauthorized alterations on the part of the professional scribes who evidently copied them. Many modern editions are, therefore, based on the Folio, which was published to honour Shakespeare posthumously and which was assembled with considerable care. Recently, though, the Quarto texts have been republished in affordable modern editions, and there has been lively debate among scholars as to their value. Those who have promoted them argue that the Folio is not necessarily more authoritative than the Quartos; they also query the very notion of an authoritative text, particularly in a period when authorship was so often collaborative. Shakespeare may have given his backing to a number of versions of his play at different times and for different occasions. And all the texts we have are reconstructions of one kind or another: some have been lengthened, others apparently shortened; some have been emended by officious editors or altered inadvertently by the compositors who set them in type. Some are so garbled in places that they were almost certainly corrupted by the scribes and compositors who copied them. All are only partial reconstructions in the sense that they are texts; we can never hope to recreate the original performances of the plays. As Leah Marcus has argued, critics have frequently favoured one text over another on completely subjective grounds. In the case of *The Taming of the Shrew* she suggests that the tendency has been to valorize the more patriarchal version at the expense of a more subversively ironic one.[4]

The indeterminacy of Shakespeare's texts creates many interpretative difficulties, though from a postmodernist perspective such indeterminacy may be exciting rather than alarming. In practice, what does it mean when we come to read a Shakespeare play? First and foremost it requires us to work with a scholarly edition in which problems of textual transmission are highlighted, explained and discussed. Second, it requires us to come to terms with these problems and in some cases resolve them, however provisionally, by favouring one reading above another. On pages 92–3 is a sample from the Arden text of *Henry V* which raises some of the textual questions we might typically encounter in studying Shakespeare.

Like this sample, virtually all the pages in a new Arden edition are divided into three. First, we have the text of the play itself, then a list of textual variants, then a set of scholarly footnotes. As all reputable editions do, the Arden encourages us to follow critical convention and refer to Shakespeare's plays by act, scene and line rather than by page number: this is because pagination varies so widely from edition to edition. The passage from *Henry V* is in prose, so every line counts as a full one, but when quoting verse you need to remember that two half-lines can share the same line number.

The textual variants consist of words and phrases which appear differently in the various extant texts collated or compared by the editor. It is thought that the first Quarto text (Q1) of *Henry V* from which the other Q texts derive was reconstructed from memory by the actors of Shakespeare's company, the Lord Chamberlain's Men. As the Q text is shorter than the Folio (F) text, editors have suggested that it was based on a version cut for performance. In his introduction the New Arden editor, J. H. Walter, explains that, like most modern editions, his is based on the Folio, on the grounds that this seems the more literary version and hence the one closest to Shakespeare's original intentions. None the less, Walter acknowledges all the discrepancies between the Q and F texts in his list of variants, and he occasionally prefers a Q reading where F seems to have been altered unjustifiably by an earlier editor, or a compositor.

Responsibility for choosing between variant readings of a particular line or passage lies not just with the editor, who gives you his or her informed opinion, but with the individual reader. You may well wish to challenge the editor's reading, and argue the merits of one of the variants: there is no more reason why you should accept the opinion of an editor than you would any other kind of critic. Of course, you are favouring the Folio by default if you read an edition based on it, but this does not prevent you questioning it in specific instances, though obviously you will have to produce reasons to back up your case.

Say, for the sake of argument, that you prefer the Quarto's 'ends' to the Folio's 'end' in line 15 of the passage reprinted overleaf. '[E]nds' is arguably more logical, since it agrees with 'fingers'.

46            KING HENRY V           [ACT II.

*Bard.* Would I were with him, wheresome'er he is,
either in heaven or in hell!
*Host.* Nay, sure, he's not in hell: he's in Arthur's
bosom, if ever man went to Arthur's bosom. A'   10
made a finer end, and went away an it had been͵
any christom child; a' parted ev'n just between
twelve and one, ev'n at the turning o' th' tide:
for after I saw him fumble with the sheets and .
play with flowers and smile upon his fingers' end,   15
I knew there was but one way; for his nose was
as sharp as a pen, and a' babbled of green fields.

11. *a finer*] F 1, 2; *finer* F 3; *a fine* Capell.           15. *end*] F; *ends* Q, Capell.
17. *and a' babbled*] Theobald; *and a Table* F.

9–10. *Arthur's bosom*] The Hostess means Abraham's bosom. See *Luke* xvi. 19–31 for the whole parable of Dives and Lazarus. This parable and the Prodigal Son were popular with Falstaff. Cf. *1H4* iii. iii. 34; iv. i. 26, etc.

11. *finer end*] i.e. than going to hell.

12. *christom child*] A child in its first month after baptism during which time it wore a white robe called a chrism-cloth (chrism, the oil then used for anointing), hence an innocent babe.

12–13. *a' parted . . . tide*] A very old belief. Cf. Pliny, *Nat. Hist.* tr. Holland, 1601, II. 98, "Hereunto addeth *Aristotle* . . . that no living creature dieth but in the refluxe and ebbe of the sea ".

14–17. *fumble ... pen*] Shakespeare's version of a portion of the famous Hippocratic " facies " contained in the *Prognostics* where Hippocrates describes the signs of approaching death. Editions of the *Prognostics* were available in Greek, in Latin, French and possibly English translations accompanied by the commentaries of Galen and others. Christopher à Vega's Latin text (1552) has the following: " De manuum vero latione haec nosse oportet quibuscunque in acutis febribus . . . ante faciem feruntur vel venantur frustra, aut colli-

gunt festucas, aut stamina de vestibus euellunt, vel stipules de pariete carpunt, omnes malas esse atque lethales " (*Liber Prognosticon*, p. 76) and earlier, " Erit autem talis nasus gracilis in extremis " (p. 30).

Peter Lowe's translation of the latter runs, " hee shall esteeme it in perill and danger of death when the nose and the nostrils are extenuated and sharpened by the same Malady " (*The Presages of Diuine Hippocrates,* 1611, Sig. A4ᵛ.) Dover Wilson cites Lupton, *Thousand Notable Things,* 1578, Bk. IX, " . . . and his nose waxe sharpe—if he pull strawes, or the cloathes of his bedde . . . ". One wonders whether Galen's comment that the nose becomes " aquillinus " may have suggested a " quill " and thus inspired the immortal " sharp as a pen " as the Hostess' muddled version.

17. *a' babbled*] Theobald's famous emendation has received support from modern studies of the secretary handwriting. The original spelling was presumably " babld " (Note the F spelling " bable ", iv. i. 71), and the similarity between " t " and " b ", " e " and " d " in that handwriting makes misreading likely (see Greg, *Principles*, pp. 129, 155, 172). Thiselton, *Notulae Criticae*, 1904, p. 14, suggested " Tatld ", his point being

Sample text from scholarly (Arden) edition.

"How now, Sir John?" quoth I: "what, man!
be o' good cheer." So a' cried out "God, God,
God!" three or four times: now I, to comfort him,        20
bid him a' should not think of God, I hoped there
was no need to trouble himself with any such
thoughts yet. So a' bade me lay more clothes on
his feet: I put my hand into the bed and felt
them, and they were as cold as any stone; then I        25
felt to his knees, and so upward, and upward, and
all was as cold as any stone.

*Nym.* They say he cried out of sack.

*Host.* Ay, that a' did.

*Bard.* And of women.                                    30

*Host.* Nay, that a' did not.

*Boy.* Yes, that a' did; and said they were devils
incarnate.

*Host.* A' could never abide carnation; 'twas a colour
he never liked.                                          35

*Boy.* A' said once, the devil would have him about
women.

*Host.* A' did in some sort, indeed, handle women; but

---

19. *be o' good*] Capell; *be a good* F.          26. *upward, and upward*] Q, F 3,
Camb.; *vp-peer'd and vpward* F 1.          32. *devils*] *Deules* F.          34. Host.]
Rowe; Woman F.          36. *devil*] *Deule* F.

---

that if the capital T of the F "Table"
was in the manuscript before the
compositor, a misreading of "B"
for "T" would be highly improbable. Bradley, *The Academy*, 21
April, 1894, and *O.E.D.* "field" 14,
sought to keep the pen image by
reading "pen on a table of green
field", interpreting "green field" in
the light of a 15th century example
as "green cloth". But "babbled
of green fields" is surely more in
character with the Falstaff who
quoted the Scriptures, who heard the
chimes at midnight, and who lost his
voice hallooing of anthems. Now he
is in the valley of the shadow, the
"green pasture" of Psalm 23 might
well be on his lips.
"Babbled" may be an unconscious

reminiscence of Fox's account of
Oldcastle's trial. Oldcastle's enemies
issued a formal repentance falsely stat-
ing that it was written by Oldcastle,
and "caused it to be blown abroad by
their feed servants, friends, and babbling sir Johns". (*Acts & Monuments*
III. 338.) See further, Appendix V.
    28. *of sack*] against sack.
    32, 36. *devils*], *devil*] "Deules . . .
Deule" F. A Shakespearian spell-
ing.
    32-3. *devils incarnate*] This phrase,
a somewhat daring paradox, was
made, popular by Lodge, *Wits
Miserie*, 1596, Sig. B1ᵛ, in which he
describes the "Devils Incarnate of
this age".
    33. *incarnate*] (*a*) in the flesh, (*b*)
red.

---

You might cite the preceding plurals ('sheets'; 'flowers') in the sentence to justify your reading, or you might look elsewhere in Shakespeare's canon for a parallel. As this example shows, textual issues can be extremely time-consuming. None the less you are bound to meet cruxes of special importance in a number of plays, and how you choose to deal with them will have a significant bearing on your overall interpretation of the text. The Hostess's description of Falstaff's death in this extract is one such example; the problem lies with the seemingly nonsensical 'and a Table of green fields' in the F text of line 17.

The eighteenth-century editor, Lewis Theobald, cited in the New Arden notes, made a unilateral decision to emend the line as it appears here, substituting 'a' babbled of green fields' ('a' means 'he', as in lines 19, 21, and so on). Walter defends his decision to follow Theobald on a number of counts listed in the footnote: first, modern paleography (the study of handwriting) confirms that 'babld' in the manuscript could well have been misread as 'Table' (though one bibliographer thinks the original read 'Tatld'); second, Falstaff elsewhere speaks in language reminiscent of scripture; third, a contemporary account of the trial of Sir John Oldcastle, on whom it is thought Shakespeare based the character of Falstaff, also refers to 'babbling'. But we are finally referred to Appendix V (some Arden texts use the abbreviation 'LN' [Longer Note] for essays too detailed to be included as footnotes), in which we discover that Theobald's reading has fallen out of fashion with many critics since the 1950s. As Walter acknowledges, 'babbled' may be merely the product of eighteenth-century sentimentality, in which case our current view of Falstaff might need some revision.

Whichever way we decide, a scrupulous editor will provide us with all the arguments and counter-arguments, and it is always worth reading the footnotes for the light they shed on these and other interpretative matters. This does not mean that the editorial notes are flawless: sometimes they will omit to quote a parallel usage; at times they will seem to adopt a rather pedestrian or even pedantic approach. It can be irksome to have a perfectly comprehensible speech laboriously glossed, and translated into prosaic modern English. Occasionally, you will wish to reject the suggestions of the notes outright, or feel that they do not provide commentary on lines which seem obscure. It is important to remember that footnotes are critical interpretations rather than facts, and that consequently the annotations of different editors will not always accord with one another.

## Conclusion

It is customary for introductions to scholarly editions to begin with textual matters rather than to end with them as I have done here. It is of course logical to establish the status and authority of a text at the outset, so that the reader is aware of the difficult and sometimes arbitrary decisions an editor has had to take. I have chosen to deal with textual issues last rather than first for two reasons. The first is pragmatic: in practice we have to get to know a play in some depth before textual questions seem interesting or, indeed, meaningful. We are not in a position to make a judgment about 'babbled' versus 'Table' until we have an idea of Falstaff's character from studying the rest of the *Henry* plays. Second, by considering textual issues last I hope to qualify the point I have been making throughout this chapter and earlier ones: that we produce the sharpest insights into Shakespeare if we focus on the specific effects of his language and closely scrutinize individual speeches, lines and words. As my brief account of Shakespeare's textual history suggests, close reading needs to be undertaken self-consciously, in full awareness of the problematic status of the Shakespearean canon. The most rigorous critical analysis will take textual problems into account, historicizing and demystifying Shakespeare in this as in other regards. Most of us would be at sea without the painstaking efforts of generations of Shakespearean editors to guide us, and we would be unable to query their suggestions were it not for the exhaustive information with which they have provided us. If we decide to accept their version of the text wholesale, however, we should realize that we do so by choice and that with this, as with every other aspect of Shakespeare's language, our readings are ultimately our own.

## Notes

1. Peggy Ashcroft, 'Playing Shakespeare', *Shakespeare Survey* 40 (1988), pp. 11–19, at p. 12.
2. Randolph Quirk, 'Shakespeare and the English language', in *A New*

*Companion to Shakespeare Studies*, ed. Kenneth Muir and S. Schoenbaum (Cambridge: Cambridge University Press, 1971), pp. 67–82, at p. 67.

3. Brian Vickers, 'Shakespeare's use of rhetoric', in *A New Companion*, pp. 83–98, at p. 90.

4. Leah Marcus, 'The Shakespearean editor as Shrew-tamer', in *Shakespeare and Gender*, ed. Deborah Barker and Ivo Kamps (London: Verso, 1995), pp. 214–34.

# CHAPTER 5

# Shakespeare in context

## Introduction

Imagine that you are living four hundred years from now and that you are reading the following:

### The first day of the Edinburgh Festival

Third time lucky. It wis like Sick Boy telt us: you've got tae know what it's like tae try tae come off it before ye can actually dae it. You can only learn through failure, and what ye learn is the importance ay preparation. He could be right. Anywey, this time ah've prepared. A month's rent in advance oan this big, bare room overlooking the Links. Too many bastards ken ma Montgomery Street address. Cash oan the nail! Partin wi that poppy wis the hardest bit. The easiest wis ma last shot, taken in ma left airm this morning. Ah needed something tae keep us gaun during this period ay intense preparation. Then ah wis off like a rocket roond the Kirkgate, whizzing through ma shopping list.

Ten tins ay Heinz tomato soup, eight tins ay mushroom soup (all to be consumed cold), one large tub ay vanilla ice-cream (which will melt and be drunk), two boatils ay Milk of Magnesia, one boatil ay paracetamol, one packet ay Rinstead mouth pastilles, one boatil ay multivits, five litres ay mineral water, twelve Lucozade isotonic drinks and some magazines: soft porn, *Viz*, *Scottish Football Today*, *The Punter*, etc. The most important item hus already been procured from a visit tae the parental home; ma Ma's bottle ay valium, removed from her bathroom cabinet. Ah don't feel bad about this. She never uses them now, and if she needs them her age and gender dictate that her radge GP will prescribe them like jelly tots. I lovingly tick off all the items oan ma list. It's going tae be a hard week.[1]

How much of what you read do you think you would understand? What contextual information might be helpful in enhancing your understanding of what you read? You might want to find out more about the word 'trainspotting' and what it could mean as the title of the book from which you read; about the Edinburgh Festival; about heroin addiction, or Heinz tomato soup, or Lucozade, or valium; about Irvine Welsh the author; about the dialect in which the book is written; about the way the book was received; about the connection of the book to the film that was made of it. Four hundred years ago Shakespeare was writing his plays and today we are still reading and watching them. Irvine Welsh's fiction may not survive as long, but I use him as an example of the importance of context. To begin to understand Welsh's *Trainspotting* you need to know something of life in Britain, specifically Edinburgh, in the 1990s. Even for those of us who live in 1990s Britain the task may not be so easy. We may have difficulty with some of the terms Welsh uses (I for one have never seen a copy of *The Punter* ). If you lived and read Welsh in the 2390s then the text would only start to make proper sense if supplemented by extensive contextual information. And truly to understand Shakespeare, surely you need to know something about *his* life and times. Take, for example, the figure of Autolycus in *The Winter's Tale* who leads us nicely into a consideration of the world of the ballad-mongering pedlar. Autolycus is a salesman and an entertainer carrying a pack full of wares and thieving at every opportunity. His triumphal soliloquy is packed full of the bric-a-brac of early modern English life:

> Ha, ha! what a fool Honesty is! and Trust, his sworn brother, a very simple gentleman! I have sold all my trumpery: not a counterfeit stone, not a ribbon, glass, pomander, brooch, table-book, Ballad, knife, tape, glove, shoe-tie, bracelet, horn-ring, to keep my pack from fasting; they throng who should buy first, as if my trinkets had been hallowed and brought a benediction to the buyer: by which means I saw whose purse was best in picture; and what I saw, to my good use I remembered. My clown (who wants but something to be a reasonable man) grew so in love with the wenches' song, that he would not stir his pettitoes till he had both tune and words; which so drew the rest of the herd to me, that all

their other senses stuck in ears: you might have pinched a placket, it was senseless; 'twas nothing to geld a codpiece of a purse; I would have filed keys off that hung in chains: no hearing, no feeling, but my sir's song, and admiring the nothing of it. So that in this time of lethargy I picked and cut most of their festival purses. (*The Winter's Tale* IV.iv.596–616)

Like Welsh's list from *Trainspotting*, Autolycus' speech invites contextualization. We may know what a codpiece is – or think we do – but what of a placket or a table book? The ballads Autolycus sells are full of sensational lies (they are of 'a usurer's wife . . . brought to bed of twenty money-bags at a burden, and how she longed to eat adders' heads carbonadoed' [IV.iv. 263–6] and other such unlikely matter), but like today's tabloids the taller the stories the more likely the sales. And Autolycus represents what some critics have called 'the rise of popular print': Mopsa's 'Pray now, buy some: I love a ballad in print, a life, for then we are sure they are true' (IV.iv.261–2) reveals the simple-minded attitude of the naive and gullible dazzled by the new availability of cheap reading-matter.

Like Welsh, Shakespeare has his reasons for writing as he does. In this chapter I shall consider some of these reasons in greater depth. I shall be trying to answer the questions, Who was Shakespeare, and what were his most important formal and theatrical influences? How can we best define and determine the wider cultural context of his plays? Finally, by focusing on two specific examples, *Macbeth* and *The Tempest*, I shall try to demonstrate the importance of establishing a socio-political background for Shakespeare's work whilst acknowledging the problematic nature of a critical approach which attempts to explain the relationship between a literary text and its society. I should perhaps make clear from the outset that I am using 'context' in the sense of 'contemporary background'; this chapter will not attempt to deal with Shakespeare in his present contexts – the interpretative issues raised by, for example, a performance in modern dress or an adaptation for film.

**Who was Shakespeare?**

In an episode of the children's television series *The Herbs* the ever-daft Dill and the always perspicacious Parsley are taking part in a school quiz with Mr. Onions the schoolmaster asking the questions:

*Mr. Onions.* We will now turn to English Literature, bards for the use
of. Now, if Shakespeare were alive today what would he be
famous for?
*Parsley.* His age?
*Mr Onions.* Wrong. Dill?
*Dill.* Er? Shakespeare? I know the name. It would be on the tip
of my tongue if I had a big enough tongue. I'm just trying to
place . . .
*Mr. Onions.* Correct. His plays of course. One mark to Dill.
(from 'Parsley and Dill get their school exams with surprise results',
*The Adventures of Parsley*, Michael Bond, Film Fair Ltd, 1989)

Like Dill we certainly know the name of Shakespeare and that he
was a poet and playwright who died centuries ago. Although it is
not the purpose of this chapter to act as a substitute for the many
works that have been penned on Shakespeare's life, the thoughtful
student of Shakespeare will realize the benefits of careful consideration of the relevance of knowing something about information
and opinions on his life and should be willing to ponder the connection of that life to the play(s) being studied.

How important is knowledge of Shakespeare's life for our comprehension of what he wrote? Certainly biographical information
can add to the poignancy of some passages in the plays. For example, the anguish of the lines in *King John* (1596) spoken by
Constance, who laments the death of the young Prince Arthur,
may be deemed to come straight from the heart of William, griev-
ing for his dead son, Hamnet:

> *Constance.*  I have heard you say
> That we shall see and know our friends in heaven:
> If that be true, I shall see my boy again;
> For, since the birth of Cain, the first male child,
> To him that did but yesterday suspire,
> There was not such a gracious creature born.
> But now will canker-sorrow eat my bud,
> And chase the native beauty from his cheek,
> And he will look as hollow as a ghost,
> As dim and meagre as an ague's fit;
> And so he'll die; and, rising so again,
> When I shall meet him in the court of heaven,
> I shall not know him: therefore never, never
> Must I behold my pretty Arthur more.

> *Pandulph.*  You hold too heinous a respect of grief.
> *Constance.*  He talks to me that never had a son.
> *King Philip.*  You are as fond of grief as of your child.
> *Constance.*  Grief fills the room up of my absent child,
> Lies in his bed, walks up and down with me,
> Puts on his pretty looks, repeats his words,
> Remembers me of all his gracious parts,
> Stuffs out his vacant garments with his form;
> Then have I reason to be fond of grief.
>
> (*King John* III.iv.76–98)

This passage does seem to link directly to Shakespeare's life, but, knowing relatively little of his life, it is unlikely that we would be able to find many such passages. There is general agreement among scholars concerning the approximate dates that the plays were penned and this means that students of Shakespeare can achieve a sense both of Shakespeare's development as an author and the relation of his times to his work. However, such links can only be tentative. We must not make naive assumptions about the life from the art (e.g. Shakespeare was retiring from London in *The Tempest* [see Chapter 9]) or about the art from the life (e.g. Shakespeare was a shrewd businessman who was mean with his wife, which explains the hard-headed materialism of, for example, *The Merchant of Venice*). There is far from general agreement on the precise dates of the composition and performance of the plays. Indeed, there is a continuing controversy about many of the texts as most modern editions of the plays (Arden or Oxford for example) make plain. Yet before we turn away from the figure of Shakespeare to the texts he has left us we must acknowledge, for we simply cannot ignore, his fame.

It is Parsley who dryly makes the truly perceptive point. Though Shakespeare is over four hundred years old, he refuses to lie down and die. His fame does indeed live on. In fact, he seems healthier than ever, flourishing everywhere you care to look. I think it is safe to say that, as long as human society does not destroy itself, Shakespeare will continue to be read, interpreted, watched, listened to, pondered, translated, quoted, paraphrased, alluded to and appropriated (the list could go on). Shakespeare has become woven into our culture (and by *our* culture I don't simply mean England's culture, I mean the *world*'s culture) whether we like it or not. Personally I do like it. And I am not alone.

Let us for a moment, then, focus on the author, William Shakespeare. I hope I will be forgiven for setting to one side the interminable debate about the authorship of these remarkable plays (whilst acknowledging that some claim they were written by Francis Bacon, or the Earl of Oxford, or Christopher Marlowe, or Walter Ralegh, or Anthony Sherley, or King James, or a combination of these individuals and others).[2] Even if we admit to uncertainty as to the authorship of the plays, or some of them, it is clear that they were written in England, mainly in London, between approximately 1590 and 1612, and that contexts for them can be sought, considered and debated.

Biographies of William Shakespeare abound. They are of assorted length and reliability. Basically there are three sources of information for the biographer: (i) documentary records such as church and local government registers and a will; (ii) the dramatic and poetic works; (iii) mention of Shakespeare by his contemporaries. Here I give a potted biography derived from a number of readily available sources. The tone of certainty adopted invites some scepticism, and I hope readers will compare mine with other biographical accounts.

William Shakespeare was born on St George's Day, that is 23 April 1564. His father, John Shakespeare, was a glovemaker from Stratford-upon-Avon. His mother was Mary Arden, daughter of Robert, a prominent local Catholic. William was the third of eight children. His two older sisters and one of his younger sisters died in infancy. His three younger brothers all died in the nine years before his own death. The only sibling who survived him was Joan, who lived until 1646. At the age of eighteen William married Anne Hathaway, eight years his senior. Five months later, in May 1583, Susanna, their first child, was born. In 1585 the couple had twins, a son they named Hamnet (who tragically died at the age of 11) and a daughter they named Judith. William went to London in 1587 to avoid prosecution for stealing deer from a local gentleman's park and writing bitter ballads against him. It was in London that William made his fortune in the theatre, enabling him to acquire property in Stratford and Blackfriars. Over a period of about twenty years he wrote more than thirty plays and perhaps collaborated on a few more. In 1609 he published a collection of 154 sonnets. He retired to Stratford in 1610 where he wrote his final masterpieces *The Winter's Tale* and *The Tempest*. He died there on

St George's Day 1616, having contracted a fever after a merry meeting with fellow poets Michael Drayton and Ben Jonson at which he drank too much. Such was the life of William Shakespeare, no doubt spiced with a little legend befitting the man who has become the pivotal figure in the canon of English literature.

Before we get too distracted by a romantic view of Shakespeare's life we should remember that writers in Tudor and Stuart England needed patrons, especially at the beginning of their careers. Shakespeare was no exception. In Henry Wriothesly, third Earl of Southampton, he found one. Before he became a monumental success in the theatre Shakespeare wrote two long poems, 'Venus and Adonis' (1593) and 'The Rape of Lucrece' (1594), both of which he dedicated to Southampton. The unctuous subservience of the dedication to 'The Rape of Lucrece' serves as a good illustration of the dependence of poets on their wealthy and influential patrons:

> To the right honourable Henry Wriothesly,
> Earl of Southampton and Baron of Tichfield
> The love I dedicate to your lordship is without end; whereof this pamphlet, without beginning, is but a superfluous moiety. The warrant I have of your honourable disposition, not the worth of my untutored lines, makes it assured of acceptance. What I have done is yours; what I have to do is yours; being part in all I have, devoted yours. Were my worth greater, my duty would show greater; meantime, as it is, it is bound to your lordship, to whom I wish long life, still lengthened with happiness.
> Your lordship's in all duty,
> William Shakespeare.

This may seem excessive to the modern reader, but looking at other dedications it soon becomes apparent that this is the common mode of expression for writers at this time. So while the necessity of patronage is a context for Shakespeare, it is also a general context affecting all writers of the period. In the words of Thomas Nashe in *Pierce Pennilesse* (1592): 'This is the lamentable condition of our times, that men of art must seek alms of cormorants, and those that deserve best, be kept under by dunces, who count it a policy to keep them bare, because they should follow their books the better.' Shakespeare wrote his longer poems during a period (1592–4) when plague had closed the theatres.

When they reopened, Shakespeare was able to make his money from dramatic writing once more and could avoid the need to seek the 'alms of cormorants'. In the same year (1599) that arguably the greatest Elizabethan poet, Edmund Spenser, died penniless in a London back street, William Shakespeare and The Lord Chamberlain's Men opened the Globe Theatre. Shakespeare astutely acquired shares in the enterprise. During the reign of James I the company changed its name to The King's Men. Shakespeare and his company now had the patronage of the King himself.

Let us now turn from the man to the texts. After all, I believe that writers would like to be remembered for their works, not their lives, otherwise why would they write at all? Shakespeare was keenly aware of death, but was confident of the immortality of his writing. Take Sonnet 18 for example:

> Shall I compare thee to a summer's day?
> Thou art more lovely and more temperate:
> Rough winds do shake the darling buds of May,
> And summer's lease hath all too short a date:
> Sometime too hot the eye of heaven shines,
> And often is his gold complexion dimm'd;
> And every fair from fair sometimes declines,
> By chance or nature's changing course untrimm'd;
> But thy eternal summer shall not fade,
> Nor lose possession of that fair thou owest;
> Nor shall Death brag thou wander'st in his shade,
> When in eternal lines to time thou grow'st:
> > So long as men can breathe, or eyes can see,
> > So long lives this, and this gives life to thee.

My quoting and your reading of these lines suggest his confidence is justified.

## Formal and theatrical contexts

Why did Shakespeare write as he did? What were his contemporaries such as Marlowe, Fletcher, Jonson, Spenser, Middleton, Webster, Sidney, Ralegh (not forgetting the monarchs Elizabeth and James) writing? Sonnet 18 draws attention to the often formal nature of the literary writing of the period. Though Shakespeare sometimes broke away from these ordered constraints through the employment of freer blank verse, and even freer prose, he often uses highly patterned language in the plays. A good example can be found in *Romeo and Juliet*, when the 'star-cross'd lovers' first exchange words and kisses.

> *Romeo.* If I profane with my unworthiest hand
> This holy shrine, the gentle sin is this
> My lips, two blushing pilgrims, ready stand,
> To smooth that rough touch with a tender kiss.
> *Juliet.* Good pilgrim, you do wrong your hand too much
> Which mannerly devotion shows in this.
> For saints have hands that pilgrims hands do touch
> And palm to palm is holy palmer's kiss.
> *Romeo.* Have not saints lips, and holy palmers too?
> *Juliet.* Ay pilgrim, lips that they must use in prayer.
> *Romeo.* Oh then, dear saint, let lips do what hands do!
> They pray; grant thou, lest faith turn to despair.
> *Juliet.* Saints do not move, though grant for prayers' sake.
> *Romeo.* Then move not while my prayer's effect I take.
> [*He kisses her*]
> (I.v.92–105)

The religious imagery of the exchange is enriched by the sonnet form into which their words fall. Their nascent love is given the poet's formal stamp of approval. As the lovers continue speaking, we can pick out the opening lines of a new sonnet in which they even begin to share lines.

This second sonnet is abruptly interrupted by Juliet's coarse nurse:

> *Romeo.* Thus from my lips, by thine, my sin is purg'd.
> *Juliet.* Then have my lips the sin that they have took.
> *Romeo.* Sin from my lips? O trespass sweetly urg'd.
> Give me my sin again.    [*He kisses her*]
> *Juliet.* You kiss by th' book.
> *Nurse.* Madam, your mother craves a word with you.
> (I.v.106–10)

The stark contrast between the lovers' devotional language and the nurse's materialistic 'he that can lay hold of her/ Shall have the chinks' (I.v.115–16) is matched by the changing pattern of the dialogue. Awareness of literary form and convention provides a context in this case which can only enhance our appreciation of the passage and the play as a whole.

The sonnet in *Romeo and Juliet* is just one example of a context in which contextualization helps us. Katherine Armstrong has discussed at greater length in the previous chapter the different rhetorical modes of Shakespeare's writing, and how a knowledge of them assists our close reading of his plays. It is perhaps still more vital that we understand Shakespeare's relationship with the genres he used. How does Shakespeare exploit and adapt the received genres of the day: history, tragedy, comedy, romance and pastoral? In the character of Polonius Shakespeare seems to ridicule the tendency to pigeonhole literary works, suggesting that generic categorizations should be taken with a grain of salt:

> [They are t]he best actors in the world, either for tragedy, comedy, history, pastoral, pastoral-comical, historical-pastoral, tragical-historical, tragical-comical-historical-pastoral, scene individable, or poem unlimited. (*Hamlet* II.ii.392–6)

But we must remember who is speaking. Polonius is continually getting himself tied in the knots of his own verbosity. Shakespeare's sense of generic convention is revealed more reliably in the words of Horatio who speaks after his close friend Hamlet's death:

> give order that these bodies
> High on a stage be placed to the view;
> And let me speak to th' yet unknowing world
> How these things came about. So shall you hear
> Of accidental judgments, casual slaughters;
> Of deaths put on by cunning and forc'd cause;
> And, in this upshot, purposes mistook
> Fall'n on th' inventors' heads – all this can I
> Truly deliver.
> (*Hamlet* V.ii.369–78)

Since we, as readers and audience, are not part of the 'unknowing world' Horatio refers to, we are in a position to set his account against what we have seen and heard. His comments concentrate our attention on the overall action of the play and fix firmly in our minds and hearts the sense of loss and tragedy.

Any conscientious student of Shakespeare should endeavour to learn about the theatrical as well as the literary conventions of the period. This includes the physical nature of the playhouse and its environs, with the opportunities it offered performers, and the limitations it imposed on them. A study of the practicalities of stage business faced by those performing *Macbeth*, for example, can alert one to the importance of properties, such as the cauldron and the feasting table, in a way that attention to the text alone would miss. (See Chapter 6 for a fuller discussion of Shakespeare's theatre.)

## The wider context

How far is it possible to establish a more general cultural context for the works of William Shakespeare? Can we talk of an 'Elizabethan world picture' as E. M. W. Tillyard famously did in his book of that name. The medieval concept of the great chain of being does survive in some of Shakespeare's plays. The oft-quoted words of Ulysses in *Troilus and Cressida* succinctly express the essence of this notion of cosmic order:

> The heavens themselves, the planets, and this centre,
> Observe degree, priority, and place,
> Insisture, course, proportion, season, form,
> Office, and custom, all in line of order.
> And therefore is the glorious planet Sol
> In noble eminence enthroned and sphered
> Amidst the other; whose medicinable eye
> Corrects the influence of evil planets,
> And posts like the commandment of a king,
> Sans check, to good or bad. But when the planets
> In evil mixture to disorder wander,
> What plagues and what portents, what mutiny,
> What raging of the sea, shaking of earth,
> Commotion in the winds, frights, changes, horrors,
> Divert and crack, rend and deracinate
> The unity and married calm of states
> Quite from their fixture! O, when degree is shak'd,
> Which is the ladder of all high designs,
> The enterprise is sick. How could communities,

Degrees in schools, and brotherhoods in cities,
Peaceful commerce from dividable shores,
The primogenity and due of birth,
Prerogative of age, crowns, sceptres, laurels,
But by degree stand in authentic place?
Take but degree away, untune that string,
And hark what discord follows. Each thing melts
In mere oppugnancy; the bounded waters
Should lift their bosoms higher than the shores,
And make a sop of all this solid globe;
Strength should be lord of imbecility,
And the rude son should strike his father dead;
Force should be right – or rather, right and wrong,
Between whose endless jars justice resides,
Should lose their names, and so should justice too.
Then everything includes itself in power,
Power into will, will into appetite,
And appetite, an universal wolf,
So doubly seconded with will and power,
Must make perforce an universal prey,
And last eat up himself. Great Agamemnon,
This chaos, when degree is suffocate,
Follows the choking.

(I.iii.85–126)

Yet Shakespeare was not a medieval man. He lived and wrote at a time which many scholars now choose to call the early modern period. Beliefs which had been unquestioningly held *were* being questioned. Power, will and individualism were threatening accepted notions of degree and authority; the individual was becoming as or more important than the social order. There was a rising tide of cynicism about the harmony of the spheres which Shakespeare gave a body and a voice to in characters such as Edmund, the appealing bastard son of Gloucester in *King Lear*. His father displays a medieval tendency to see a correspondence between activities in the heavens and human affairs:

These late eclipses in the sun and moon portend no good to us: though the wisdom of Nature can reason thus, yet Nature finds itself scourg'd by the sequent effects. Love cools, friendship falls off, brothers divide: in cities, mutinies; in countries, discord; in palaces, treason; and the bond crack'd 'twixt son and father. This villain of mine comes under the prediction; there's son against father: the King falls from bias of nature; there's father against child. We have seen the best of our time: machinations, hollowness, treachery, and all ruinous disorders follow us disquietly to our graves.

(*King Lear* I.ii.100–11)

When the perplexed Gloucester leaves the stage following this outburst Edmund shows his disdain for this explanation of the disarray in the kingdom:

This is the excellent foppery of the world, that, when we are sick in fortune, often the surfeits of our own behaviour, we make guilty of our disasters the sun, the moon, and stars; as if we were villains on necessity, fools by heavenly compulsion, knaves, thieves, and treachers by spherical predominance, drunkards, liars, and adulterers by an enforc'd obedience of planetary influence; and all that we are evil in, by a divine thrusting on. An admirable evasion of whoremaster man, to lay his goatish disposition to the charge of a star! My father compounded with my mother under the dragon's tail, and my nativity was under *Ursa major*; so that it follows I am rough and lecherous. Fut! I should have been that I am had the maidenliest star in the firmament twinkled on my bastardizing.

(*King Lear* I.ii.115–30)

Like Marlowe's Dr Faustus before him, Edmund refuses to be constrained or limited by the circumstances into which he is born. For him existence precedes essence, not the other way round. He is one of the first modern anti-heroes, to be famously followed by Milton's Lucifer in *Paradise Lost* (1667). Individuals like Shakespeare's Edmund, Marlowe's Faustus and Milton's Lucifer will not accept the ordained order. They rebel against it. In *King Lear* chaos spreads outward from Lear's first misjudged actions and it is by no means thwarted, repudiated or contained by the forces of order, justice and love, as it seems to be in *Macbeth*. In *King Lear* the ordered society seems to be permanently cracked open, whereas in *Macbeth* the forces of order rally against the tyrant Macbeth and ultimately destroy him. Malcolm regains control and establishes once again a sense of hierarchy with himself at the top and deserving Earls below him. Malcolm closes the play with a commanding speech which stresses the re-establishment of

109

order and pattern and clearly identifies the unleashed chaos and
evil with the Macbeths:

> We shall not spend large expense of time,
> Before we reckon with your several loves,
> And make us even with you. My Thanes and kinsmen,
> Henceforth be Earls; the first that ever Scotland
> In such an honour nam'd. What's more to do,
> Which would be planted newly with the time, –
> As calling home our exil'd friends abroad,
> That fled the snares of watchful tyranny;
> Producing forth the cruel ministers
> Of this dead butcher, and his fiend-like Queen,
> Who, as 'tis thought, by self and violent hands
> Took of her life; – this, and what needful else
> That calls upon us, by the grace of Grace,
> We will perform in measure, time and place.
> So thanks to all at once, and to each one,
> Whom we invite to see us crown'd at Scone.
>
> (*Macbeth* V.ix.26–41)

In *King Lear*, though Edmund is defeated at the end of the play
in a ritualistic duel by the legitimate Edgar, the consequences of
his villainy are not prevented, for as he is led away Lear enters
with the body of the slain Cordelia. Edmund's 'some good I mean
to do/ Despite of mine own nature' (V.iii.242–3) is immediately
contradicted by Lear's despairing 'Howl, howl, howl!' (V.iii.256).
The trio of Albany, Kent and Edgar who end the play are unable
to muster much enthusiasm for their task of ruling in the fifteen
and a half lines which follow Lear's death. The state is gored and
has to be sustained, but there is no suggestion that it will or can be
healed. Kent is clearly suicidal: 'I have a journey, sir, shortly to go;/
My master calls me, I must not say no' (V.iii.320–1). Edgar also
succumbs to 'the weight of this sad time', which, he says, 'we must
obey' (V.iii.322). The final lines of the play are spoken by Edgar:
'the oldest hath borne most: we that are young/ Shall never see so
much, nor live so long.' There is a sense that no one will live as
long as Lear, and this can be related to a general sense of foreboding in the period, a sense that the world was winding down and
collapsing. Economic uncertainty, religious conflict and political
instability seemed to be mirrored in the cosmos itself. The

discovery in 1572 of a new star in the heavens which then disappeared was a truly frightening event for Elizabethans.[3] We may interpret the phenomenon as a supernova, but to the Elizabethans it was a worrying sign of the mutability of the heavens themselves. The previously accepted order of the spheres was evidently crumbling and few, if any, certainties remained, about either the human or the divine order. The rise of cynical, Machiavellian figures who wilfully exercised their power and did not accept such notions as the divine right of kings we can see in the figure of Northumberland in *Richard II*, or Iago in *Othello*, or Richard of Gloucester in *Richard III*. These characters follow no one; they serve only themselves. Unlike the Vice figures in the medieval mystery plays, they are not motivated simply by evil. They are not just devilish, but are given *human* motivations and exercise great intelligence in their machinations. Yet as I have suggested in my discussion of Edmund in *King Lear*, we find these nihilistic, self-serving villains strangely admirable and attractive. Why? Perhaps because they seem so modern.

It appears that social harmony and political proportion are re-established in *Macbeth*, though we should note that Macduff stands in relation to Malcolm at the end of the play as Macbeth did to Duncan at the beginning. In performance the actor playing Malcolm might deliver his speech hesitantly, as though dishing out honours in a pathetic attempt to assert his authority.

*King Lear* represents the bleakest vision in Shakespeare's dramatic output. The questions that will not go away in this play seem to be: 'How bad can it get?' 'Will it continue to get worse?' And the answer that keeps contradicting the promised endings of justice and hope is one of increasing despair.

I have focused here on one of the general contexts in which we can set Shakespeare's writing. There are many others. In this section I shall briefly suggest other contexts about which modern students could, and probably should, acquire some knowledge. These suggestions are of course only a tip of that vast iceberg we term 'context'.

First, there is Shakespeare's relation to the popular culture of his times. In some plays there is so much song that to appreciate the play fully we need to discover as much about the songs as we can.[4] Shakespeare often adapts popular songs of the time and his plays frequently contain dancing or jigging along with the singing and music. In *Twelfth Night* songs contribute to characterization,

as when Orsino calls for a 'dying air', when Feste offers a love
song, and when Sir Andrew begs for 'a song of good life' (i.e. a
drinking song). Significantly, the misanthropic and pompous
Malvolio, steward of Olivia's house, is determined to put an end
to the late-night high spirits of Toby and his crew:

> *Malvolio.* My masters, are you mad? Or what are you?
> Have you no wit, manners, nor honesty, but to gabble
> like tinkers at this time of night? Do ye make an alehouse
> of my lady's house, that ye squeak out your cozier's
> catches without any mitigation or remorse of voice?
> Is there no respect of place, persons, nor time in you?
> (*Twelfth Night* II.iii.85–91)

Malvolio's haughty disapproval galls Sir Toby into a humorous
revenge which, however, in its excesses eventually disturbs the
audience. There is no escaping the fact that Malvolio *is* treated
cruelly, to the point of imprisonment and torture. Yet reference to
the political context of *Twelfth Night* helps us to recognize that
where Sir Toby is a caricature of a dissipated country knight,
Malvolio is a caricature of a priggish puritan. The temperamental
and philosophical opposition (and social gulf) between them is
encapsulated in Toby's rude reply to Malvolio's reproof:

> Art any more than a steward? Dost thou think because thou art
> virtuous, there shall be no more cakes and ale?
> (*Twelfth Night* II.iii.110–11)

Maria calls Malvolio 'a kind of puritan' (II.iii.134) and he stands
totally at odds with Sir Toby's belly-led life. Between them they
communicate the notion of a society with many currents running
through it.

Shakespeare's art was the product of elite as well as popular
influences. The Renaissance was so called because of the rebirth of
interest in Europe's cultural roots in ancient Greece and Rome.
Like many Renaissance authors, Shakespeare exploits the rich
tapestry of classical mythology. Twentieth-century audiences may
have largely forgotten the story of the Olympian lovers Venus, the
goddess of love, and Mars, the god of war, but in *Antony and
Cleopatra* Shakespeare re-embodies these figures from a Greco-
Roman mythology in Antony and Cleopatra, extraordinarily

passionate lovers who reject the material and the political, the clayey human realm, and enter a new dimension, rising 'dolphin-like' above 'the element they lived in'.[5]

## Socio-political contexts: two examples

As elsewhere in this book, I shall conclude my discussion by focusing on a few specific examples. As I have argued, contextualization deepens and enhances our understanding of Shakespeare, but how such contextualization might be practised in a class discussion or an essay needs further clarification.

Both internal and external evidence suggests that *Macbeth* was written with the audience of King James I of England and VI of Scotland very much in mind. Banquo is the ancestor of the Stuart line and the procession of kings across the stage in front of the bemused Macbeth bridges the generation gap between James and Banquo. The eight kings (the last in fact a queen) would have been: Robert II, Robert III, James I, James II, James III, James IV, James V and Mary Queen of Scots (who holds the mirror for James VI of Scotland and I of England). The play is obsessed with witchcraft, as was James, who wrote a study of the subject entitled *Dæmonologie* (1597). Like James's treatise, Shakespeare's play lingers on the sordid details of necromancy and witchcraft. The following list of ingredients would grace any ghoulish cook-book:

> Scale of dragon, tooth of wolf;
> Witches' mummy; maw, and gulf,
> Of the ravin'd salt-sea shark;
> Root of hemlock, digg'd i' th' dark;
> Liver of blaspheming Jew;
> Gall of goat, and slips of yew,
> Sliver'd in the moon's eclipse;
> Nose of Turk, and Tartar's lips;
> Finger of birth-strangled babe,
> Ditch-deliver'd by a drab,
> Make the gruel thick and slab.
> (*Macbeth* IV.i.22–31)

The play has acquired a sinister reputation from its association with the occult, and it has proved especially magnetic for contextual critics recently – Garry Wills being one example. Wills's *Witches and Jesuits* (1995) is a concerted and successful effort to bind *Macbeth* to its contemporary context, that is to James I's England in the wake of the Gunpowder plot of 1605. Wills paints a convincing portrait of a king and a society enthralled and obsessed by political conspiracy, jesuitical equivocation and necromancy. He sets the play in the context of other 'Gunpowder plays' and James's own writing on witches and plots. As Wills says: '*Macbeth* looks like a different play when we consider it in this context, in conjunction with these other artefacts.'[6] How might a student use such information in an essay or presentation? Well, one might include it without suggesting that it 'accounts' for the play, and conclude by pointing out that the political agenda is by no means clear: Shakespeare could have been indulging James or subtly critiquing his propensity to blame social and political conflict on the supernatural. This indicates a capacity to assimilate context and contextual/materialist criticism, while remaining sceptical of it.

Another example of how both to highlight context and problematize it is suggested by *The Tempest*. To the least informed reader *The Tempest* reflects the influence of Renaissance travel and exploration, particularly of the New World. Virtually all modern editors note that a collection of contemporary pamphlets about the Bermudas had a direct impact on Shakespeare's play.[7]

Many consider *The Tempest* to be Shakespeare's final play and none of the thirty-six which precede it more amply demonstrates the fascinating and complex relation of context to text. The accidental discovery of the Americas in 1492 by Christopher Columbus heralded an age of exploration and empire-building by the major European powers, especially Spain, Portugal, France and England. Half the world was up for grabs, and to be sure it was grabbed very quickly. Shakespeare's play reverberates with questions of possession and power bound up with New World colonization, but we must be aware of the limited explanatory value of the Bermuda pamphlets, and how they give us little assistance in understanding one of the most enigmatic aspects of the text, the portrayal of Caliban.

What of Caliban? I ask this because his character presents us with an interesting contextual case study. The figure of Caliban can be looked at in many historical and literary contexts, but one which strongly suggests itself is connected with the debate over his name, which is a near anagram of 'cannibal', but may also be derived from 'Carib', meaning a native of the Caribbean. The name itself seems to signify something. That Caliban can be seen as a type of native New World denizen should not mean our investigation should end there. Admiring contemporary accounts of native peoples such as the one to be found in Montaigne's essay 'Of Cannibals' provide a pertinent context for Caliban, though he has been seen as far more than a type of noble savage.

Certainly Ariel and Caliban appear as two sides of a single coin, the former associated with thin air and the latter with the heavy earth. Caliban is a variation on the wild man of medieval and Elizabethan pageant. There are accounts of Elizabeth herself taming wild men in moments of public theatre.[8] Caliban is a variation on this wild man, though he is not simply subjugated. He does, to some extent, rebel and have his own voice, and he sometimes speaks with the beauty of poetry:

> Be not afeard, the isle is full of noises,
> Sounds and sweet airs, that give delight, and hurt not.
> Sometimes a thousand twangling instruments
> Will hum about mine eares; and sometime voices,
> That, if I then had wak'd after long sleep,
> Will make me sleep again: and then, in dreaming,
> The clouds methought would open, and show riches
> Ready to drop on me; that, when I wak'd,
> I cried to dream again.
>
> (*The Tempest* III.ii.132–41)

This gives the lie to Caliban's earlier 'You taught me language; and the profit on't/ Is, I know how to curse. The red plague rid you/ For learning me your language!' (I.ii.365–7). Caliban may be bitter and vengeful, but he has some finer qualities. Like one of his predecessors, the wild figure of Lust in Spenser's *Faerie Queene* (Book IV, Canto Seven), Caliban functions as a moral example. He is part of a darkness we must acknowledge as ours, a warning of the monstrosity we become if we lose control of our baser element. Miranda and Ferdinand do not choose the naked lust that Caliban displayed when he tried to rape Prospero's daughter. The two rapt lovers are temperately playing chess together when Prospero unveils them to an astonished audience.

Shakespeare's reading was wide and varied. Because of the complexity of Caliban's literary parentage we should be cautious in our investigations of context. Alden and Virginia Vaughan claim that one explanation of Caliban's name has flourished ever since, in the late eighteenth century, a particular edition of the work was published with annotations by Richard Farmer, Master of Emmanuel College, Cambridge.[9] Farmer states bluntly that 'The metathesis in Caliban from Canibal [sic] is evident.' But Caliban may not be intended to be seen as a cannibal. As we have seen, the name could derive from Carib, and the play can be contextualized by reference to seventeenth-century events in the Caribbean – shipwrecks on Bermuda particularly. There seems to be no intention in the play to present Caliban as a man-eater, the distinguishing feature of cannibals. What Caliban most wants, like Ariel, is freedom, not flesh. Before we condemn him as an utter savage, let us remember Caliban's poetry and even his bravery in daring to oppose Prospero. Caliban seems to possess something to admire, especially when we set him against the Machiavellian cynicism of the 'civilized' Antonio and Alonso. If you read the text in Frank Kermode's Arden edition, you may be influenced by his view of Caliban's symbolic function in the play, but you will also be presented with a variety of contextual readings and background texts, and be able to develop your own ideas about Caliban and the question of context more broadly. To avoid being over-influenced by one critical opinion, make sure you take an interest in the different editions. Read the different introductions, once you have read the play carefully yourself. Be wary of any one view, because what might seem obvious as an interpretation of a play, or a moment in a play, may be traced to a particular interpretation in history which was adopted for particular reasons. To locate Caliban's various etymological and historical contexts is not necessarily to resolve them, for as Vaughan and Vaughan say of the various perspectives and opinions on Caliban, 'the diversity . . . precludes consensus.'[10] You won't find many more decisive statements of indecisiveness.

Studying Shakespeare should, I think, involve a continuing effort to contextualize and hence to deepen one's understanding of the text. To read Shakespeare is, inevitably, to contextualize. Even confining one's reading to Shakespeare produces contextualizations. When I am reading *Hamlet*, for instance, I am contextualizing my understanding of *Othello*. (Think of 'friendship' or 'reputation' in both plays, for instance.) None the less, the debate about the relevance of context, whether biographical, literary or historical, to Shakespeare's work, continues as an essential part of the discipline we call literary criticism. And even that debate is only part of the question of context, for there is another context to think about: your own.

## Conclusion

I would like to end on a note of caution. Text is a word derived from the Latin word *textus*, from which we also get the terms textile and texture. A text is produced from a weave of materials. The pursuit of context (the Latin *'con'* meaning 'with') is the pursuit of what materials go to make up a text. Seeking and establishing context is a way of teasing out the various threads of the text. In the richly woven fabric of Shakespeare's plays there are many threads to be appreciated, but let us not lose sight of the overall beauty of the pattern. We do not wish to be left with an unravelled mess. A contextual approach should aim at completeness; it would be a pity if our attention to detail meant we lost sight of the whole.

## Notes

1. Irvine Welsh, *Trainspotting* (London: Minerva, 1993), pp. 14–15.
2. John Michell's 272-page *Who Wrote Shakespeare?* (London: Thames and Hudson, 1996) testifies to the continuing interest in, and considerable doubt over, the authorship of the plays. Michell concludes his book with the observation that 'Who wrote Shakespeare [is] a perfect mystery, dangerously addictive but very worthwhile looking into.'
3. See *The Cambridge Companion to Shakespeare Studies*, ed. Stanley Wells (Cambridge: Cambridge University Press, 1986), p. 31.
4. For example, in *The Winter's Tale* Shakespeare uses six songs which are discussed on pages 172–4 of the Arden edition edited by J. H. P. Pafford.
5. Cleopatra uses these words to describe Antony to Dolabella (V.ii.88–9), but they might equally apply to her own reputation (see Enobarbus at II.iii.200ff).
6. Garry Wills, *Witches and Jesuits* (Oxford: Oxford University Press, 1995).
7. See Sylvester Jourdain, *A Discovery of the Bermudas* (1610) and Strachey's *True Reportory of the Wracke*. Both appear in the appendices

of the Arden edition of the play edited by Frank Kermode (1954; London: Routledge, 1988).

8. Alden T. Vaughan and Virginia Mason Vaughan, *Shakespeare's Caliban: A cultural history* (Cambridge: Cambridge University Press, 1991), pp. 66–7.

9. *Ibid.*, p. 30.

10. *Ibid.*, p. 54.

# CHAPTER 6

# Shakespeare in performance

## Prologue

You can get an enormous amount from the interpretations of
Shakespeare in performance, whether other people's or your
own. As we discussed in Chapter 2, going to see productions of
Shakespeare will almost certainly benefit your understanding of
the written texts. Seeing and hearing a performance by real people
in a particular setting is a marvellously direct way of engaging with
a Shakespearean play. Performance of a play brings it to life. The
move from page to stage means that the words of the play-text
become only one part among many in the complex medium of
theatrical performance. Julian Hilton observes:

> Performance draws on a uniquely wide range of disciplines and skills:
> electrics, electronics, architecture, carpentry, painting, graphic and
> scenic design, computing (for lighting and accounting), financial man-
> agement, marketing, music, acoustics, acting, dancing, singing, and so
> on and so forth. Yet performance is not solely about displaying range: it
> is also concerned with aesthetic, intellectual and social integration. It
> encourages the integration of theory and practice; it combines psycho-
> motoric, affective and cognitive learning; it unites art with technology;
> it bonds performers with audiences. This combination of range and
> integration makes it the classic humanist discipline.[1]

It is not only the integration of different skills and disciplines which
makes performance so compelling. The immediacy of performance
produces the excitement of a live experiment. The audience gather

119

like guinea-pigs to play their part in the testing laboratory of performance science. Each staging is unique, and its effects are measured
by the collective and the individual responses of those gathered. As
Hilton says: 'the process by which a single, coherent performance is
constructed out of the infinite range of possibilities open to it is one
analogous to classic scientific method.'[2]

It is in the combination of aural and visual effects that the attractiveness and power of theatre as an art-form lies. When reading we
are unlikely to neglect the words spoken, but we may be less able
to piece out the action of the play; we may find it difficult to
envisage what is happening as the words are spoken. Human
beings often communicate through other means than words, and it
is these non-verbal communications which performance realizes.
To indicate the importance of considering non-verbal channels of
communication at work in the theatre it may be useful to turn to
the memorable expression of the centrality of gesture in human
affairs and interaction made by Michel de Montaigne in his marvellous essay *An Apologie of Raymond Sebond*:

> What doe we with our hands? Doe we not sue and entreat, promis and
> performe, call men unto us and discharge them, bid them farwell and
> be gone, threaten, pray, beseech, deny, refuse, demand, admire, num-
> ber, confesse, repent, feare, bee ashamed, doubt, instruct, command,
> incite, encourage, sweare, witnesse, accuse, condemne, absolve, injurie,
> despise, defie, despight, flatter, applaud, blesse, humble, mocke, recon-
> cile, recommend, exalt, shew gladnesse, rejoyce, complaine, waile,
> sorrow, discomfort, dispaire, cry out, forbid, declare silence and
> astonishment? And what not? With so great variation, and amplifying,
> as if they would contend with the tongue. And with our head, doe we
> not invite and call to us, discharge and send away, avow, disavow, belie,
> welcome, honour, worship, disdaine, demand, direct, rejoyce, affirme,
> deny, complaine, cherish, blandish, chide, yeeld, submit, brag, boast,
> threaten, exhort, warrant, assure, and enquire? What doe we with our
> eye-lids? and with our shoulders? To conclude, there is no motion, nor
> jesture that doth not speake, and speakes in a language very easie, and
> without any teaching to be understood: nay, which is more, it is a
> language common and publike to all: whereby it followeth (seeing the
> varietie, and severall use it hath from others) that this must rather be
> deemed the proper and peculiar speech of humane nature.

Montaigne expresses the notion that the human body has a
language of its own and that we are always communicating,

non-verbally, through it. With our hands, with our heads, with our eye-lids and even our shoulders we speak a natural language of gesture. Montaigne goes so far as to suggest that the variation and amplification of this body language means that it 'would contend with the tongue'. The theatrical medium is a combination of the language of the tongue and the language of the body, of speech and gesture, and both languages must be studied. And it is not just gesture that can signify meaning in the theatre. We might add that stature, physiognomy, mask, costume, properties, lighting, set-design, music and noise can all be used by players and directors of Shakespeare in performance.

The success of Shakespeare's drama is at least partly due to his employment of the combinations of the verbal and visual and the imagined and the literal, which his chosen medium, the theatre, offers. One might think of Lear, wild storms of passion thundering in his head as he braves the tempestuous weather, or of Malvolio ridiculously strutting around the stage in his cross-gartered yellow stockings, grinning like an imbecile, as Olivia flatly states she thinks him mad. Shakespeare in performance, especially good performance, can make us laugh and cry; something that seldom occurs when we read. I remember being moved to tears when watching and listening to Warren Mitchell and Trevor Baxter playing Gloucester and Lear in Leeds in October 1995. The scene where the recently blinded Gloucester meets the mad Lear is perhaps the most pitiful in the play. The sorry spectacle of their meeting was augmented in this production by doleful music underscoring their words and a beautifully constructed waterfall at the rear of the stage dribbling its waters down in an effective visual and aural evocation of weeping. The experience, for me, was intense and moving, and that is the all-important difference that performance (and willing imaginations, and, dare I say it, hearts) can make. Performance can make the difference between a work that lives and breathes and one that sits dead on the page.

However, live theatre is just one aspect of Shakespeare in performance to be considered in this chapter. I shall also discuss Shakespeare's use of the theatrical metaphor and its added resonance in the theatre; contemporary performances; performance history; and participation in performance as a method of learning.

## The theatrical metaphor

Shakespeare's plays confront us with the theatricality of life, and the life-like qualities of the theatre, or dramatic enactment. There are moments in the plays when Shakespeare seems more concerned with contemplating the theatrical medium he employs than with developing 'character' or 'plot'. Take the following exchange between Falstaff and Prince Hal in *Henry IV, Part One*:

> *Prince.* Do thou stand for my father and examine me upon the
> particulars of my life.
> *Falstaff.* Shall I? Content! This chair shall be my state, this dagger my
> sceptre, and this cushion my crown.
> *Prince.* Thy state is taken for a joint-stool, thy golden sceptre for a
> leaden dagger, and thy precious rich crown for a pitiful bald
> crown.
> *Falstaff.* Well, and the fire of grace be not quite out of thee, now shalt
> thou be moved. Give me a cup of sack to make my eyes look
> red, that it may be thought I have wept, for I must speak in
> passion, and I will do it in King Cambyses' vein.
> *Prince.* Well, here is my leg.
> *Falstaff.* And here is my speech. Stand aside, nobility.
> *Hostess.* O Jesu, this is excellent sport, i'faith.
> *Falstaff.* Weep not, sweet Queen, for trickling tears are vain.
> *Hostess.* O the Father, how he holds his countenance!
> *Falstaff.* For God's sake, lords, convey my tristful Queen,
> For tears do stop the floodgates of her eyes.
> *Hostess.* O Jesu, he doth it as like one of these harlotry players as ever
> I see!
>
> (*Henry IV, Part One* II.iv.371–91)

This passage highlights the importance of the complicity of the audience in the success of the dramatic venture. The audience must participate in the illusion of theatre or the dramatic enterprise will flounder. Like those gathered at the unveiling of Hermione in *The Winter's Tale* we must 'awake our faith', a faith in the transforming power of the human mind. Falstaff ridicules nobility by playing the king, and he has his audience, both on and off stage, in fits of laughter. The comic effect here, where Falstaff exposes the theatre as illusion, rests on ridiculing, through overacting, the seriousness of the subject. The subject is of course kingship. Moreover, when we try to visualize the passage on the stage we quickly realize the value of experiencing Shakespeare in performance in order fully to appreciate the complexities of the text – in this case, its comic complexities.

There are occasions when Shakespeare is even blunter in his use of theatrical metaphor:

> *Duke Senior.* Thou seest we are not all alone unhappy:
> This wide and universal theatre
> Presents more woeful pageants than the scene
> Wherein we play in.
> *Jaques.* All the world's a stage,
> And all the men and women merely players;
> They have their exits and their entrances,
> And one man in his time plays many parts,
> His acts being seven ages.
>
> (*As You Like It* II.vii. 136–43)

The speech invites all of us, player and audience alike, to see ourselves as actors making our entrances and exits and playing our many parts.

Shakespeare's use of the theatrical metaphor often seems tinged with melancholy, as in the figure of Feste in *Twelfth Night* with his sad songs of death in the midst of festive comedy. Feste closes the play with a song which ends with the lines 'our play is done / And we'll strive to please you every day.' It is not easy to entertain and perform, indeed it is hard work, and few audiences perhaps, are as receptive, indulgent and tolerant as Theseus in *A Midsummer Night's Dream*, who wryly observes during the mechanicals' farcical tragedy of *Pyramus and Thisbe* that 'the best in this kind [actors] are but shadows; and the worst are no worse, if imagination amend them' (V.i.208–9). Hippolyta's witty response, 'It must be your imagination then, and not theirs', provides a suitably terse expression of the theatrical truth, that the audience must be willing to help if the performance is to succeed. In this case a lot of help is needed as Bottom, Quince and the others seem determined to destroy any illusion by announcing their roles in the real (though really fictional) world defined by their profession:

> In this same interlude it doth befall
> That I, one Snout by name, present a wall
>
> (V.i.154–5)

> Then know that I as Snug the joiner am
> A lion fell
>
> (V.i.218–19)

With the audience's collusion, fine comedy results.

The humble plea for indulgence and forgiveness of the players in *A Midsummer Night's Dream* is made in lines which also suggest the brevity of the play and indeed of life itself. As Theseus says, 'No epilogue, I pray you; for your play needs no excuse. Never excuse; for when the players are all dead, there need none to be blamed' (V.i.341–3). While Nick Bottom and Peter Quince, Snug, Snout, Flute and Starveling conclude their ridiculous and hilarious entertainment by dancing their riotous Bergomask, Theseus reflects that 'This palpable-gross play hath well beguil'd/ The heavy gait of night' (V.i.355–6). Though a play might pass the time, it is itself subject to time and cannot outlast the duration of its performance.

The metaphor of life as ephemeral theatre also features in the tragedies, as in Macbeth's memorable coupling of the ephemeral passion of the player on the stage with the seeming futility of existence:

> *Macbeth.* Tomorrow, and tomorrow, and tomorrow
> Creeps in this petty pace from day to day,
> To the last syllable of recorded time;
> And all our yesterdays have lighted fools
> The way to dusty death. Out, out, brief candle!
> Life's but a walking shadow, a poor player
> That struts and frets his hour upon the stage
> And then is heard no more. It is a tale
> Told by an idiot, full of sound and fury
> Signifying nothing.
>
> (*Macbeth* V.v.19–28)

Shakespeare is making a comparison that cuts to the quick of our lives, and watching actors playing parts delivering these lines can only enhance their meaning and increase the potency of their effect upon us. Paradoxically, though the actor who plays Macbeth himself struts and frets to tell his tale, the audience will be reluctant to view all his efforts as futile and meaningless, a reluctance which underscores the depth of Macbeth's own despair.

The theatrical metaphor is, then, central in Shakespeare's work and, being so central, it arguably demands that the student be aware that the medium Shakespeare has chosen and works through is that of dramatic performance. Shakespeare's imagination is a theatrical imagination. We can assume that when he wrote his plays Shakespeare thought of bodies in movement on the stage, acting and reacting to what is said and done. The plays work through action and words, and one of the repeated messages is that the realm of human social life is similar to the world of the stage. On the stage we see a constant flux of actors playing parts, suggesting that self and identity are essentially unstable concepts and that we are nothing more than a shadowy composition of the different roles we play.

Allusion to the theatrical medium can have extremely complex effects. Take the following:

*Cleopatra.* Now, Iras, what think'st thou?
Thou an Egyptian puppet shall be shown
In Rome as well as I. Mechanic slaves
With greasy aprons, rules and hammers shall
Uplift us to the view. In their thick breaths,
Rank of gross diet, shall we be enclouded
And forced to drink their vapour.
*Iras.* The gods forbid!
*Cleopatra.* Nay, 'tis most certain, Iras. Saucy lictors
Will catch at us like strumpets, and scald rhymers
Ballad us out o' tune. The quick comedians
Extemporally will stage us and present
Our Alexandrian revels; Antony
Shall be brought drunken forth; and I shall see
Some squeaking Cleopatra boy my greatness
I' th' posture of a whore.
(*Antony and Cleopatra* V.ii.206–19)

With immense irony the fate Cleopatra fears is enacted as the boy-actor on the early seventeenth-century stage delivers these lines to a theatre full of unwashed groundlings. Cleopatra's greatness *is* 'boyed', though the play also presents her as divine, regal, strong, cunning and above all, by this stage of the play, resolute. She is constant, *not* shifting, demonstrating the true qualities of tragic heroism. There is a gorgeous playful ambiguity in Shakespeare's art here, which an awareness of performance possibilities and a knowledge of theatrical history can only accentuate.

There are few characters in drama more puzzling and mysterious than Hamlet, the irresolute-scholar philosopher who is also
very much an actor. Hamlet delivers what many consider
Shakespeare's clearest observations on performance practice,
just before the central play-within-a-play in III.ii:

> *Hamlet.* Speak the speech, I pray you, as I pronounced it to you,
> trippingly on the tongue; but if you mouth it as many of your
> players do, I had lief the town-crier spoke my lines. Nor do
> not saw the air too much with your hand, thus, but use all
> gently; for in the very torrent, tempest, and as I may say,
> whirlwind of your passion, you must acquire and beget a
> temperance that may give it smoothness. O, it offends me to
> the soul to hear a robustious periwig-pated fellow tear a
> passion to tatters, to very rags, to split the ears of the
> groundlings, who for the most part are capable of nothing but
> inexplicable dumb-shows and noise. I would have such a
> fellow whipped for o'erdoing Termagant. it out-Herods
> Herod. Pray you avoid it.
> *1st Player.* I warrant your honour.
> *Hamlet.* Be not too tame neither, but let your own discretion be your
> tutor. Suit the action to the word, the word to the action, with
> this special observance, that you o'erstep not the modesty of
> nature. For anything so o'erdone is from the purpose of
> playing, whose end, both at the first and now, was and is to
> hold as 'twere the mirror up to nature; to show virtue her
> feature, scorn her own image, and the very age and body of
> the time his form and pressure.
>
> (*Hamlet* III.ii.1–24)

The appeal here is for feeling and emotion, but in the correct proportions. The actors are instructed to 'use all gently' and told that
they must 'acquire and beget a temperance' as the best way
to ensure that the highest passion is successfully represented.
(Shakespeare would presumably not subscribe to the modern notion
of 'method' acting which holds that the actor must become the
character being played as far as possible.) The actors are warned
against playing to the groundlings, who are in turn roundly crit-
icized. The concern is for balance, with the most stress placed on
avoiding 'o'erdoing' the role set down in the script. It is through this
middle way that 'the purpose of playing' is realized. Hamlet's blunt
and famous expression of that purpose remains remarkably true of

the acting most admired in our own time, and Shakespearean acting in particular demands a willingness to moderate between the formality of his language and the need for naturalism. Shakespeare's drama seems able, in performance, to make points of contemporary relevance and thereby Shakespearean acting can continue to show the 'very age and body of the time his form and pressure'.

Hamlet's advice leads us directly into the scene at the very heart of the play. Hamlet and Horatio hope to expose Claudius's guilt by confronting him with the image of his own murderous deed, a play in which a man kills his brother, the king, by pouring poison into his ear as he sleeps in his garden. Hamlet feels he can use the play to produce a particular effect in his target-audience. That is, Hamlet hopes to stir Claudius's conscience. The murder itself becomes emblematically fixed as a core image of the play – a central symbol of corruption. The foul and unnatural murder is hauntingly described in Act I by the ghost, mimed in Act III as the dumb show, and then performed by the players in *The Mousetrap*, with Hamlet's added commentary on the action (it is also echoed in the poisonings of Act 5):

*Lucianus.* Thoughts black, hands apt, drugs fit, and time agreeing,
Confederated season, else no creature seeing,
Thou mixture rank, of midnight weeds collected,
With Hecate's ban thrice blasted, thrice infected,
Thy natural magic and dire property
On wholesome life usurps immediately.
*Pours the poison in the sleeper's ears.*
*Hamlet.* A poisons him i' th' garden for his estate. His name's
Gonzago. The story is extant, and written in very choice
Italian. You shall see anon how the murderer gets the love of
Gonzago's wife.
*Ophelia.* The King rises.
*Hamlet.* What, frighted with false fire?
*Queen.* How fares my lord?
*Polonius.* Give o'er the play.
*King.* Give me some light. Away.
*Polonius.* Lights, lights, lights. *Exeunt all but Hamlet and Horatio*
(*Hamlet* III.ii.249–64)

The reaction from Claudius is revealing, especially to the fixed eyes of Hamlet and Horatio. They have seen enough to be convinced of his guilt. Hamlet is performing brilliantly in this scene and he moves from successfully playing on Claudius's conscience to a virtuoso display with Rosencrantz and Guildenstern (whom he accuses, ironically, of trying to play *him* like a recorder) and then to manipulating Polonius, whom he plays with consummate and remorseless skill:

*Polonius.* My lord, the Queen would speak with you, and presently.
*Hamlet.* Do you see yonder cloud that's almost in shape of a camel?
*Polonius.* By th' mass and 'tis – like a camel indeed.
*Hamlet.* Methinks it is like a weasel.
*Polonius.* It is backed like a weasel.
*Hamlet.* Or like a whale.
*Polonius.* Very like a whale.
*Hamlet.* Then I will come to my mother by and by.

(III.iii.365–74)

Hamlet is typical of many Shakespearean characters in both undercutting yet implicitly asserting the truth of the theatrical medium, and in simultaneously acknowledging that life is like a play quite as much as any play can resemble life.

## Contemporary performance

In Chapter 5 I discussed the need to reconstruct the original social and political subtexts of the plays in order to understand them better. I would now like to consider the theatrical metaphor in terms of Shakespeare's contemporary context. The most fascinating aspect of the life/theatre comparison is that it works both ways. Just as the actor on the stage holds up a mirror to nature (or life), so the individuals within a society, from the lowest to the highest, can be seen to be enacting roles. In Shakespeare's plays nobody is spared the comparison; indeed kings, whether good or bad, are commonly shown as actors presenting a mask to the world which conceals their true visage. Prince Hal's early soliloquy in *Henry IV, Part One* ('yet herein will I imitate the sun' [I.ii.190–210]) alerts the audience to the artifice which is finally stripped away at the end of *Henry IV, Part Two* when, as king, Hal publicly rejects the crestfallen Falstaff:

I know thee not, old man. Fall to thy prayers.
How ill white hairs become a fool and jester!
I have long dreamt of such a kind of man,
So surfeit-swell'd, so old, and so profane;
But, being awak'd, I do despise my dream.
Make less thy body hence, and more thy grace;
Leave gormandizing; know the grave doth gape
For thee thrice wider than for other men –
Reply not to me with a fool-born jest;
Presume not that I am the thing I was,
For God doth know, so shall the world perceive,
That I have turn'd away my former self.
(*Henry IV, Part Two* V.iv.48–59)

The thematic concern with the education of a prince is played out in the figure of Hal who is to become the epic ruler, Henry V. The theme is a crucial concern of many texts of the period, including Shakespeare's plays. When the topic, obviously sensitive to authorities who depend upon the notion of unquestioned hierarchical structures, is debated in a medium which allows the enactment of events such as the deposition of a king, as in *Richard II*, it is not difficult to appreciate the risks involved for those who have anything to do with this art. Theatre is deeply political.[3] The education of Hal in *Henry IV, Part One* and *Henry IV, Part Two*, which culminates in *Henry V* with the worthy king who trounces foreign opponents against the odds, provides the tonic for the controversial portrayal of bad rulers ousted. Shakespeare presents us with many examples of tyrants and bad rulers: Richard II, Richard III, Angelo, Macbeth, Lear, Leontes. Yet Shakespeare seems to have successfully negotiated the difficulty of placing questions of authority and degree before his audiences in enthralling and entertaining stories, without unduly antagonizing those in power.

A celebrated instance of the power and dangers of early modern performance is that of *Richard II* and its possible connection with the rebellion in 1601 of the Earl of Essex. The play climaxes with the spectacle of the deposition of a weak and corrupt monarch. On 7 February 1601 a specially comissioned performance of the play at the Globe Theatre is thought to have incited opposition to Elizabeth I, so helping the Earl of Essex to launch his rebellion. Elizabeth's famous remark, 'I am Richard II. Know ye not that?' suggests that she did not fail to see the link, and she was unimpressed by the fact that 'this tragedie was played forty times in open streets and houses'. As this example illustrates, an awareness of the political pressures on artists such as Shakespeare and his playfellows can throw up fascinating perspectives, making us aware of ironies to which we may well otherwise be oblivious.

## Performance history

Gāmini Sālgado's *Eyewitnesses of Shakespeare*[4] provides some fascinating information on the history of Shakespeare in performance. Here you will find accounts of theatrical rivalries and reports of *Hamlet* performed on ships (p. 28), praise for the boy-actor who played Desdemona in *Othello* at Oxford (p. 30) and for the production of *Macbeth* at the Globe Theatre (see Figure 6.1) in 1610 (p. 31), details about the tragic fire which destroyed the Globe Theatre in 1613 (p. 34), and extracts from puritan texts condemning the theatre for promoting vice (p. 39). The book throws up some extraordinary moments in stage history: one actor playing Macduff actually accidentally killed Macbeth on stage in a duel by piercing him in the eye, for example (pp. 55–6). Sālgado also highlights some of the great names of Shakespearean acting: MacReady, Kemble, Garrick, Burbage, Siddons, Terry.

As Sālgado's book shows, the performance history of Shakespeare's plays is a topic in its own right. If we briefly consider just one aspect of performance, that of stage business, it soon becomes clear that stage performance, though arguably the most ephemeral of art-forms, can generate customs and traditions which become intimately connected with a Shakespearean text. Famous productions, or moments in them, establish themselves as interpretational conventions, and directors and actors working in the theatre inevitably come to situate themselves in relation to these past performances. Whether or not Macbeth drops his cup on seeing Banquo's ghost at the banquet (III.iv.92) (and whether the cup is wooden, pewter or glass); whether Hamlet's sword sticks in the stage when he swears to avenge the ghost (I.v.164); whether Othello's words 'let it alone' (III.iii.292) refer to Desdemona's handkerchief or her attempts to soothe his fevered brow, are questions which need to be resolved in performance, and theatrical precedent is likely to influence how this is achieved.

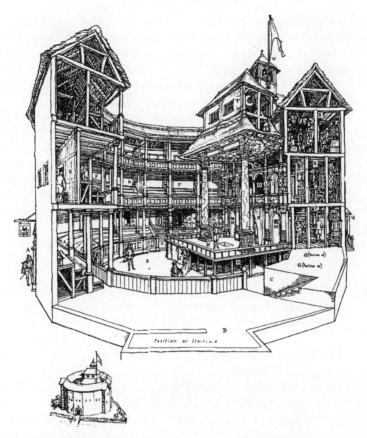

The Globe Playhouse 1599–1613 – A conjectural reconstruction

KEY

| | |
|---|---|
| AA | Main entrance |
| B | The Yard |
| CC | Entrances to lowest gallery |
| D | Entrance to staircase and upper galleries |
| E | Corridor serving the different section of the middle gallery |
| F | Middle gallery ('Twopenny Rooms') |
| G | 'Gentlemen's Rooms' or 'Lords' Rooms' |
| H | The stage |
| J | The hanging being put up round the stage |
| K | The 'Hell' under the stage |
| L | The stage trap, leading down to the Hell |
| MM | Stage doors |
| N | Curtained 'place behind the stage' |
| O | Gallery above the stage, used as required sometimes by musicians, sometimes by spectators, and often as part of the play |
| P | Back-stage area (the tiring-house) |
| Q | Tiring-house door |
| R | Dressing-rooms |
| S | Wardrobe and storage |
| T | The hut housing the machine for lower enthroned gods, etc., to the stage |
| U | The 'Heavens' |
| W | Hoisting the playhouse flag |

*Figure 6.1* The first Globe Theatre. (*Source*: from a reconstruction drawing by C. Walter Hodges in his book *The Globe Restored*, second edition, Oxford University Press, 1968.)

Each play has its own history of past performances, many of which have been recorded in some form and can be experienced by us through a multitude of media (see Chapter 7). Take *King Lear*, for example. In the late seventeenth century Nahum Tate decided to rewrite Shakespeare's play, giving it an ending which totally changed the play. In Tate's version Lear and Cordelia are saved from death by Albany and Edgar. The revised play ends with a celebration of the faithful love of Edgar and Cordelia, who are treated as god and goddess. In contrast to the muted resignation of his Shakespearean original, Tate's Edgar proudly pronounces that 'W' are past the fire and now must shine to Ages'. He and Cordelia are described as a 'celestial pair' and will clearly rule happily while Lear retires with the honest and loyal Kent. The play concludes with the following words from Edgar to Cordelia:

> Divine Cordelia, all the Gods can witness
> How much thy Love to Empire I prefer!
> Thy bright Example shall convince the World
> (Whatever Storms or Fortune are decreed)
> That Truth and Vertue shall at last succeed.[5]

Remarkably, Tate's version held the stage for 170 years, until Shakespeare's bleak ending was restored in the 1830s. Why should the 1830s have produced an audience ready for a reversal of Tate's revisions? Perhaps at the start of the Age of Reform fears of social disintegration made audiences more pessimistic or less confident of the future and therefore willing to accept Shakespeare's original. One hundred and seventy years on again, at the turn of the twenty-first century, we cannot imagine replacing Shakespeare's apocalyptic image of horror with Tate's sugar-sweet ending – though Disney may yet try. The despair of the original ending of *King Lear* seems perfectly acceptable in our times, perhaps because we're more inured to stage and screen violence.

Though Tate's revisions are radical we must accept that all performances inevitably 'change' a play, or make of it something new. The texts themselves are not stable; most of the plays are extant in several versions (see Chapter 4). Decisions have to be made about which words are going to be used and which omitted. Will the order of the words on the page be preserved, or will one speech be transposed with another for added impact? These are only the most obvious of the many questions that must be resolved in staging a Shakespearean play. Performance requires actors and directors to turn the text into something living, but also something which bears a relation to the original – though precisely what the relation should be is often difficult to determine. Performance is different from just playing or rehearsing, as anyone who has ever appeared in a production, or delivered a class presentation, or indeed taken a driving test, will know. Performance is the real thing, and in the end it rests on a series of decisions about the text and its interpretation. But why leave the decisions and the interpretations to others? If you move from the audience to the stage, from spectatorship to participation, your engagement with the play will be even more immediate and enriching.

## Acting and learning

The reason why plays have always been potentially controversial is that they go beyond words and do so publicly. A play is full of sights and sounds, often powerfully symbolic in themselves. Take Hamlet holding Yorick's skull. This is an image we see recreated again and again in our culture. It has been used widely (to sell lager and on the cover of a book of Winnie the Pooh quotations, to name but two examples). It is one of the great images of dramatic art. As he holds the skull Hamlet says:

> Alas poor Yorick. I knew him, Horatio, a fellow of infinite jest, of most excellent fancy. He hath bore me on his back a thousand times, and now – how abhorred in my imagination it is. My gorge rises at it. Here hung those lips that I have kissed I know not how oft.
>
> (V.i.178–83)

The impact of seeing a man holding a skull while saying these words has surely been crucial in fixing this moment from *Hamlet* in our collective consciousness. Shakespeare is drawing on a common image of melancholic meditation, which you can find in much of the art of the period. The shocking sound of a spade on gravel and splintering bone; the sight of a man standing in a half-

133

dug grave joking about decomposition: the materialities of the gravediggers' scene contribute inestimably to the poignancy of the jesting dialogue.

As Simon Shepherd expresses it in his essay 'Acting against bardom: Some utopian thoughts on workshops': 'One quality of the dramatic text which almost always disappears, in exercises or commentary, is the excitement generated by speed, suspense, thrills.'[6] It is our responsibility as students of Shakespeare's craft to do what we can to recover these missing thrills. Unless we have access to the plays in performance we will have to make enormous efforts to imagine what certain scenes – the street brawls in *Romeo and Juliet*, for example, or the appearance of Banquo's ghost – might be like in the theatre. There are many ways to engage with Shakespeare in performance, ranging from reading aloud passages of the text alone or with others and working out the practicalities of staging particular scenes to attending live performances, listening to audio-tapes, or watching videos. (See Chapter 7 for a further discussion.)

I now wish briefly to illustrate two methods of employing performance in class situations in order to enhance our understanding of the plays. My first example, from *The Winter's Tale*, uses a method called 'actioning' to focus on the moment when the formidable Paulina confronts the tyrant Leontes with his wife's new-born baby, and he retorts that the child is not his. As I illustrate below, having cast the scene the students should attempt to translate the words that the character speaks into a performative statement, that is, a statement that accomplishes something, a speech-act. As well as reading his or her lines the actor playing each character should speak the speech-act while using their body to reinforce the utterance through (perhaps exaggerated for effect) gesture. I have given suggested interpretations of the speech-acts inherent in the lines in square brackets following the spoken words. When students become involved in the actions which, in performance, necessarily go along with the words, their appreciation of the dynamics of the scene increases. One of the first things performance methods of learning like this helps to clarify is how many people are involved in a scene and how many props are necessary. Here we have at least half-a-dozen people, perhaps many more, on the stage with a new-born baby (perhaps represented by a doll prop) in the midst of the hubbub:

*Enter* Paulina [*carrying a baby, with* Antigonus, *lords and servants, who try to prevent her*].

| | |
|---|---|
| *A lord.* | You must not enter. [I forbid you] |
| *Paulina.* | Nay rather, good my lords, be second to me: [I enlist you] |
| | Fear you his tyrannous passion more, alas, [I shame you] |
| | Than the queen's life? a gracious innocent soul, |
| | More free than he is jealous. [I praise the queen] |
| *Antigonus.* | That's enough. [I rebuke you] |
| *Servant.* | Madam, he hath not slept to-night, commanded |
| | None should come at him. [I explain (why you must go)] |
| *Paulina.* | Not so hot, good sir; [I calm you] |
| | I come to bring him sleep. 'Tis such as you, |
| | That creep like shadows by him, and do sigh |
| | At each his needless heavings; such as you [I accuse you] |
| | Nourish the cause of his awaking. I |
| | Do come with words as medicinal as true, |
| | Honest, as either, to purge him of that humour |
| | That presses him from sleep. [I announce my mission] |
| *Leontes.* | What noise is there, ho? [I enquire] |
| *Paulina.* | No noise, my lord; but needful conference |
| | About some gossips for your highness. [I correct you] |
| *Leontes.* | How! [I express astonishment] |
| | Away with that audacious lady! Antigonus, [I command] |
| | I charg'd thee that she should not come about me. |
| | [I complain] |
| | I knew she would. [I grumble] |
| *Antigonus.* | I told her so, my lord, |
| | On your displeasure's peril and on mine |
| | She should not visit you. [I exonerate myself] |
| *Leontes.* | What! canst not rule her? [I taunt you] |
| *Paulina.* | From all dishonesty he can: in this – [I defend Antigonus] |
| | Unless he take the course that you have done, |
| | Commit me from committing honour – trust it, |
| | [I instruct Leontes] |
| | He shall not rule me. |
| *Antigonus.* | La you now, you hear: |
| | When she will take the rein I let her run; |
| | But she'll not stumble. [I praise Paulina] |

*Paulina.* Good my liege, I come, – [I introduce
And I beseech you hear me, who professes [myself as:
Myself your loyal servant, your physician, [physician]
Your most obedient counsellor, yet that dares
[counsellor]
Less appear so, in comforting your evils,
Than such as most seem yours; – I say, I come
From your good queen. [Hermione's ambassador]
*Leontes.* Good queen! [I ridicule your words]
*Paulina.* Good queen, my lord, good queen: I say good queen,
And would by combat make her good, so were I
A man, the worst about you. [I correct you and
challenge you]
*Leontes.* Force her hence. [I order Lords]
*Paulina.* Let him that makes but trifles of his eyes [I threaten
Lords]
First hand me: on mine own accord I'll off;
[I announce errand]
But first, I'll do my errand. The good queen [I give
you child]
(For she is good) hath brought you forth a daughter;
Here 'tis; [*Laying down the child*] commends it to your
blessing.

(*The Winter's Tale* II.iii.26–66)

The enacted speech-acts would serve alone as a mime or dumb-show for this scene. The dumb-show popular in Elizabethan and Jacobean theatre (and illustrated in *Hamlet* [III.ii]) was action without words, action which clearly speaks a language independent of words. That so much can be and is clearly communicated without verbal language is made clear through 'actioning' a scene as above. Performance releases the non-verbal communication latent in the text and therefore makes a significant contribution to our comprehension of it.

Status games are a further example of the difference even a limited amount of performance makes. Try dealing out cards randomly and secretly from a deck, one to each group member. Participants should be told to move about the room behaving to others according to their status as defined by their card (with Ace the lowest of the low and King, well, King). You will probably find that people soon start to behave differently, with 2's and 3's skulking shamefully and Kings and Queens swaggering confidently in the foreground. A simple exercise like this quickly demonstrates that status, or perceived status, can profoundly affect the manner in which one moves and speaks, and this in turn will depend on whom you speak to and whether you perceive them to be of equal, higher or lower status than you are.

Take the following exchange:

*Lucio.* What news, Friar, of the Duke?
*Duke.* I know none: can you tell me of any?
*Lucio.* Some say he is with the Emperor of Russia; other some he is in Rome: but where is he, think you?
*Duke.* I know not where: but wheresoever, I wish him well.
*Lucio.* It was a mad fantastical trick of him to steal from the state, and usurp the beggary he was never born to. Lord Angelo dukes it well in his absence: he puts transgression to 't . . .

*(Measure for Measure* III.i.338–44)

Lucio goes on to bemoan Angelo's harsh application of a long-neglected law, by which sex outside marriage is punishable by death, but soon returns to making critical and slanderous comments about the Duke himself:

*Lucio.* Why, what a ruthless thing is this in him [Angelo], for the rebellion of a codpiece to take away the life of a man! Would the Duke that is absent have done this? Ere he would have hanged a man for the getting a hundred bastards, he would have paid for the nursing a thousand. He had some feeling of the sport, he knew the service; and that instructed him to mercy.
*Duke.* I never heart the absent Duke much detected for women. He was not inclined that way.
*Lucio.* O sir, you are deceived.
*Duke.* 'Tis not possible.
*Lucio.* Who, not the Duke? Yes, your beggar of fifty: and his use was to put a ducat in her clack-dish: the Duke had crotchets in him. He would be drunk too; that let me inform you.
*Duke.* You do him wrong surely.

*(Measure for Measure* III.i.360–74)

Lucio is ignorant of the proper status of the man he is talking to and herein lies the comedy of the scene. The Duke becomes temporarily trapped by the role he is playing and can do little to defend himself from Lucio's comic and bawdy assault. Reading the scene might be entertaining, but how much more comedy is offered through an enactment in which the Duke uncomfortably squirms in the disguise of a holy man while, presumably unaware of his mistake, Lucio spins his smutty slander. The effect in performance is delicious for the audience, who can fully enjoy the non-verbal elements of the situation which we must endeavour to imagine when reading: the attitudes, faces, gestures and bodily interactions of the two actors who speak the above words.

That we can become trapped by an adopted role is evident, but Shakespeare is also fascinated by the notion of individual selves under strain, often cast in roles they find themselves unable to play effectively. Coriolanus, for example, is destroyed by his excessive pride and honour combined with his inability to play politics. He considers himself a fixed and unalterable thing. His firm sense of self makes him incapable of reconciling honour with the shifting behaviour and demands of the increasingly powerful plebiscite of Rome. He is torn apart by the fact that although those he serves, the common people, demand that he pay them lip-service, he cannot. They are out to save their skin, he to save his identity. Though he tries to dissemble he is unable to indulge in the commonplace duplicity of the politician and, in a magnificent irony, must therefore turn on Rome itself. His fellow nobles implore him to flatter the common crowd, but Coriolanus has only disdain for them. The strain of playing a role is too much for him, as the following passage illustrates:

*Coriolanus.* You have put me now to such a part which never
            I shall discharge to th' life.
*Cominius.* Come, come, we'll prompt you.
*Volumnia.* I prithee now, sweet son, as thou hast said
            My praises made thee first a soldier, so,
            To have my praise for this, perform a part
            Thou hast not done before.
*Coriolanus.* Well, I must do't.
            Away, my disposition, and possess me
            Some harlot's spirit! My throat of war be turned,
            Which quired with my drum, into a pipe
            Small as an eunuch or the virgin voice
            That babies lull asleep! The smiles of knaves
            Tent in my cheeks, and schoolboys' tears take up
            The glasses of my sight! A beggar's tongue

Make motion through my lips, and my armed knees,
Who bowed but in my stirrup, bend like his
That hath received an alms! I will not do't;
Lest I surcease to honour mine own truth,
And by my body's action teach my mind
A most inherent baseness.

(III.ii.105–23)

Ironically, Coriolanus's dedication to his true self, a self lacking in deceit, leads to his tragedy and therefore implies the need for deceit in human society. One must surrender to the role-playing nature of life, to the necessary impermanence of self, otherwise one will end up like Coriolanus, destroyed by the changeable world.

## Theatre of dreams

Puck closes *A Midsummer Night's Dream* with a speech which contains the following lines:

If we shadows have offended,
Think but this, and all is mended,
That you have but slumber'd here
While these visions did appear.
And this weak and idle theme,
No more yielding than a dream.

(IV.i.410–15)

Shakespeare's drama frequently functions as dreamscape and we are alerted again and again to the unreality of what we witness, especially in the comedies and romances. In his late plays, *The Tempest* and *The Winter's Tale*, Shakespeare is partly concerned with a consideration of his art, the art of the theatre, and partly with the idea that theatre, like life, may be no more substantial than a dream. Prospero is an artist who, through his learning, is able to command spirits (actors) and events (plot). Similarly, though more tyrannically, Leontes tries to impose his perception of truth on others. His hubris (excessive pride) when he contradicts the oracle of Apollo is immediately punished by the gods. It is Paulina who restores his bride Hermione to him sixteen years later. As she seems to bring the statue to life with her command

'Music, awake her; strike!' (V.iii.98) the audience, both on stage and beyond, are encouraged to lay aside their scepticism and confront the wonder of theatrical art in a moment which resembles a religious sacrament:

> *Paulina.* Either forbear,
> Quit presently the chapel, or resolve you
> For more amazement. If you can behold it,
> I'll make the statue move indeed; descend,
> And take you by the hand: but then you'll think
> (Which I protest against) I am assisted
> By wicked powers.
>
> (V.iii.85–90)

Leontes, who has most to gain from awaking his faith, reacts to the descending Hermione with an emotional statement which could be read as Shakespeare's defence of dramatic art from the encroachments of a suspicious and litigious state:

> O, she's warm
> If this be magic, let it be an art
> Lawful as eating.
>
> (V.iii.109–11)

Perhaps Shakespeare had half an eye here on the puritans, who called for the closure of the theatres (partly because they were dens of ill-repute and partly because the puritans mistrusted theatrical representations and fictions as lies).[7] Paulina speaks to all who hear, stage characters and wider audience, when she says: 'It is requir'd/ You do awake your faith' (V.iii.94–5). Hermione's transformation from art to life is so wonderful that we want to believe in it – and in the theatrical enterprise itself, perhaps.

Yet Shakespeare goes out of his way to remind us that he is dealing in dreams and stories, that a tale is being told, and a pretty tall tale at that. Early in the play the young Mamillius, Prince of Sicilia, claims 'A sad tale's best for winter: I have one/ Of sprites and goblins' (II.i.25–6). He begins the tale at his mother's request:

> *Hermione.* Let's have that, good sir.
> Come on, sit down, come on, and do your best
> To fright me with your sprites: you're powerful at it.

*Mamillius.* There was a man –
*Hermione.* Nay, come sit down: then on.
*Mamillius.* Dwelt by a churchyard: I will tell it softly,
Yon crickets shall not hear it.
*Hermione.* Come on then,
And giv't me in mine ear.
[*Enter* LEONTES, *with* ANTIGONUS, *Lords, and others.*]
(II.i.26–32)

Shakespeare is undoubtedly a great storyteller. He is, like the ill-fated Mamillius, 'powerful at it' and we, like Hermione in this scene, crave his words. The less we care whether the plays are 'realistic' or 'plausible' the more readily we can enter what the contemporary American playwright David Mamet has described as 'the national dream-life' of the theatre.[8] The phrase 'national dream-life' seems particularly appropriate as a description of what Shakespeare's plays have become for us. For one of the great effects of theatre is that of a shared audience experience:

Lead us from hence, where we may leisurely
Each one demand, and answer to his part
Perform'd in this wide gap of time, since first
We were dissever'd: hastily lead away. *Exeunt.*
(*The Winter's Tale* V.iii.152–5)

By pursuing the relation of Shakespeare's plays to performance, whether by considering the use of theatrical metaphor in the plays, or studying contemporary staging and performance history, or contemplating and responding to actual or recorded performances, or performing the plays yourself, you can only broaden and deepen your understanding and appreciation of Shakespeare's dramatic dream.

## Notes

1. Julian Hilton, *Performance* (London: Macmillan, 1987), p. 127.
2. *Ibid.*
3. See Jonathon Dollimore and Alan Sinfield, *Political Shakespeare* (Manchester: Manchester University Press, 1985), especially Dollimore's introductory chapter, pp. 2–17.

141

4. Gāmini Sālgado, *Eyewitnesses of Shakespeare* (London: Chatto and Windus for Sussex University Press, 1975).
5. Elizabeth Home, *The First English Actresses* (Cambridge: Cambridge University Press, 1992), p. 120.
6. Shepherd's essay appears in *Shakespeare in the Changing Curriculum*, eds. Lesley Aers and Nigel Wheale (London: Routledge, 1991), pp. 88–107.
7. See Barbara Freedman's article 'Elizabethan protest, plague, and plays: Rereading the "Documents of Control"', *English Literary Renaissance*, Vol. 26 (Winter 1996), 17–45.
8. David Mamet, *Writing in Restaurants* (London: Faber and Faber, 1988), p. 8.

# CHAPTER 7

# Multimedia Shakespeare

## Mediating Shakespeare

In this chapter you will be encouraged to find your own preferred medium for familiarizing yourself with Shakespeare's plays and researching more deeply into them. You will also be encouraged to think about where you are getting your information on Shakespeare, how it is transmitted, how reliable the source is, how it is presented and what context it is set in.

Your choice is wide and varied. A mix of media will no doubt be of most value. You might find videos of film versions useful, or prefer audio-tapes as they allow you to follow the text in your own edition. Critical and contextual material is also widely available in video and audio form. I have cited some examples of different audio-visual resources to illustrate the benefits of their use. The latest interactive media (as opposed to the linear materials which assume a more passive audience) are necessarily, by definition, dependent on the choices of the individual user. These media – CD-ROM, Internet, world wide web – must be explored, in the main, by oneself. I am happy here to indicate a little of what is out there, but you must use these interfaces yourself, choosing your own pathways through the already considerable amount of material. Shifts in teaching and learning over the next few years are likely to be from passive to active learning, from static to dynamic presentation, from real to virtual objects and from single to multiple media. Multimedia is likely to have a deep impact on our society and will be applied in various areas: business, government, communication, entertainment and education. The implications for the study of Shakespeare are beginning to become apparent. The combination of different media controlled by a personal computer will open up varied and exciting possibilities and opportunities in Shakespeare studies.

For many centuries the most advanced and powerful media for recording and transmitting information has been the book. The history of the book is a fascinating topic in itself. Though books have become relatively cheaper and cheaper to produce in larger and larger numbers, the basic technology (leaves of paper bound together and protected by a cover) has remained largely unchanged over the centuries. But we are living in an age of huge technological development and the manner in which text is transmitted is now changing.

'Multimedia' refers to 'information presented or stored in a combination of different forms, using graphics, text, sound, video, and animation'.[1] Multimedia is, then, media integration, with interactive computing providing the interface for the user. A useful representation of this integration of media is provided in Figure 7.1.

One reason why Shakespearean drama is so amenable to the latest technology might be that the theatrical medium is working to a very similar model which might be expressed as follows (see Figure 7.2).

One notable difference in the two models seems to be the degree of interaction possible in the theatre, though an audience

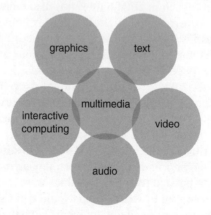

*Figure 7.1*   Multimedia model.

144

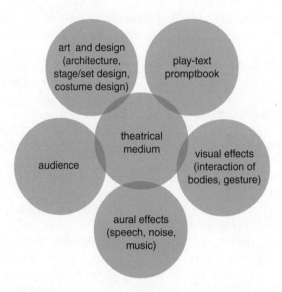

*Figure 7.2*   Theatrical medium model.

certainly reacts by laughing, crying or applauding, and indeed, judging from some contemporary accounts the theatre of early modern England was a more riotous place than it generally is now. In fact, though it is fairly rare, audience members do occasionally react in a manner which can directly affect the experience of the play for others and in some cases alter the performance of a play, but this is the exception rather than the rule in the theatre. With multimedia educational resources the capacity for 'audience' inter- action is an integral part of the way it works.

In addition to the happy correlation between the components integrated in multimedia and in the theatre, the fact is that avail- able information on Shakespeare is presented and stored in a com- bination of different forms: different versions of the plays and poems either singly or collected; illustrated books; printed crit- icism; audio-tape performances, workshops and discussions; film and video-tape performances, workshops and discussions; theatri- cal architecture; costume design; paintings; animation; and lately, interactive CD-ROM packages and web-sites on the Internet.

Multimedia developments offer the opportunity to make soft- ware links between texts, images and sounds. These links are called hyper-media, and they provide multimedia presentations with characteristic flexibility as they allow for interaction in the learning process. Interactive multimedia, as opposed to linear media, place you in control of the material, allowing you to move freely through the hyper-linked images, sound and video clips in a given program. Predefined areas, usually highlighted by use of colour, underlining or capital letters, are known as *hotspots*. These hotspots provide the hyper-links and open associated files which might consist of audio, graphic or video clips, or perhaps a new window filled with more information and more hyper-links. Hyper-link hotspots enable you to follow your own pathways, while making it easy to retrace your steps and branch out anew if you so wish. The student who uses multimedia technology is transformed from a passive recipient of others' materials into an active producer of their own educational information.

When we study any of Shakespeare's plays we should be aware, as I pointed out in Chapter 5, that there are questions surrounding the text. In some cases there are a number of versions, and amongst versions there are different states (the result of proof-reading corrections introduced during print-runs, for example). Versions of the plays were not collected and published together, as a book, until seven years after Shakespeare's death. During Shakespeare's lifetime the plays were not circulating widely as literary works to be read and re-read. The plays were working in another medium than the printed word; they were working for listeners and viewers, for a theatrical audience. This fact means that Shakespeare is well placed to continue his dominance of English literary studies in the age of multimedia. Consider the multiple ways that Shakespeare is mediated to us: through endless allusion in poetry and prose; through sculpture, opera, cartoon and painting; through drama which borrows from, adapts and transforms the plays; through film and television adaptations. And these different offshoots of Shakespeare spring so naturally because his dramatic art was a multimedia project which combined poetry and prose, song and soliloquy, dance, pageant, procession, ritual combat, spectacle, and music both festive and solemn. The Shakespearean masque, for example, combines different elements (sculpture, music, painting, costume, set design) in a demonstration of the multimedia imagination at work. Take the scene in *The Tempest* where Prospero, with

Ariel's help, conjurs up Juno, Ceres and a host of nymphs to dance for the soon-to-be-wed Ferdinand and Miranda (IV.i).

The plays could be said to consist of many voices in multiple registers. Though Shakespeare's reputation is connected with the towering passion of King Lear's poetry, his fool's wisdom is communicating at a different, though perhaps no less profound level, the level of proverbial song and the folklore of saws and maxims:

> Have more than thou showest,
> Speak less than thou knowest,
> Lend less than thou owest,
> Ride more than thou goest,
> Learn more than thou trowest,
> Set less than thou throwest,
> Leave thy drink and thy whore,
> And keep in-a-door,
> And thou shalt have more
> Than two tens to a score.
>                         (I.iv.116–25)

Shakespeare's contemporary audience was a mixed one, ranging from the 'groundlings' who stood to the wealthy occupants of the expensive seats. One way that Shakespearean drama works is by presenting a range of different voices and registers of speech which enable the plays to communicate on multiple levels, thus appealing to this varied audience.

## Text

Throughout this book we have discussed Shakespeare's writing, but part of the phenomenon of Shakespeare is the amount of writing he has inspired. One of the ways that Shakespeare is mediated to us is through the writings of others who have responded to his work. Take the romantic poet John Keats writing in 1818 about his experience 'On Sitting Down to Read *King Lear* Once Again':

> once again, the fierce dispute
> Betwixt damnation and impassioned clay
> Must I burn through, once more humbly assay
> The bitter-sweet of this Shakespearian fruit:

Chief Poet! and ye clouds of Albion,
Begetters of our deep eternal theme!
When through the old oak forest I am gone,
Let me not wander in a barren dream,
But, when I am consumed in the fire,
Give me new Phoenix wings to fly at my desire.

Critical editions of Shakespeare's plays tend to give quite a lot of information on possible sources of, and influences behind, the work, but part of the wonder of Shakespeare is the influence his work has had on other creative writers. Some plays have inspired more than others. *The Tempest* seems to appeal particularly to poets, novelists, illustrators, animators and film-makers as a source of inspiration. Keats is certainly not alone amongst creative artists in praising and pondering Shakespeare. But of what interest is material inspired by Shakespeare to the student of Shakespeare? Keats's lines, though post-dating the play by over two hundred years, can provide us with a useful departure for a discussion of *King Lear*, Shakespeare and tragedy. Keats deliberately chooses to write about the reading experience as a trial by fire as he describes *King Lear* as a book he must 'burn through'. His use of the image of the mythical winged Phoenix, rising from the ashes, concludes the sonnet triumphally. The effort of 'once more humbly assay-[ing]' the work is rewarded by the purging cathartic effect.

Keats does convey his sense of the universe of *King Lear* with his mention of 'Albion' and 'deep eternal theme' and 'old oak forest'; a sense, that is, of ancient Britain. This suggests a feature of Shakespeare's plays which is worth noting here. In most of the plays Shakespeare has successfully created a unique world peopled with denizens all its own. Think of Illyria in *Twelfth Night*, or Othello's fortified Cyprus. Think of the woods of *A Midsummer Night's Dream* or the woods in *Titus Andronicus*. Think of Falstaff's Eastcheap or Hamlet's Elsinore. Think of Cleopatra's Egypt or the Rome of Coriolanus. Each play takes place in its own world or worlds though these are by no means firmly fixed by Shakespeare. Shakespeare's plays function rhetorically, not realistically. The stage was a bare one, leaving open questions of setting for the audience to imaginatively infer. What is the kind of island we imagine when we read or hear the following exchange?

*Adrian.* The air breathes upon us here most sweetly.
*Sebastian.* As if it had lungs, and rotten ones.
*Antonio.* Or as 'twere perfumed by a fen.
*Gonzalo.* Here is everything advantageous to life.
*Antonio.* True; save means to live.
*Sebastian.* Of that there's none, or little.
*Gonzalo.* How lush and lusty the grass looks! how green!
*Antonio.* The ground indeed is tawny.
*Sebastian.* With an eye of green in 't.
(*The Tempest* II.i.46–54)

Just as the separate characters reveal different dispositions and suggest that the island is whatever you make it, so different artists coming into contact with the plays will have to construct these worlds imaginatively as they will. It is the limitless imaginative variety offered by these Shakespearean worlds that makes them so suitable for multimedia exploration. For our sense of the kind of world we are in when we are in a Shakespearean play will be more than a matter of words; it will have much to do with non-verbal modes of signification such as music and other sound effects, costume and props.

One way of responding to the plays is with a piece of improvized writing of your own. You could try following Keats and write a poetical response to the experience of reading (or reading once again) a particular play. Or you might find it stimulating to take ten or so lines from a play and try to write a paraphrase of the extract. Looking at your version and the original try to determine what is missing from your version, and what you have altered. You will find that a simple exercise like this helps you to focus on the detail of the text.

**Art and graphics**

The play scene in *Hamlet* was a common topic for students at art college in the nineteenth century. In Daniel Maclise's oil of this scene painted in 1842 we can see in the background tapestries depicting Biblical scenes, the 'Temptation in the Garden of Eden', the 'Expulsion', the 'Sacrifice of Abel' and 'Cain Murdering Abel'. All these tapestries speak to the wary eye. Shakespeare's audience would have been familiar with the allegorical and emblematic medium of tapestry and dramatic tableaux, but we have some

*The Play Scene in 'Hamlet'* by Daniel Maclise. (*Source*: The Tate Gallery, London.)

work to do to reopen our channels of thought in this particular medium. The most moving moment in the tragedy of *Romeo and Juliet* comes when the two young lovers lie dead in the silent tomb of the Capulets at the end of the play. The play is working here through a static, one might say painterly, image of sacrifice.

When words are being used in the plays there is nearly always a linked image we need to consider. As students of Shakespeare we should always be asking ourselves what is the visual image that accompanies the words read, and are the 'meanings' of image and word complementary or in conflict? In *Richard III* we see Richard appear 'aloft, between two Bishops', pietistically carrying a prayer book. His cynical show of religious faith achieves the desired response from his audience. In this case the visual and the verbal messages are in collision, and Richard is made more sinister by his hypocritical manipulation of image:

> *Mayor.* See, where his grace stands, 'tween two clergymen!
> *Buckingham.* Two props of virtue for a Christian Prince,
>            To stay him from the fall of vanity:

150

And see, a book of prayer in his hand –
True ornaments to know a holy man.
Famous Plantagenet, most gracious Prince,
Lend favourable ear to our requests;
And pardon us the interruption
Of thy devotion and right Christian zeal.
(*Richard III* III.vii.94–102)

Many artists have responded to Shakespeare through their painting as a recent exhibition from the Tate Gallery Collection at Norwich Castle Museum made clear.[2] Artists such as Thomas Stothard, James Sant, Robert Huskisson, Ford Madox Brown, William Holman Hunt, John Singer Sargent, Henry Wallis and William Orpen were displayed alongside Maclise's work. Perhaps the most famous painting in the exhibition was the 1851 oil by Sir John Everett Millais of Ophelia drowning. This scene is based on the speech by Gertrude in which she describes the tragic demise of Ophelia, and indeed it is so well known that it is difficult to contemplate her death without conjuring up the symbolic detail of the pre-Raphaelite masterpiece.

Some plays have received more attention than others. Indeed, some characters, or incidents, have been interpreted and portrayed on so many occasions that the history of their representation becomes a sizeable study in themself (for example Ophelia's drowning, the play scene in *Hamlet*, or Caliban).

In the case of the series of short, animated films (*The Animated Tales*) the artistic response to Shakespearean text has been a collaborative one. Teams of animators, painters, artist and musicians from Britain and Russia have worked on half-hour long interpretations of a number of the plays, consulting literary, educational and academic advisers to assist in the production of memorable and enjoyable versions.[3]

### Recorded Shakespeare

Thomas Edison made the first sound recording in 1877 when he spoke 'Mary had a little lamb . . . ' into his phonograph. We take this technology for granted but should appreciate the vast storehouse of interpretation that the capacity to record sound presents us with. Sound archives provide immediate access to particular performances of the plays. The easiest way in is to trust a professional. It may not be easy to trust an actor, but there are actors who can make us see things for the first time, or who give us a tingle of excitement and emotion. Richard Burton is one of these actors for me. I find listening to his voice an experience in itself, and when he is delivering Shakespeare the experience can be searing. Now it may not be the most up-to-date medium, but the old vinyl LP of *Coriolanus* featuring Richard Burton which I found in the college library proved to be an eye-opening rendition. I had read the play a few times as an undergraduate and subsequently. I had always been impressed with the poetry, but had never felt any sympathy for the eponymous hero, Caius Martius or 'Coriolanus'. Burton's performance on the crackly LPs was of such vigour, the words burst on my ears. The battle speeches of Coriolanus, delivered with such speed, energy and aggression against the background of the hue and cry of the crowd, left a particularly lasting impression. I can still hear Burton's strains when I read:

> Those are they
> That most are willing. If any such be here –
> As it were sin to doubt – that love this painting
> Wherein you see me smeared; if any fear
> Lesser his person than an ill report;
> If any think brave death outweighs bad life,
> And that his country's dearer than himself;
> Let him alone, or so many so minded
> Wave thus, to express his disposition,
> And follow Marcius.
>> *They all shout, and wave their swords; take him up in their arms, and cast up their caps.*
> O me alone! Make you a sword of me?
>> (*Coriolanus* I.vi.67–76)

Richard Briars's Polonius is another example of an audio recording that I find entertaining and enlightening. His performance, as part of the Renaissance Theatre Company audio production of the play, was a comic masterpiece. The way he drew out the 'brevity is the soul of wit' speech, with a stuttering style, was both deeply frustrating and highly amusing. The character of Polonius was imbued with a well-intentioned incompetence (though I did wonder how much of my newfound tolerance for the role was a result of Briars's association in my mind with the benevolent, jumper-wearing Tom Good of *The Good Life*).

Audio-recordings not only bring the voices of Shakespeare's plays to life, they can also lead us into a finer contemplation of the music, song and sound effects of a play. Listening to *Twelfth Night* on tape assists us in realizing the abundant variety of music and song employed as the play ranges from the mournful 'Come away death' to the exuberant 'what is love?'.

Audio-tape discussions of the plays are also available.[4] These generally consist of one or two academics discussing aspects of the chosen play and can provide students with an alternative means of engaging with vital questions and topics surrounding the text. The appeal of audio-tapes is that one can listen to them while doing some other task. In the case of the plays themselves audio-recordings offer a good opportunity for the student to follow the play in their own copy of the text. And of course, one can always stop and rewind the tape at any point if one so desires.

### Shakespeare on film and video

The first moving images made by Thomas Edison in 1893 were only fifteen seconds long and could be viewed by only one person at a time. Just over thirty years later, in 1927, the first Hollywood movie with a sound-track was shown, and colour film became available in the 1930s. The development of this technology through the twentieth century has had, and continues to have, a huge effect on the way that Shakespearean drama is represented to us.

Once a performance of a Shakespeare play is filmed it is in some sense fixed. Unlike theatre which is always ephemeral (though conventions develop and are often difficult to shift) 'film is fixture, establishing itself as another kind of text'.[5] In Orson Welles's *Othello*, before we even hear any words spoken, we have five minutes of mood-setting music and memorable images. A sombre piano accompanies the spectacle of Iago being hoisted up the castle walls in a cage while the dead bodies of Othello and Desdemona are borne through the citadel. The effect is immediate, and not dependent on words at all. We have a vision of the play's end and an atmosphere of fear and anxiety is conveyed through the startling contrast of light and shadow combined with the solemn sound track.

Similar effects can be noted in all film versions. With recorded film it is possible to compare and contrast the treatment of the same play by different directors at different times. Take Laurence Olivier's 1944 film of *Henry V* and compare it with Kenneth Branagh's 1989 version, for example. Olivier's film was made in an England embroiled in war and its dedication itself reveals much of the effect Olivier was aiming for:

> To
> THE COMMANDOS
> and
> AIRBORNE TROOPS
> of
> GREAT BRITAIN
> the spirit of whose ancestors
> it has been humbly attempted
> to recapture in some ensuing scenes
> THIS FILM IS DEDICATED

The film is a patriotic celebration of British military bravery and most of the more disturbing moments of the play are cut. Branagh's version, in contrast, presents a very different play. As Branagh himself wrote, 'in my own performance, I tried to realise the qualities of introspection, fear, doubt and anger which I believed the text indicated.'[6] *Henry V* provides just one example of a Shakespeare play which has inspired famous film versions. Indeed, for many, Shakespeare is more likely to be experienced through film than through text. We might pause here for a moment to consider the words of Anthony Davies on this matter:

> Scholars of Shakespeare as literature seem rarely to venture into the domain of Shakespearean film criticism. This is puzzling insofar as both the published text and the film exist – unlike the staged performance – as objects, and it is likely that over the years more people will form an idea of Shakespeare's *Romeo and Juliet* or *Hamlet* from the respective films of Zeffirelli and Olivier than will do so from any encounter with printed text.[7]

What Davies says seems highly probable, and the implications for Shakespeare scholars must be considered. But whatever our reservations about the ascendancy of film interpretations of Shakespeare we should not be blinded to the fact that recorded audio and video versions of the plays represent a valuable resource to students, so long as these recordings are used thoughtfully and in conjunction with a concerted engagement with the texts themselves. Here are the words of a student who produced written and oral work of a high standard when he studied at Chester:

> When I was revising I ideally wanted to know certain plays like the back of my hand. So I continually re-read them and kept watching the videos. It sounds a bit of a traditional way of learning but I felt more secure drumming the basics into my head and then going on to deeper subjects. I felt that way I was better prepared to handle questions from any angle. The alternative was to revise certain topics, which seemed a high-risk strategy. (Richard Hulse)

Thorough familiarity does indeed prepare you well to address any question and recorded performances are useful in making the material familiar. But also recorded performances, like live performances, can throw up totally unexpected interpretations which contradict your notions concerning a particular play. As in discussion, contradiction should cause you to ponder your ideas and defend or modify them.

Not only are there many video versions of the plays available, in addition there are other videos that can be of practical use. The Open University series of taped workshops (mentioned in Chapter 2) are helpful in bringing out aspects of performance which the student may have difficulty realizing. To take one example, the *Antony and Cleopatra* workshop[8] introduced by Cicely Palser Havely concentrates on Act IV scene iv of the play, a short scene in which Antony, in taking his leave of Cleopatra puts on his armour to do battle with Octavius Caesar. The four actors involved in the scene, playing Antony, Cleopatra, Eros and Charmian, have to figure out, with the help of the director John Russell Brown, exactly what they are doing at each moment. Even though the scene is less than forty lines long, there is plenty of work to be done. James Laurenson, playing Antony, remarks that the scene is 'very proppy' and this is apparent as the actors struggle to co-ordinate the stage business of arming Antony with the text they must speak. The scene must look a little muddled, which is a difficult thing to arrange and rehearse. The intimacy of doing a job together, strapping up the buckles of Antony's armour, must be conveyed with an emotional undercurrent. The following lines look rather blank on the page, but the workshop brings such moments to life:

*Cleopatra.* Nay, I'll help too.
What's this for?
*Antony.* Ah, let be, let be! thou art
The armourer of my heart: false, false: this, this.
*Cleopatra.* Sooth, la, I'll help: thus it must be.

(IV.iv.5–8)

Through the action of the workshop a line like 'thus it must be' suddenly achieves a double resonance, describing at once the fiddly matter of buckling a strap while also expressing a sense of unfolding fate and impending doom. The workshop also makes apparent the awkwardness of entrances and exits, both aspects of performance too easily neglected when reading.

## Interactive computing

In recent years there has been a phenomenal growth in the use of personal computers in higher education. The combination of the emergence of multimedia and the burgeoning of global digital networks means that most students of Shakespeare in higher education are now presented with new and exciting opportunities. In the final section of this chapter I aim to indicate something of the impact of these developments on Shakespeare studies, and I will be citing specific examples to illustrate the extent of the changing picture.

The range of Shakespeare-related materials already available on CD-ROM can be illustrated by a description of a number of available packages. *The BBC Shakespeare on CD-ROM* consists of substantial extracts from the BBC TV productions, complete audio performances, the definitive Alexander text of the plays and video and audio interviews with actors, directors and critics. At the time of writing three titles are available: *Romeo and Juliet*, *Macbeth* and *A Midsummer Night's Dream*. These offer the student some interactivity, but are generally aimed at the school market, as is the *Karaoke Shakespeare CD-ROM* from Cambridge. Titles available in this series include *Macbeth*, *A Midsummer Night's Dream*, *Romeo and Juliet* and *Twelfth Night*. These disks offer the student the prospect of reading a selected character's part.

Electronic archives are of more use and interest to students in higher education. One notable example of an electronic archive is *The World Shakespeare Bibliography on CD-ROM 1990–1993*,[9] which contains over 12,000 records of material on Shakespeare (books, articles, book reviews, dissertations, theatrical productions, reviews of productions, audio-visual materials and electronic media) cited in over seventy languages. Annual updates are planned to extend this bibliography so that the period 1900 to the present day is contained on one disk. The package features rapid search and retrieval functions with straightforward screen commands.

Another package which is breaking into new educational areas is the fascinating Pilot CD-ROM produced by The Open University and BBC Shakespeare Multimedia Research Group in collaboration with the University of Alberta, Routledge, the Royal Academy of Dramatic Art and University College Chester. This package contains a number of exciting new features in that it:

- Is interactive. The student takes text and follows it through to performance by interacting as director, editor, actor, designer, or from different perspectives in the audience.
- Uses three distinctive innovative performances with a range of lighting, set designs, costumes and playing spaces.
- Features interviews with scholars and performance experts from around the world.

Other electronic packages are more text-based, such as the *Arden Shakespeare CD-ROM: Texts and Sources for Shakespeare Studies*.[10] Designed to help users engage with both texts and sources, this CD-ROM consists of an integrated database which includes:

- the complete modern text of every Shakespeare play from the Arden 2 edition,
- facsimile images of each page of first Folio and early Quarto texts,
- poems and sonnets,
- a selection of texts to facilitate a variety of research, such as:

Bullough's *Narrative and Dramatic Sources of Shakespeare*, Bevington's *Shakespeare* bibliography, Abbot's *A Shakespearian Grammar*, Onions and Eagleson's *A Shakespeare Glossary* and Partridge's *Shakespeare's Bawdy*.

With its wide range of search facilities this package provides students with a flexible research tool with promising potential. The designers have opted to resist the temptation to make use of multimedia's capacity to integrate other media such as graphics, video and audio, preferring instead to concentrate on the text. At first this seems disappointing, especially given the Arden 3 series' predilection for plates demonstrating artistic interpretations and performance history. The reason, it seems, is one of capacity. No doubt as the ability to store more data on less software develops, products will offer more and more material, integrating a combination of media.

A characteristic of this CD-ROM is that it has been 'specifically tailored by a distinguished group of international scholars and is uniquely designed for higher level research across the entire

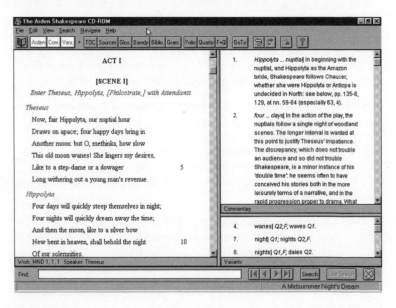

Sample screen showing Arden text, commentary and variants. (*Source*: taken from *The Arden Shakespeare CD-ROM*. Copyright © Thomas Nelson and Sons Limited, 1997.)

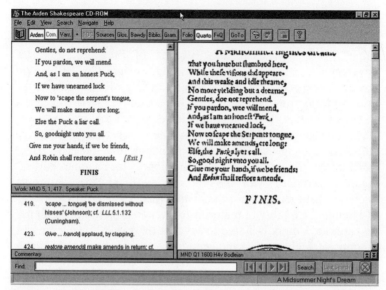

Sample screen showing Arden text, commentary and Quarto version. (*Source*: taken from *The Arden Shakespeare CD-ROM*. Copyright © Thomas Nelson and Sons Limited, 1997.)

corpus' (to quote the publicity material). Some illustrations of sample pages from the disk with annotations to indicate their potential use are shown above.

As well as the intriguing development of CD-ROM technology there is the ever-expanding Internet. You can visit University College Chester English Department's home page by accessing: http://www.chester.ac.uk/. Select Academic Departments, select English Department, select Internet Resources in English, select Shakespeare and you will be given a choice of the following:

- A Guide to Shakespeare on the Internet by Terry Gray
- Complete Works of William Shakespeare
- Oregon Shakespeare Festival
- Search Program for Shakespeare's poetry
- Shakespeare, companies, festivals and productions
- The Shakespeare Homepage
- Shakespeare Resources on the Internet
- Shakespeare Web Server

Directing people on which pathways to follow would be wholly counter to the exciting spirit of cybersurfing. To be sure there are frustrations, but there are also moments of enjoyment and education. During my own brief (30-minute) surf round these screens I came across the mysterious persona of Prospero, who had developed a web-site entitled Was Shakespeare Gay? I also discovered designs of the Cockpit theatre by Inigo Jones being rebuilt at the International Shakespeare Globe Centre.

The Internet is ideally suited to Shakespeare's role-playing world. Those engaging with Shakespeare on the Internet can assume roles while also feeling that they are participating in a collective educational enterprise rather than studying alone. One becomes part of a complex audience with the opportunity to engage with other audience members and not the private reader alone with a book.

Though the quality of material encountered on the Internet may be variable, I think it is safe to say that there will be an increasing amount of high-quality and genuinely useful material available. Indeed, publishers are now offering Shakespeare on-line. Chadwyck Healey have recently made available a literary database of Editions and Adaptations of Shakespeare which includes eleven major editions of the plays from the First Folio to the Cambridge edition of 1863–6 and twenty-four separate contemporary printings of individual plays plus more than one hundred adaptations, sequels and burlesques from the seventeenth, eighteenth and nineteenth centuries. All these texts are produced in full, with all accompanying matter as well as a facsimile of the title-pages, illustrations and a selection of other pages. Combined with search fields which can be browsed, this collection represents a formidable learning resource and is presumably a sign of things to come in Shakespeare studies – and indeed in education generally. The student can sit at the terminal and access an array of texts which would otherwise be inaccessible.

The learning process will become increasingly interactive and intertextual in the lively future of multimedia Shakespeare, as dynamic and changing digital networks are used and contributed to by students around the globe.

**Notes**

1. Simon Collin, *The Way Multimedia Works* (London: Dorling Kindersley, 1994), p. 124.

2. *Art as Theatre: Shakespeare and theatre in British painting from Hogarth to Sargent*, Norwich Castle Museum, 3 February–14 April 1996.

3. *Shakespeare Animated Films Ltd*, Moscow and Cardiff (Soyuzmultifilm/Christmas Films with S4C Channel 4 Wales), Series Producer and Director: Dave Edwards.

4. The *Sussex Tapes* (Sussex Publications Limited, London) and *Norwich Tapes* (Norwich Tapes Limited, Buckingham) are both useful series.

5. Anthony Davies, *Filming Shakespeare's Plays* (Cambridge: Cambridge University Press, 1988), p. 3.

6. Kenneth Branagh makes this claim in the Introduction to *Henry V by William Shakespeare: A screen adaptation by Kenneth Branagh* (London: Chatto and Windus, 1989), pp. 9–10.

7. Anthony Davies, *Filming Shakespeare's Plays*, p. 4.

8. *Antony and Cleopatra* Workshop, Open University/BBC, Educational Enterprises Ltd, Milton Keynes, 1984.

9. *The World Shakespeare Bibliography on CD-ROM* is published by Cambridge University Press in association with The Folger Shakespeare Library, Washington DC, and edited by James L. Harner, Texas A and M University.

10. Consultant Editor: Professor Jonathan Bate, University of Liverpool.

# CHAPTER 8

# Shakespeare and criticism

## Introduction

It would be impossible to write a systematic or otherwise useful overview of four centuries of Shakespeare criticism within the confines of a single chapter. Rather than producing a series of general reflections, or attempting to summarize the principal insights of a tiny selection of critics, I propose to focus here on the criticism of a single play and use it as a case-study. I hope thereby to suggest some ways in which students of Shakespeare can find their bearings in the vast and diverse body of secondary material he has inspired. My aim is to show how criticism on Shakespeare can be used to inform, rather than swamp, our own responses to him.

I have chosen *Measure for Measure* for my case-study, since it is so often hailed as the Shakespearean text which speaks most intimately to the preoccupations of our own times. As Graham Nicholls puts it, 'The play's complex treatment of complex questions, its attack on moral absolutism, have meant that this play is the easiest to ascribe to Shakespeare Our Contemporary.'[1] T. F. Wharton is still more definite: '*Measure for Measure* is currently Shakespeare's most popular play.'[2] Wharton bases his claim on the number of revivals of *Measure for Measure* in the international theatre: seven major productions in 1981 alone. The statistic may be evidence of the play's popularity with directors rather than with audiences or students, but it does seem that since the 1970s *Measure for Measure* has engaged the attention of critics as or more frequently than any other of Shakespeare's plays. It seems

163

uniquely controversial: as Darryl J. Gless says, 'Perhaps more than any other Shakespearean play, it has elicited and continues to elicit interpretations that violently conflict.'[3]

Given its frequent stagings and now central place in the canon, many students are likely to be familiar with *Measure for Measure*. Nevertheless, it is not essential to have prior knowledge of the text in order to read and understand this chapter, for it will be used here as a vehicle for the examination of Shakespeare criticism, rather than as a subject for exposition in its own right. I shall begin, however, with a brief account of the plot in order to highlight those aspects of the play which have attracted most attention from critics.

**Plot summary**

*Measure for Measure* is set in Vienna. The ruler of the city, Duke Vincentio, is suddenly impatient with the sexual promiscuity of his people and with his own shortcomings, and decides to abrogate his powers temporarily to Angelo, a young nobleman noted for his personal integrity. The Duke appears to leave Vienna, though in fact he remains, disguised as a friar, in order to witness Angelo's conduct in office. Angelo immediately institutes a clean-up campaign of the local brothels and taverns, and arrests a young man, Claudio, for sleeping with his fiancée, Julietta, before marriage. Claudio's sister, Isabella, is a novice at the nearby convent of St Clare, and his friend, Lucio, persuades her to go to Angelo and plead for her brother's pardon: under the revived law against fornication, Claudio has been sentenced to death.

Angelo is unmoved by Isabella's pleas, but he rapidly becomes attracted to her. Soon he offers to release Claudio if Isabella will agree to sleep with him. Appalled and terrified, Isabella refuses, and goes to visit Claudio in prison where he begs her, unsuccessfully, to comply with Angelo's demand.

At this point the Duke, still in disguise, offers Isabella a solution. Angelo was once betrothed to a lady named Mariana, but he broke off the engagement (which would have been legally binding in this historical period) when she lost her dowry. Mariana remains in love with Angelo, and the Duke knows she will agree to substitute herself for Isabella in a meeting with Angelo after dark in the ducal gardens. Mariana does indeed fall in with this plot, as does Isabella; technically there is no moral problem about the substitution (or 'bed trick') since Mariana and Angelo are betrothed.

The Duke appears to be foiled when Angelo fails to keep his side of the bargain and reissues the order for Claudio's execution. However, the Duke intervenes again, persuading the prison authorities to substitute another head for Claudio's. A condemned murderer, Barnardine, is first proposed, but fortunately for the Duke a fellow prisoner, Ragozine, dies suddenly from natural causes, and his head is a better match for Claudio's.

The Duke now announces his return to Vienna, and summons Angelo to the city gate. There Isabella accuses Angelo of murder, adultery, hypocrisy and rape, and by appearing to discount these claims the Duke allows Angelo to incriminate himself further by his denials. He continues to support Angelo in the face of further accusations from Mariana. Escalus, who arguably represents Justice in the play, calls for the mysterious friar to be brought forward, and challenges him for having provoked Isabella and Mariana to slander Angelo. The Duke momentarily leaves the scene, and re-enters in his old disguise. Just as he is accused of conspiracy he reveals his true identity, and by doing so exposes Angelo's deceit. In a puzzling, paradoxical finale, the Duke marries Angelo and Mariana, reprieves Angelo from a sentence of execution, and proposes marriage to Isabella. The comic ending is arguably therefore only achieved through the implausible manipulations of the Duke, and at the expense of not resolving the ethical issues raised by the play. Angelo is forgiven, and Isabella appears to renounce a life of chastity; the Duke, who is in a sense responsible for what has happened, somehow emerges as an agent of love and reconciliation.

### Criticism of *Measure for Measure*

For all the recent interest in Shakespeare's dramatic structures and historical contexts, it is the quality of his poetry, the realism of many of his characters, and the interest of his themes, whether philosophical, psychological or political, which has made him the focus of such consistent attention from generations of critics. In the case of *Measure for Measure* certain speeches have been virtually canonized in their own right, in particular two speeches

STUDYING SHAKESPEARE: A PRACTICAL GUIDE

which argue the respective merits of death and life (III.i.5–41; III.i.117–31). Other parts of the play are equally memorable when encountered in context: for example, the Duke's initial musings about government (I.i.3–21), Isabella's defence of her chastity (II.iv.99–104) and Angelo's agonized self-recriminations (II.ii.162–87). In terms of characterization, the irresolvable ambiguities of the three principal characters have been the chief stimuli to debate. The Duke has been variously perceived as a Prospero-like semi-divine, a Machiavel and a fascinating enigma. Angelo is an astonishingly credible blend of self-righteousness, guilt, repression and cruelty. Likewise, Isabella combines naivety, principle, masochism and egotism. The interaction of these and the rest of the characters in the play produces a rich, complex exploration of power, ethics and sexuality which seems as pertinent today as it must have been to its original Jacobean audience.

Not surprisingly, then, interest in *Measure for Measure* has increased exponentially in the last hundred years or so and, as with any Shakespearean text, strategies are needed in order to chart a way through the wealth of critical material it has generated. In the sections which follow I describe a range of methods for organizing one's critical reading, beginning at an introductory level, and working up to the kind of research one might attempt in the preparation of an extended essay or dissertation. It goes without saying that before you begin your critical reading you ought to have read the primary text more than once, and have a clear grasp of the plot, the central themes, and the evident motivation of the characters.

## Critical guides and introductions

All the serial critical introductions to literary texts, such as Macmillan's *Casebooks* and *New Casebooks*, Edward Arnold's *Studies in English Literature*, Macmillan's *The Critics Debate*, Harvester's *New Critical Guides* and Norton's *Modern Critical Interpretations*, include studies of *Measure for Measure*, and indeed the rest of Shakespeare's plays. Most academic libraries will stock the full range, and some guides are relatively inexpensive to buy; this ready availability makes them very valuable to the student.

Often, however, a particular critical text will feature in more than one guide, and the guides themselves may overlap in their discussions of the play. This can be frustrating if you want to explore less 'mainstream' critical approaches. On the other hand, a guide is just that, and it is unreasonable to expect it to do more than introduce you to the secondary literature. Though these books tend to summarize earlier critics, or offer very selective extracts from them, they are often written or edited by eminent specialists in their field and provide very useful overviews of the material on a given text.

Relying on a single guide is probably unwise, since it is likely to lead to rather superficial written work. However, reading a number of guides can be a very efficient way of working, particularly when you are being asked to write to frequent deadlines and do not have a number of weeks to research your essays in depth. By comparing a variety of reputable introductory books (be guided by the publisher in deciding which are reputable – an established publisher is an indication that the book is worth reading), you will notice that certain critics are cited repeatedly, and you will begin to form a mental picture of the most significant works of criticism on a particular play.

In the case of *Measure for Measure*, comparison of the contents pages, bibliographies and 'Suggested Further Reading' sections in various introductory guides suggests that critics are fairly unanimous about the indispensability of certain critical texts: E. M. W. Tillyard's *Shakespeare's Problem Plays* (1950), for instance, or Roy Battenhouse's '*Measure for Measure* and the Christian doctrine of the atonement', published in the *Papers of the Modern Language Association* (*PMLA*) in 1946.[4] Both these texts are also referenced in J. W. Lever's introduction to the Arden *Measure for Measure*, which is another indication of their importance. Similarly, by consulting recent introductory guides as well as older ones, you will be able to work out which books and articles are emerging as 'classics' of contemporary criticism. Literature reviews such as *Year's Work in English Studies* (*YWES*) are helpful supplements here; *YWES* appears annually and contains chapters on the secondary material published on every major period and author in English literature, Shakespeare included, in a given year. Although always a year or two 'behind', *YWES* will be more up-to-date than most critical guides in the library. The opinions of the reviewers are not to be taken as irrefutable; though all are experts, they will have their partialities and blindspots like anyone else.

They can, however, be very valuable both in directing you to particular critical texts and encouraging you to adopt a discriminating approach to them.

As I have been implying, summaries of the kind found in *YWES* (other periodical review essays are listed in the earlier chapter, 'Writing about Shakespeare') are, like the standard guides aimed at a student market, best used as a springboard for further reading, however selective that has to be. If you attach a bibliography to your essay which lists only two or three textbooks – say a *Casebook* and a Harvester *New Critical Guide* – you will convey the impression that you have done the bare minimum in terms of reading around the subject. If, however, you list three such guides, plus two or three articles and a scholarly monograph, you suggest that you have begun with some basic fact-finding and have followed it up with some more sophisticated reading on a particular aspect of the primary text.

**Further critical reading**

A rather more thorough approach to critical reading would be to identify the principal landmarks in criticism on a particular play and read them for yourself. Course reading lists are likely to give some indication of where to start, but the bibliographies in the introductory guides, along with any lists given in critical editions of the primary text, will help you to choose the critics it will be most profitable to pursue. You may well have some idea already of which ones you will find most interesting; if you found J. W. Lever useful for Shakespeare's tragedies,[5] for instance, you will be keen to discover his views on *Measure for Measure*.

When it comes to writing your essay, you will be expected to demonstrate a grasp of the secondary material without allowing the published critics to drown out your individual response to the text. This response is not a question of emotion, but of having produced your own interpretation, only partly in relation to other people's. You are not normally asked to include a literature review or survey in an essay except, perhaps, when it comes to a dissertation.

Nevertheless, it is a valuable exercise to try to write a brief survey of the critical literature for your own use, since it will clarify your thoughts about your reading and furnish you with useful material for your formal essay. One method is to pause after reaching the end of your secondary reading, or a portion of it, and write a 2–4-page report, summarizing each critical text and highlighting its chief contribution to the subject. Try to historicize the various critics, so that you convey a sense of Shakespeare's changing critical reception. Below is an example of such a literature review, produced after a week or two's reading on *Measure for Measure*. The texts discussed are easily available, some in popular anthologies such as the Macmillan *Casebook Measure for Measure*, edited by C. K. Stead, some in books which are still in print and widely used. The review uses brief parenthetical references rather than footnotes, being designed to be used alongside a bibliography (printed at the end).

---

### *Measure for Measure:* literature review

Criticism of *Measure for Measure* only becomes really illuminating from the late nineteenth century onwards, since the cynicism and graphic sexual references of the play discouraged eighteenth- and early nineteenth-century critics such as Samuel Johnson and S. T. Coleridge from paying detailed attention to it. In this review I will begin by discussing Edward Dowden's comments in *Shakspere: His mind and art* (1875; repr. 1897), and then adumbrate some of the more important critical readings of *Measure for Measure* which have appeared in the twentieth century.

In a number of ways, Dowden's treatment of *Measure for Measure* is typical of Victorian reactions to Shakespeare. The play is considered almost perfunctorily, as though it is relatively slight by comparison with Dowden's main focus, the great tragedies. Nineteenth-century commentators placed an even lower value on the so-called problem plays or late comedies than on the 'happy' comedies of the 1590s. Dowden is disappointed by the absence of 'mirth' in *Measure for Measure*; where humour is attempted (in the low-life scenes) he finds it morally distasteful. The rest of his attention is absorbed by Isabella, whose 'pure zeal' (p. 82) he admires intensely. He does not contemplate the possibility (which will occur so readily to later critics) that her chastity may derive from vanity as well as principle. He also finds no reason to question her refusal to sacrifice

---

169

herself for Claudio: 'as she had strength to accept pain and death for herself rather than dishonour, so she can reasonably accept pain and death for those who are dearest to her' (p. 83). No less approving of wifely submission than of virginal purity, Dowden sees no inconsistency in Isabella's marrying the Duke: marriage is a life as consecrated as that of holy orders. His critique of *Measure for Measure* clearly tells us more about Victorian attitudes to women and sexuality than it does about Shakespeare; none the less, his view of Isabella is interestingly similar to recent feminist defences of her commitment to selfhood.

Of earlier twentieth-century discussions of *Measure for Measure*, G. Wilson Knight's ameliorative, Christian vision of the play was among the most influential. (It is reprinted, like the extract from Dowden, in the Macmillan *Casebook*, but is also still in print in its original form, as a chapter in Wilson Knight's *The Wheel of Fire* [1930].)

For Wilson Knight, *Measure for Measure* is a profoundly Christian play in which the mercy and forgiveness of the Gospels are made to supplant the 'crudity of man's justice' through the operations of a divine ruler, the omnipotent Duke. Wilson Knight argues not only that *Measure for Measure* is ethically coherent, but that it is founded on a biblically sanctioned notion of justice. His essay demonstrates convincingly that it is possible to read the play not as a dark, problematic study in hypocrisy but as an assertion of the New Testament values, charity and forbearance.

Wilson Knight's reading of the play reflects Leavisite concerns with structural unity and balance as well as morality: 'no play of Shakespeare shows more thoughtful care, more deliberate purpose, more consummate skill in structural technique.' This is a welcome corrective to the tendency of much criticism, before and since, to regard the play as structurally flawed. Yet Wilson Knight was mainly influential for suggesting that Shakespeare wrote from a doctrinal perspective. Whereas A. C. Bradley's *Shakespearean Tragedy* (1904) had offered an almost secular, humanist Shakespeare, Wilson Knight presented *Measure for Measure* as a dramatic enactment of the Gospel of St Matthew: 'Judge not, that ye be not judged.' Even today, most critics regard Christian ethics as central to *Measure for Measure*, though their understanding of 'Christian ethics' can be a loose, ecumenical one. Several have attempted to develop and refine

Wilson Knight's idea of *Measure for Measure* as a parable: Roy W. Battenhouse (1946) and Nevill Coghill (1955) are singled out as important examples by J. W. Lever in his introduction to the Arden edition of the play (1965). Other critics have offered determined resistance to reading the play as a dramatized parable or a theological treatise. In reaction to Wilson Knight and partly in response to him, many mid-century writers sought to contextualize *Measure for Measure* in wider terms than merely biblical ones. From the 1940s to the 1970s, historicist critics related the play to Jacobean laws governing betrothal and adultery. As with Dowden's warm approval of Isabella, and Wilson Knight's allegorical interpretation, this trend reflected wider contemporary assumptions about Shakespeare and literature in general. Ernest Schanzer's *The Problem Plays of Shakespeare* (1963) is chiefly known to the present generation of college and university students at one remove, through the work of those who have taken issue with his exoneration of Angelo. Briefly, Schanzer argued that there was a fundamental difference between Angelo's engagement to marry Mariana, and Claudio's understanding with Julietta. The former was a contract *de futura*, a contract, which makes Angelo's reprieve at the end of the play acceptable, and Isabella's approval of the substitution of Mariana for herself much less doubtful in ethical terms.

Several critics have taken issue with Schanzer. A. D. Nuttall (1975) insists on the exact parallel between Claudio and Angelo's circumstances, and argues that far from exonerating Isabella Shakespeare deliberately problematizes her. The underlying point of Nuttall's critique is to demonstrate the play's psychological subtlety: in his view, Shakespeare means Isabella to seem compromised, however faintly.

The controversy over the laws of betrothal as represented in *Measure for Measure* is characteristic of Shakespearean criticism which pre-dates or sidesteps the advent of literary theory. Schanzer's position is that of the traditional historicist critic who seeks to illuminate the text with reference to informed assumptions about its author's intentions. In total contrast, though equally anti-theoretical, David L. Stevenson's 'Design and Structure in *Measure for Measure*' reflects the formalist preoccupations of New Criticism. Stevenson compares the play to a poem by John Donne, arguing that its construction is 'a series of intricately interrelated moral ironies and reversals . . . resolved by a final balancing out of paradox' (*Casebook*, p. 213). Though the desire to rescue *Measure for Measure* for those who prefer literary texts to be unified and highly wrought now seems misguided, an analysis such as Stevenson's is important for the contrast it provides with contemporary views of *Measure for Measure* as a notably dissonant, contradictory text.

Much recent criticism of *Measure for Measure* has tended to approach the play from the perspectives of cultural materialism and feminism. In *Political Shakespeare* (1984) Jonathan Dollimore asks why so many previous critics have assented unquestioningly to the puritanical view of Vienna expressed by the Duke; traditionally *Measure for Measure* has been interpreted as an attack on sexual licence. For Dollimore Shakespeare neither equates sexual transgression with social disorder, nor valorizes sexual transgression as a manifestation of the carnivalesque. Instead his play exposes the dependency of those in power on the demonizing of deviant behaviour, which enables them to displace ruling-class disorder onto the lower orders, and more importantly legitimizes the authoritarianism they require in order to govern.

Dollimore's personal commitment to political radicalism leads him to conclude by noting that while Shakespeare reveals disorder as essential to authority, he none the less colludes in the exploitation of deviancy in so far as he fails to give the prostitutes of Vienna a voice or presence in his play. Dollimore's refusal to recuperate Shakespeare in terms of liberal values is, therefore, implicitly feminist as well as materialist. In *Still Harping on Daughters* (1983) Lisa Jardine offers a more overtly feminist analysis of Isabella in *Measure for Measure*, arguing that Isabella fails to conform to the type of the submissive female hero. Unlike so many female saints, Isabella refuses martyrdom, neither fleeing from Angelo nor yielding to him. Because she will not martyr herself, and will not sacrifice her honour either, her virtue, according to Jardine, is placed in question. For Jardine, *Measure for Measure* is based on the principle that female sexuality is both wrong and uncontrollable: Isabella seeks to conform to an ideal of chastity, yet betrays 'an obsessive fear of her own sexuality in general' (p. 192).

*Literature review: Bibliography*

Roy W. Battenhouse, '*Measure for Measure* and the Christian doctrine of the atonement', *PMLA* 61 (1946), 1029–59.
A. C. Bradley, *Shakespearean Tragedy* (1904; repr. London: Macmillan, 1978).
Nevill Coghill, 'Comic form in *Measure for Measure*', *Shakespeare Survey* 8 (1955), 14–27.
Jonathan Dollimore, 'Transgression and surveillance in *Measure for Measure*', in *Political Shakespeare*, ed. Jonathan Dollimore and Alan Sinfield (Manchester: Manchester University Press, 1985), pp. 72–87.
Edward Dowden, *Shakspere: A critical study of his mind and art* (1875; repr. London: Kegan Paul, Trench, Trubner, 1897).
Lisa Jardine, *Still Harping on Daughters: Women and drama in the age of Shakespeare* (Brighton: Harvester Press, 1983).
G. Wilson Knight, *The Wheel of Fire* (1930; repr. Oxford: Oxford University Press, 1977).
J. W. Lever, 'Introduction' to the Arden edition of *Measure for Measure* (London: Methuen, 1965).
A. D. Nuttall, '*Measure for Measure*: The bed-trick', *Shakespeare Survey* 28 (1975), repr. in *The Stoic in Love: Selected essays on literature and ideas* (Hemel Hempstead: Harvester Wheatsheaf, 1989), pp. 41–8.
Ernest Schanzer, *The Problem Plays of Shakespeare* (London: Routledge and Kegan Paul, 1963).
C. K. Stead, *Shakespeare: Measure for Measure: A casebook* (London: Macmillan, 1971).
David L. Stevenson, 'Design and structure in *Measure for Measure*', repr. in Stead, *Casebook*, pp. 213–32.

This summary makes no attempt to be comprehensive, ignoring a number of major critical issues raised by *Measure for Measure* as well as many important commentators on it. It is arguably reductive to attempt to represent subtle arguments in so few words. However, such a review is not aiming at coverage of all the available material, but rather is seeking to demonstrate a grasp of the central ideas of certain earlier critics. By producing such a review you are learning to assimilate and condense the arguments of other writers, the study skill which was recommended in Chapter 3.

## In-depth research

Reading a range of major critics on a single play is obviously more demanding and less superficial than relying on a selection of textbook-level critical guides, and making your own decisions about which critical texts are worth studying is more satisfying than trusting someone else's judgment. It suggests even more initiative to use indices and online searches to produce a bibliography of all material published on a text in a given period of years and work from that, and it is advisable to do so if you are producing an extended essay or dissertation. The MLA bibliography on CD-ROM, for example, lists 204 critical essays on *Measure for Measure* published between January 1980 and November 1995, and gives the title, author and source of each. No academic library will be able to provide all of these, but no student is likely to want to read them all anyway. Having printed out the entries, or those in a 'selection field' (everything on a particular character, for instance), the hard copy can be gone through with a highlighter pen to identify the texts which seem most relevant to your project, and which texts, within that narrower spectrum, your library is likely to hold.

The advantage of such research is that it enables you to pursue a particular aspect of the text, or a particular critical approach to it independently. Having had your curiosity aroused by Jardine's critique of the patriarchal values latent in the play's portrayal of Isabella, for example, you can discover the ways in which subsequent critics have developed and extended the debate about Shakespeare's supposed misogyny in this play. For instance, the database can be scanned for texts whose titles mention Isabella by name, or contain other relevant search terms. The very first page of entries on *Measure for Measure* throws up a dissertation on 'Representations of power and women in *Measure for Measure* and selected sources',[6] and an article by Karl F. Zender entitled 'Isabella's choice';[7] the next lists an article by Laura Lunger Knoppers entitled '(En)gendering shame: *Measure for Measure* and the spectacles of power'.[8]

The disadvantage of electronic databases is, of course, the unmanageable volume of material they tend to uncover. Reading even a small proportion of 204 texts on *Measure for Measure* sounds impossible, and the chances of writing anything remotely original seem hopeless, having discovered what has been written already. Assimilating most of the criticism on a course reading list or a short bibliography makes one feel reasonably confident of one's grasp of a subject, but being confronted by a 35-page printout can have a psychological effect equivalent to trailing last in a marathon.

Once you start to track down and read particular texts, however, you will probably find yourself pleasantly surprised. Relatively few will make a substantial or revolutionary contribution to knowledge about the play, and most will be reducible to a few significant points. You will be able to discount the majority of articles and books altogether, either because they focus on an aspect of the play which does not greatly interest you, or because their theoretical approach is incompatible with yours. At the same time, a good number of critics will turn out to be really perceptive and suggestive, making the exercise of conducting a search manifestly worthwhile.

Whether you have resolutely read as little criticism as you can, or tried to trace the history of the play's critical reception, or confined yourself to reading as widely as possible in criticism from the last ten years, it is by no means unlikely that you will still have something original to say about your primary text. Students produce innovative and imaginative ideas all the time; writing critical essays is like cooking, in that there are an almost infinite number of ways of combining ingredients and inventing new recipes. It is worth remembering that you probably have more time to ponder a particular text than your tutor or lecturer does, and enjoy the advantage of encountering it for only the first or second time. Even if you doubt your ability to write a startingly original analysis of the play as a whole, you may well find yourself making detailed observations on its language which are yours alone.

To demonstrate what I mean, I will end this chapter with a critical essay of my own on *Measure for Measure*, which was written after a few weeks' study of the text itself and its secondary literature, past and recent. The subject of the essay is a familiar one: the relationship between ethical principles and practice in the play. The conflict between justice and mercy, and the disparity between those ideals and the sin-ridden society of Vienna, are among the most heavily discussed issues in criticism on *Measure for Measure*. In terms of its general argument the essay makes no advances on the insights of earlier writers: Ernest Schanzer and

G. Wilson Knight, for example, long ago identified the relationship between justice and mercy (which is parallel to the relationship between absolutism and relativism) as the central theme of *Measure for Measure*, and many commentators have expressed unease with the ethical implications of the comic resolution. Where the essay does try to be imaginative is at the level of close reading; it shows that Shakespeare's concern with ethics is reflected at the level of individual lines and phrases.

### *Measure for Measure:* **sample essay**

---

'Heaven doth with us as we with torches do' (I.i.32): Ethics into practice in *Measure for Measure*

This essay seeks to engage with a question which has been central to criticism of Shakespeare's *Measure for Measure* from the beginning of the nineteenth century: how to respond to a comedy whose happy ending is achieved at the expense of resolving the ethical conflicts it raises.[9] Critics as diverse as E. M. W. Tillyard, Rosalind Miles and Harriet Hawkins have identified this apparent failure as the reason why *Measure for Measure* is customarily regarded as a 'problem' play.[10] In what follows I shall argue that Shakespeare's deliberate intention is to demonstrate the impossibility of acting in accordance with rigid moral principles, given the complexities and contradictions of 'real life'. I shall be seeking to show that ethical compromise is not forced on Shakespeare by the conventions of his comic form, but is the main theme of his play, which asserts the value of negotiation, flexibility and forgiveness as opposed to zealotry, absolutism and punishment.

Many commentators have drawn attention to the seamy, even sordid nature of the Vienna depicted in *Measure for Measure*. W. W. Lawrence regarded it as 'degenerate';[11] more recently, Nigel Alexander has found it nearly 'consumed' by 'lust';[12] and many recent productions, notably the BBC television *Measure for Measure* first broadcast in October 1995, have set the play in a red-light world of sleaze and sexual violence. By contrast, Jonathan Dollimore has recently objected to the alacrity with which generations of critics have accepted the Duke's, and Angelo's, puritanical disapproval of the city.

Dollimore argues, following Michel Foucault, [13] that those in authority actually depend on the demonizing of sexual and social dissidence, since such dissidence legitimizes the surveillance and repression essential to the exercise and maintenance of power. In other words, it is in the interests of the Duke and Angelo to identify the lower orders with debauchery and corruption (thereby displacing their own sexual guilt onto their social subordinates), since this justifies them in disciplining those they rule, and hence in ruling absolutely.

Dollimore's interpretation is persuasive, yet like others it cannot account for the ending of the play except as evidence of Shakespeare's willingness to sacrifice ethics for the sake of comic resolution. The final scenes ask us to trust the Duke, even though we have seen that he is responsible for much of the sexual exploitation and repression which took place in his 'absence'. Yet I would argue that Shakespeare's failure to confront the implications of the Duke's conduct directly is not an unconscious evasion but a deliberate strategy by which he once again addresses his central concern, the disparity between ethical ideals and the way in which individuals conduct themselves in reality. And though for Shakespeare, as for Foucault and Dollimore, power is corrupt, in *Measure for Measure* there is also scope for individuals – particularly, perhaps, the powerful – to recognize their shortcomings and learn to forgive themselves and others.

There is no doubt that *Measure for Measure* portrays a society which falls far short of the ideals to which some of its characters aspire. Even a casual conversation between drinking mates reveals an inevitable gulf between principles and practice: 'There's not a soldier of us all that, in the thanksgiving before meat, do relish the petition well that prays for peace' (I.ii.14–16). And Vienna is still imperfect at the end of the play, as dissatisfied critics have pointed out. Yet all the principal characters in the play are forced at some stage to confront the difficulties of reconciling their principles with their messy, problematic circumstances, and some of them have to try to make sense of the relationship between their personal ethics and the demands of their office. Neither task is simple: absolutes are rendered meaningless in a world of irrationality and impulse, and the demands of office expose the individual's moral failings and threaten to corrupt further in their turn. As Darryl J. Gless observes, *Measure for Measure* has been regarded as structurally weak by many critics, flawed by its inability to reconcile justice and mercy, except in a manifestly contrived way.[14] But to see this as Shakespeare's point – that compromises, imperfections and failures are characteristic of human action – is, perhaps, to redeem the play for those who find it unsatisfactory in ethical, and hence comic, terms.

The idea of ethical compromise applies to virtually all the characters in the play. Escalus, for example, who is introduced as the ultimate source of wisdom on the subject of government, is unable to resolve the classic ethical dilemma faced by those who are required to carry out orders they consider absurd. The conflict between his instinct and his reason is acutely painful to him:

> *Esc.* It grieves me for the death of Claudio,
> But there's no remedy.
> *Justice.* Lord Angelo is severe.
> *Esc.* It is but needful.
> Mercy is not itself, that oft looks so;
> Pardon is still the nurse of second woe.
> But yet, poor Claudio! There is no remedy.
> (II.i.266–71)

The split is signalled by the fact that these remarks are addressed to a hitherto silent 'Justice', as if Escalus, previously the chief representative of justice in the play, is dissociating himself mentally from a law he now regards as retributive. His anxiety further reveals itself in his unconvincing attempt to interpret Angelo's actions as merciful: 'Mercy is not itself, that oft looks so.' Despite the intellectual effort behind it, the speech actually suggests that justice can be antithetical to mercy as well as its corollary. It also indicates that for Escalus mercy is *prior* to justice, for he tries to argue that Angelo's justice is in fact mercy, in a guise human beings will be apt to misrecognize. His own conventional pieties do not convince Escalus, his broken syntax conveying his inability to come to terms with a justice manifestly inimical to mercy: 'But yet, poor Claudio! There is no remedy.' And we notice that what requires a remedy here is not sin, but justice itself, harsh, inhuman and unbending.

The pressures of office for Escalus, and his discomfort with the rigid letter of the law, mirror subsequent moments in the play when human behaviour renders moral truisms inadequate. Most famously, in the last scene mercy and forgiveness are made to seem ambiguous

when their object is incapable of mercy himself. For certain characters, however, moral absolutes are attractive precisely because they
appear to simplify or solve the business of making ethical judgments.
Isabella's asceticism springs from naive idealism; as a novice she craves
'strict restraint' (I.iv.4), and she is almost enthusiastic in picturing
herself as a martyr:

> That is, were I under the terms of death,
> Th' impression of keen whips I'd wear as rubies,
> And strip myself to death as to a bed
> That longing have been sick for . . .
>
> (II.iv.100–4)

Yet the very intensity of the speech is revealing. There is a sublimi-
nal sexual longing here which is not masochistic in any straightforward sense: Isabella conceives of self-denial as thrillingly erotic, which
is not quite the same as saying that she invites Angelo's sadism. Her
language, rich in the iconography of medieval Christianity – and the
sado-masochistic imagery of St Sebastian in particular – is above all
passionate, and it is the mutuality of her passion and her chastity
which is chiefly suggested; her evident unconscious desire for sexual
humiliation is only secondary. Unlike Escalus, however, Isabella does
not realize that simple moral binaries elude her: her very integrity is a
kind of egotism which blinds her to her weaknesses.

Given her stated commitment to an ethic of absolute sexual purity,
it is not surprising that Isabella is shocked and disappointed by the
evidence of human frailty she sees in Angelo:

> man, proud man,
> Dress'd in a little brief authority,
> Most ignorant of what he's most assur'd –
> His glassy essence – like an angry ape
> Plays such fantastic tricks before high heaven
> As makes the angels weep . . .
>
> (II.ii.117–22)

Yet one of the play's major ironies is that Angelo shares exactly the
craving for moral perfection – and the fascination with punishment –
which we see more transparently in Isabella. His first speech in office
is chillingly austere:

> We must not make a scarecrow of the law,
> Setting it up to fear the birds of prey,
> And let it keep one shape till custom make it
> Their perch and not their terror.
>
> (II.i.1–4)

However, the fact that he expresses this belief as an imperative to be enforced ('We must . . .'), coupled with his rather stilted, self-conscious delivery, underlines his consciousness of the problems of upholding the law in the face of habitual civic indiscipline. With hindsight we might wonder whether his own, somewhat dubious, past (his abandonment of Mariana) has contributed to his present need for moral absolutes. When the Duke first relinquishes his power, Angelo is filled with self-doubt: 'Let there be some more test made of my metal, / Before so noble and so great a figure / Be stamp'd on it' (I.i.49–51). And his first action is to withdraw with Escalus, in order to discuss the extent to which they can or should act on their new powers.

The complications and resolution of the play's comic structure will require Isabella and Angelo to recognize the limitations – and inherent self-contradictions – of their respective ethical stances. Isabella has to return to the ordinary world the very moment she attempts to renounce it, and Angelo taunts her with the inconsistency of her argument regarding Claudio:

> Which had you rather, that the most just law
> Now took your brother's life; or, to redeem him,
> Give up your body to such sweet uncleanness
> As she that he hath stain'd?
>
> (II.iv.52)

In other words, if she will not sin to save Claudio's life, she must concede that Claudio deserves to die for committing the same sin. When Angelo himself is forced to acknowledge the gulf between his moral convictions and his actual behaviour, he feels a sense of unbearable loss: 'so deep sticks it in my penitent heart / That I crave death more willingly than mercy' (V.i.473–4). Interestingly, though, neither Isabella nor Angelo will formally repudiate their ideals; quite the reverse. Angelo declares that death would be preferable to a life of conscious sin, and Isabella, notoriously, does not voice her acceptance of the Duke's marriage proposal.

One character in *Measure for Measure*, the Duke, is conscious from the outset of the discrepancy between his sense of what is morally right and his actual conduct. He appears, therefore, to offer a model for those who struggle to put their principles into practice, for he manages to confront his own weaknesses as well as other people's. He begins the action by explaining that he will not presume to talk of political philosophy to an expert such as Escalus, and says he is so sharply aware of his past failings that he feels unqualified to institute more rigorous laws in Vienna. He appoints Angelo in his stead, on the grounds that Angelo has an unblemished reputation. Yet although the Duke's humility looks initially like true virtue, the voluntary relinquishing of power by a ruler is by no means clear-cut in moral terms – it is the root of the tragedy in *King Lear*, for instance – and for all that he wishes to see a more exacting moral order imposed on Vienna, the Duke's motives remain dark and mysterious throughout the play. In retrospect his language suggests that he was more interested in testing Angelo's virtue than in harnessing it: 'Hence we shall see / If power change purpose, what our seemers be' (I.iii.53–4). The anatomizing satirist is actually closer to an *agent provocateur*.

To be sure, the Duke's eagerness to expose the failings of his successor is subsequently mitigated by his determination to treat Angelo with mercy. Yet once again the effect is also disquieting: mercy towards Angelo necessarily involves injustice for his victims. Though the Duke may be intended as a model for others who struggle to maintain their integrity in the face of pressures from within and without, his judgments are more pragmatic than noble. Like Escalus, Isabella and Angelo, the Duke falls short of the standard to which he initially aspires.

Questions of ethical compromise are also raised in relation to the minor characters, most of whom are manifest sinners. Lucio marvels at a governor who would seek to stamp out extramarital sex, and his language is as unanswerable as Sir Toby Belch's defence of 'cakes and ale' (*Twelfth Night* II.iii.115): 'Yes, in good sooth, the vice is of a great kindred; it is well allied; but it is impossible to extirp it quite, friar, till eating and drinking be put down' (III.ii.97–9). Though elsewhere Lucio is portrayed as a deeply unreliable commentator, this argument seems irrefutable: who can deny that sexuality is part of the natural order of things? In general the play portrays a world of cheerful vice; as Pompey puts it, 'The valiant heart's not whipt out of his trade' (II.i.253), and the usual response of the citizens to the imposition of the law against adultery is indignation. 'Why, here's a change indeed in the commonwealth!' exclaims the bawd Mistress Overdone, and she asks, 'What shall become of me?' (I.ii.96–7). The resentful grumbling of Pompey is matched by Claudio's more articulate baulking at Angelo's severity:

> this new governor
> Awakes me all the enrolled penalties
> Which have, like unscour'd armour, hung by th' wall
> So long, that nineteen zodiacs have gone round,
> And none of them been worn.
>
> (I.ii.154–8)

The inference is that Angelo's puritanism is militant, even cruel, and the simple eloquence with which Claudio and Juliet speak of each other is an implicit comment on the brutality of their punisher.

As I have indicated, there are no examples of unproblematic virtue or vice in *Measure for Measure*. Claudio's unconscious recognition that Angelo's desire for chastity is a putting on of armour anticipates the audience's subsequent discovery that chastity is indeed something for which Angelo must struggle. He is innately sinful, as he admits, and as Isabella is quick to exploit: 'Else let my brother die, / If not a feodary but only he / Owe and succeed thy weakness' (II.iv.121–3). Angelo, she argues, has no right to single out Claudio for special punishment, given that frailty is the condition of all men, Angelo included. The choice of 'feodary' to describe Claudio is sly, insinuating that he is Angelo's accomplice in sin. Though Angelo attempts to implicate Isabella likewise ('Nay, call us ten times frail' [II.iv.127]), she rejects the idea: for her, women are vulnerable objects of male lust, not subjects of their own: 'Ay, as the glasses where they view themselves, / Which are as easy broke as they make forms' (II.iv.124–5).

Yet however fiercely Isabella resists Angelo's attack on her chastity, and however intransigently he defends his decision to execute Claudio, their confrontation undermines them both. Isabella will shortly find a less fastidious substitute to satisfy Angelo's lust, and her defiant 'More than our brother is our chastity' (II.iv.184) sounds hysterical rather than resolute. The dialogue is one example of a series of episodes in which characters realize they are far from morally invincible and that in any case an uncompromising personal ethic cannot equip them to deal with the complexities of life itself.

Nevertheless, there is a baffling contradiction in a text which, on the one hand, seeks to show that those in authority cannot consider themselves above the law, and on the other, insists that human frailty is natural and inevitable. The point of satire is to expose vice and hypocrisy, and the Duke's plot does just that. The point of comedy, however, is to celebrate renewal and forgiveness, and in the end *Measure for Measure* indeed seems to shrug its shoulders, and offer a tolerant view of human weakness. Angelo – and Claudio – are allowed to live.

Critics are on the whole in accord in regarding the ending of the play as unsatisfactory. Perhaps their dissatisfaction derives from this fundamental contradiction between satire and comedy, which is also an ethical contradiction between absolutes and compromise. It is not just Isabella and Angelo who have to question the practical usefulness of their rigid principles; the audience too has to come to terms with the knowledge that ethical ideals are impossible to maintain in practice. Inevitably, those in authority are as imperfect as those they rule, and power often makes them more so.

To resist or resent the ending of *Measure for Measure* is, however, to blame Shakespeare for the moral inconsistencies he acknowledges and accepts as an inevitable aspect of human affairs. 'Remedy' is a recurring word in this play, and an appropriate term for the improvisatory ethic which the characters learn to practise. Vice cannot be prevented in Duke Vincentio's Vienna, only cured. Shakespeare's title, *Measure for Measure*, is most obviously a reference to the similarities between Claudio's situation and that of his accuser, and is sometimes regarded by critics as an allusion to the bible's 'An eye for an eye' (Exodus 21.24). Yet 'measure' implies moderation as well as retribution, and it evokes the image of blind justice tempering punishment with mercy just as much as it makes ironic allusion to the rigours of the law. The play can, and has, been read as a gloss on Matthew 7.1–2: 'Judge not, that ye be not judged. For with what judgement ye judge, ye shall be judged: and with what measure ye mete, it shall be measured to you again.' There are no wholly irredeemable characters in *Measure for Measure* (even the murderer, Barnardine, has a 'reckless[ness]' [IV.ii.141] which makes him human and sympathetic), and no wholly virtuous characters either. Yet the end of the play is not a failure but an affirmation: it makes the best of its flawed world and fallen men and women, and expects its audience likewise to come to terms with the reality of a world in which ethical absolutism is neither possible nor ultimately, perhaps, very desirable.

## Conclusion

This example follows the advice on essay-writing commonly given to students at school and college or university and expounded in Chapter 3 of this book. It has a focused argument, a clear structure (with an introduction, a longer expository section and a conclusion), and it quotes amply but briefly from the play. It also exemplifies the various ways in which critical reading can enhance one's own response to the primary text. First, references to particular critics are used to back up assertions which might otherwise lack credibility: that Vienna is 'sordid', for instance. Second, and less explicitly, a knowledge of the critical background informs the essay at the most fundamental level, helping the writer to identify the issues which can and should be addressed. Third, the essay locates itself in relation to the range of critical responses to *Measure for Measure*, demonstrating an awareness of, and a degree of independence from, previous interpretations of the text. The general tendency among critics to regard the play as poorly constructed is mentioned not only in the introduction but also in the main body of the essay and again in the conclusion. And though it reflects the longstanding debate over the equivocal morality of *Measure for Measure*, the essay also intervenes in that debate by suggesting that compromise is not forced on Shakespeare but deliberately pursued by him. Fourth, this example illustrates the very limited extent to which you need to cite other critics directly in your essays. While Dollimore is discussed at some length, his critique being directly relevant to the essay's argument, there are only residual traces of the other criticism covered by the literature review. Though a dissertation would probably require you to provide a fairly thorough and inclusive analysis of the relevant secondary literature, references to critics should be kept relatively brief in short essays, where the remit is to present your own interpretation of the text. Last, the essay contains a number of close readings which are evidence of an active engagement with the text and hence, again, a reasonable degree of critical independence. Examining and analyzing specific words, phrases and lines is one of the clearest ways to demonstrate that you have thought intelligently about the text and have ideas of your own to communicate.

Just as the heading 'Shakespeare and Criticism' covers an astonishing range of responses and approaches, so the ways in which such criticism can be classified and used are many. By setting out to read around your subject with some awareness of the kinds of criticism available you will make efficient use of your time and read with greater scepticism and discrimination. As you extend your reading, your essays will become more informed and authoritative, and more carefully thought out. Hopefully, though, your increased familiarity with the critics will eventually effect an important change in the way you perceive them. In coming to recognize that you are only the latest in a long, diverse history of Shakespearean commentators, your attitude towards them should gradually become less deferential, and you will begin to view them more questioningly and sceptically. This model is not just pedagogically but politically sounder than one in which, by using criticism as a reservoir of ideas, the student not only risks plagiarism, but effectively submits to a relationship of dependency and inequality. Reading criticism should be a form of dialogue, dissent being just as important in this context as it is in the seminar or the tutorial. The need for critical self-consciousness and self-reflection will be one of the key themes in the next chapter.

## Notes

1. Graham Nicholls, *Measure for Measure: Text and performance* (London: Macmillan, 1986), p. 10.
2. T. F. Wharton, *Measure for Measure: The critics debate* (London: Macmillan, 1989), p. 9.
3. Darryl J. Gless, *Measure for Measure, the Law and the Convent* (Princeton, NJ: Princeton University Press, 1979), p. 3.
4. E. M. W. Tillyard, *Shakespeare's Problem Plays* (1950; repr. London: Penguin, 1965); Roy W. Battenhouse, '*Measure for Measure* and the Christian doctrine of the atonement', *PMLA* 61 (1946), 1029–59.
5. J. W. Lever, *The Tragedy of State* (London: Methuen, 1971).
6. Lorraine Francis Kuziw, 'Representations of power and women in *Measure for Measure* and selected sources'. Diss, New York University, 1993.
7. Karl F. Zender, 'Isabella's choice', *Philological Quarterly* 73 (1994), 77–93.
8. Laura Lunger Knoppers, '(En)gendering shame: *Measure for Measure* and the spectacles of power', *English Literary Renaissance* 23 (1993), 450–71.

9. S. T. Coleridge, for example, argued that 'the pardon and marriage of Angelo not merely baffles the strong indignant claim of justice – (for cruelty, with lust and damnable baseness, cannot be forgiven, because we cannot conceive them as being morally repented of;) but it is likewise degrading to the character of woman' (*Lectures on Shakspeare and Other Poets and Dramatists* [London: Dent, 1907], p. 84).

10. Tillyard, *Shakespeare's Problem Plays*, p. 131; Rosalind Miles, *The Problem of Measure for Measure: A historical investigation* (London: Vision, 1976), pp. 254–5; Harriet Hawkins, *Measure for Measure* (Brighton: Harvester Press, 1987), p. 93.

11. W. W. Lawrence, 'Real life and artifice' (125), in *Measure for Measure: A Casebook*, ed. C. K. Stead (London: Macmillan, 1971), pp. 122–37.

12. Nigel Alexander, *Shakespeare: Measure for Measure* (London: Edward Arnold, 1975), p. 26.

13. See, for example, Michel Foucault's *Discipline and Punish: The birth of the prison*, trans. Alan Sheridan (1977; repr. Harmondsworth: Penguin, 1991).

14. Gless, *Measure for Measure, the Law and the Convent*, p. 5.

# CHAPTER 9

# Shakespeare and theory

## Introduction

The boundaries between criticism and theory are often blurred, but the theorist can perhaps be distinguished from the critic by a determination to critique the assumptions governing his or her interpretations of a text. Admittedly, this can be carried to absurd lengths; I recently attended a conference on the application of theory in literary studies, and recall that the most contentious moment of the two days was when someone asked if the word 'theory' should appear in the programme of the conference with a capital 'T' or not. This seems to me to demonstrate the pitfalls of an obsession with theory: the danger of not seeing the wood for the trees, or in this instance the T's.

A reliable source tells us that theory means a 'Systematic conception or statement of the principles of something; abstract knowledge, or the formulation of it: often used as implying more or less unsupported hypothesis: distinguished from or opposed to practice' (*Oxford English Dictionary*). In this last definition there's the rub, for literary studies at least. Theory is hypothetical, not practical, and as such can appear hopelessly irrelevant to what actually happens when we read Shakespeare.

Yet every reading of Shakespeare or any author, however instinctive and unreflecting, has theoretical implications, even if they remain unconscious and unarticulated. In this chapter I want to engage you in a brief consideration of two poles of the art (or science) of literary criticism, subjectivity and objectivity, in order to focus on one of the most vexed questions for modern critical theory: the relationship between text and context. To help to avoid too much speculation (what Iago calls 'mere prattle without practice' [*Othello* I.i.26]), I will employ concrete examples from the plays to illuminate this central theoretical issue raised by the opposition between subjectivity and objectivity, the extent to which we can and should historicize or contextualize when interpreting literary texts. Following this, Katherine Armstrong will offer a reading of *The Tempest* which demonstrates how we can put a particular kind of historicist theory, materialist feminism, into practice and, in doing so, reflect not only on the literary text itself but on the implications of our approach to it.

### Where is meaning?

Shakespeare's plays are collections of words which require a reader to bring them to life and give them meaning. The object of the Shakespearean text (which is, as we saw at the end of Chapter 4, by no means a thoroughly stable object) is repeatedly colliding with the subject experiencing it. Does the meaning of the text lie in the text itself, or in me, the subject who reads it? For the New Critics of the 1950s and 1960s, the function of criticism was to discover the inherent meaning of the literary text, a meaning which transcended history. In contrast, historicist approaches to literature stress the grounding in history of both text and reader, each being the product of particular material conditions. The first kind of criticism assumes that the text contains objective meaning, available to any reader perceptive and determined enough to uncover it. The second kind of criticism assumes that the meaning of any text is at least in part subjective, dependent on the value-judgments, assumptions and prior experiences of its author and reader. In what follows I will explore ahistoricist ideas of reading and criticism, and their theoretical (or antitheoretical) implications; I will also outline the position of New Historicist critics, and explain why they place such importance on the contextualization of not just the text but the reader as well.

### Is meaning subjective or objective?

Most people tend to respond initially to literature on a personal level, a level which seems to lack any theoretical awareness. For instance, they are likely to comment on Shakespeare's characters as if they were real human beings and make judgments about their attractiveness or otherwise. 'I can't stand Lady Macbeth'; 'Isn't Hamlet weird?'; 'I can't figure out what motivates Iago'; 'I think Orsino's a fop': these are not uncommon reactions to the complexities of the Shakespearean text. Treating dramatic characters as if they were real people may be irrational, but we find it difficult to resist it. As Howard Felperin argues:

> the traditionally mimetic ambitions of literature in general and drama in particular encourage us to consider its characters and plots as if they were actions performed by human beings with past and ongoing lives no less 'real' for being invisible or unavailable to us, and still in some sense 'there' while remaining unrepresented.[1]

I, for one, certainly do not wish to dismiss this mode of interpretation out of hand: a great deal of our satisfaction with Shakespeare comes from our sense that his characters' experiences are relevant to our own. However, we must always remember that we are reading fictions, and that all characters are fictional constructs. It is therefore pointless to try to answer questions such as 'how many children had Lady Macbeth?'[2] or 'what happens to the Fool after he disappears from Lear's side?' The kind of truth we find in a Shakespeare text will be subjective or imaginative rather than objective or literal.

Another common response to Shakespeare is to feel that there is a special timelessness about his writing. We seize on strings of words that we might put in our commonplace books (if we had the time to keep them). These are the quotations which seem to require no contextualization or effort of interpretation but which speak directly to us across the centuries. Shakespeare seems full of enduring wisdom. Take Hamlet's outburst:

> How weary, stale, flat, and unprofitable
> Seem to me all the uses of this world!
> (I.ii.133–4)

We surely need no specialist knowledge to recognize this as a universal statement of despair. But as students of literature we seek meanings other than the obvious or superficial; we endeavour, among other things, to produce readings which are sensitive to context. When we compare his comment about the 'uses of this world' with Hamlet's earlier discussion of the term 'seem' (I.ii.76–86), or with his later meditations ('there is nothing either good or bad but thinking makes it so' [II.ii.249–50]; 'O God, I could be bounded in a nutshell and count myself a king of infinite space – were it not that I have bad dreams' [II.ii.254–6]; 'to me, what is this quintessence of dust?' [II.ii.308]), we start to build an image of Hamlet not as suicidal depressive but as introspective, melancholic philosopher. And perhaps we go back to 'seem *to me*' with more of an eye for the loaded subjectivity and relativity of the statement. Hamlet may be sad, but he is also self-consciously aware of how he feels, and thus to some extent detached from his feelings; he could even be said to be performing them. The words may seem timeless, but it is Hamlet who speaks them in a play that is his tragedy, and our knowledge of this context profoundly influences our reading of what he says.

Even though Hamlet can scarcely be considered typical or representative of the average reader or theatre-goer, most people identify none the less with his despair. Whether they are right to do so is, however, questionable, since few people nowadays are likely to understand its exact nature. To do so we would need to inform ourselves about other representations of melancholy in Shakespeare's time. Robert Burton's *Anatomy of Melancholy* (1621), for example, is an enquiry into a topic which was clearly of great interest in early modern Europe, and it shows us that melancholy was viewed by contemporaries as a pathological state. Knowing Burton's work, we can assume that Shakespeare's audience would have identified Hamlet as an outstanding example of the melancholic man. Garbed in 'customary suits of solemn black' (I.ii.78), the solitary, brooding individual called Hamlet has his parallels (and variants) in other Shakespearean plays. Romeo pining for Rosaline at the opening of *Romeo and Juliet* is very much the melancholic lover, while the absolute discontent of Jaques in *As You Like It* is remarkably similar to Hamlet's 'this most excellent canopy the air . . . appeareth nothing to me but a foul and pestilent congregation of vapours' (II.ii.299–303) and 'Denmark's a prison' (II.ii.243):

> Invest me in my motley. Give me leave
> To speak my mind, and I will through and through

Cleanse the foul body of th'infected world,
If they will patiently receive my medicine.
(*As You Like It* II.vii.58–61)

Shakespeare's own characters, then, illustrate the inevitable subjectivity – the pull of the self – involved in any act of judgment or interpretation. Hamlet's despair takes an historically specific form, and is expressed in words and symptoms available only to men (and not women) of a particular class in a particular period. And just as it occurs to Hamlet to compare Denmark to a prison because the metaphor was a commonplace way to describe a sense of spiritual confinement in the early seventeenth century (compare, for example, John Donne's 'Else a great Prince in Prison lies'),[3] so our responses to Shakespeare's plays are inevitably historically conditioned and subjective. Recently many literary critics have tried to be 'up front' about the extent to which their responses to texts are influenced by their personal values, expectations and experiences, arguing that although we may not be able to escape subjectivity entirely, we can attempt to understand the origins of our responses and recognize that they, too, like any literary text, are historically produced. For one thing this self-analysis may enable us to take a step backwards from our initial reading and appreciate more fully those of other readers. For another it allows us to perceive the limitations of our readings, and precisely how they are conditioned by our beliefs and assumptions.

Rather than assuming that we can explain the plays once and for all we might instead want to use them to, among other things, explain ourselves. In this way the tables can be turned on us and the plays become the means to knowledge of ourselves and our society. As the critic Harold Bloom writes, 'The most bewildering of Shakespearean achievements is to have suggested more contexts for explaining us than we are capable of supplying for explaining his characters.'[4]

As so often, Shakespeare himself anticipated the direction his critics would take. Although I have argued that a sense of self is crucial to Hamlet and to his uncle, many of Shakespeare's characters voice the notion that, when stripped of their context, they lose their identity. The plays frequently question whether personal identity is any more than a matter of role, status, ceremony and

191

habit. Shakespeare raises this issue in an early play, *Richard II*, when Richard soliloquizes in prison:

> Thus play I in one person many people,
> And none contented. Sometimes am I king;
> Then treasons make me wish myself a beggar,
> And so I am. Then crushing penury
> Persuades me I was better when a king;
> Then am I king'd again, and by and by
> Think that I am unking'd by Bolingbroke,
> And straight am nothing. But whate'er I be,
> Nor I, nor any man that but man is
> With nothing shall be pleas'd, till he be eas'd
> With being nothing.
>
> (V.v.31–41)

And this theme recurs again and again in the plays. We might think not only of Hamlet's repetitive 'to me' comments, but of King Lear with his 'Who is it that can tell me who I am?' (I.iv.227), Iago's 'I am not what I am' (*Othello* I.i.65), Viola's 'I am not that I play' (*Twelfth Night* I.v.185), Bottom's transformation in *A Midsummer Night's Dream*, or Richard III's deceptions and seemings. Coriolanus is ironically destroyed by his constancy and permanence of character in a play which seems to explore the impossibility of establishing once and for all a single identity and character. Indeed, the refusal to role-play, to act, to dissemble here leads to catastrophe. Coriolanus realizes this when he changes his mind at the request of his mother Volumnia:

> O my mother, mother! O!
> You have won a happy victory to Rome;
> But for your son, believe it, O, believe it,
> Most dangerously you have with him prevail'd,
> If not most mortal to him. But let it come.
>
> (V.iii.185–9)

Shakespeare repeatedly problematizes the notion of self and character with the implication that it is not only the actors in the plays who play roles but those sitting in the audience too. (See Chapter 6 for a fuller discussion of this issue.)

## Context

As the foregoing discussion has shown, we cannot escape history any more than Shakespeare himself or his characters could escape it. This claim forms the central plank in the critical theory known as New Historicism, and since it ultimately derives from the political philosophy of Karl Marx it is worth beginning with what Marx himself has to say on the subject:

> Men make their own history, but they do not make it just as they please; they do not make it under circumstances chosen by themselves, but under circumstances directly encountered, given and transmitted from the past. The tradition of all dead generations weighs like a nightmare on the brain of the living. And just when they seemed engaged in revolutionising themselves and things, in creating something that has never yet existed, precisely in such periods of revolutionary crisis they anxiously conjure up the spirits of the past to their service and borrow from them names, battle cries and costumes in order to present the new scene of world history in this time-honoured disguise and this borrowed language.[5]

Everywhere you care to look, from Northern Ireland to Serbia to Rwanda, Marx's view is confirmed. History haunts us. We cannot be rid of it or pretend that it has died. And history certainly haunts literature. Like the ghost of Hamlet's father, believed to have been played originally by Shakespeare himself, history haunts Shakespeare's work and our study of it. We should read closely and respond personally, yes, but part of that close reading and personal engagement should involve digging down, like gravediggers, and discovering the past, like Yorick's skull, producing plenty of food for present (and future) thought.

To understand how a reading can be enhanced, deepened and even altered by contextualizing or historicizing the literary text, consider the example of Autolycus in *The Winter's Tale*. When I first read this play, I was immediately enchanted by Autolycus's high spirits and trickery. I felt he was a truly unique creation. His role as a ballad-seller particularly caught my imagination, and so I began researching the phenomenon of the broadside ballad in early modern England. In a book entitled *The Elizabethan Underworld*[6] I was fascinated to discover a reprint of a pamphlet 'imprinted at London by Thomas Scarlet for Cutberd Burbie' in 1592 entitled 'Thirde and last Part of Conny-catching. With the new devised Art of Foole-taking. The like Cosenages and Villenies never before discovered'. The pamphlet contained the following description:

> This trade, or rather unsufferable loitering quality, in singing of ballads and songs at the doors of such houses where plays are used, as also in open markets and other places of this City, where is most resort; which is nothing else but a sly fetch to draw many together, who, listening unto a harmless ditty, afterward walk home to their houses with heavy hearts.[7]

The reason for the audience's heavy hearts, it was revealed, lay in the fact that their purses had been stolen as they listened, transfixed, to the ballad-singing. This seems to describe the activities of characters very like Autolycus (see the earlier discussion in Chapter 5), and suggests that Shakespeare's lovable rogue was not a wholly original creation.

The cony-catching pamphlet helps to put the figure of Autolycus in focus, though it could hardly be said to 'explain' his function and dramatic significance in the play. What the pamphlet does provide is a glimpse of the material culture which produced the play *The Winter's Tale*, and its remarkable blend of myth and social realism.

Grasping history as Hamlet grasps Yorick's skull is literally impossible, but as my examples from *Hamlet* and *The Winter's Tale* suggest, partial, provisional attempts can and should be made to interpret Shakespeare in context. The most famous of the recent critical approaches which encourage us to dig in the dirt of the past is New Historicism, a branch of criticism whose most famous practitioners include such names as Stephen Greenblatt, Louis Montrose, Stephen Orgel and Patricia Parker. In his brief account of New Historicism Louis Montrose explains that:

> the newer historical criticism is *new* in its refusal of unproblematized distinctions between 'literature' and 'history', between 'text' and 'context'; new in resisting a prevalent tendency to posit and privilege a unified and autonomous individual – whether an Author or a work – to be set against a social or literary background. Briefly and too simply characterized, its collective project is to resituate canonical literary texts among the multiple forms of writing, and in relation to the non-discursive practice and institutions, of the social formation in which

those texts have been produced – while, at the same time, recognizing that this project of historical resituation is necessarily the textual construction of critics who are themselves historical subjects.[8]

In other words, texts should not be considered as objects in an autonomous aesthetic realm, but as products of specific social and economic conditions. And as we have seen, readers and critics are subject to the same pressures, so that their interpretations of texts are no more free of history than the texts themselves. Andrew Bennett and Nicholas Royle elaborate on this idea by suggesting that:

> What is new about new historicism in particular is its recognition that history is the 'history of the present', that history is in the making, that, rather than being monumental and closed, history is radically open to transformation and rewriting.[9]

We shall see what this means in practical terms when we reflect on *The Tempest*, and the possibilities of reclaiming from patriarchy this most canonical of texts by bringing feminist critical approaches to bear on it (see the section on 'Shakespeare and Feminism: *The Tempest*', below).

Bennett and Royle have brought us full circle. The most recent and influential historicist approach to literature, whilst encouraging readers to be aware of the text's historicity, is equally insistent that the reader develops and maintains a self-conscious understanding of his or her own embeddedness in history. In New Historicism, object and subject are irretrievably bound up with one another.

### Text and context

So where does this leave us as readers of Shakespeare? It leaves us negotiating between ourselves and the text, aware that the play we are studying is woven into one historical context and that we are woven into another, that any critique or interpretation we encounter is woven into yet other contexts, and that all of them are only partially knowable. Our understanding of Shakespeare is, like our understanding of ourselves, inevitably fragmentary. Yet we need not despair at having lost the certainties of New Criticism, which thought we could reach a definitive interpretation of a text, or of 'old' historicism, which saw the literary text as a transparent window onto history, as opposed to a mediating and mediated reflection – and part – of it. In place of the old certainties we have, with New Historicism, an exhilarating openness as to what historicization might involve. For instance, in Stephen Greenblatt's *Learning to Curse*, an obscure reference to Claude Duret's report in *Thresor de l'histoire des langves de cest univers* (1607) ('that the Indians, fearing that their secrets would be recorded and revealed, would not approach certain trees whose leaves the Spanish used for paper') provides a compelling context for Caliban's notion that Prospero's power resides in his books.[10] Here an obscure text far removed from traditional ideas of the literary is used to shed light on an aspect of Shakespeare's play which we may well have overlooked in the past. And contextualization has not reduced the text to history or denied its aesthetic function; rather it has offered us a new way of reading, and a new way of understanding the interplay between literature and society.

This would seem a good point at which to turn from the theoretical issues raised by historicist criticism to the practicalities of interpreting an individual text in the light of what we can determine about Shakespeare's society, and also what we recognize as our own historically determined preoccupations and preconceptions. My introduction has foregrounded the need to reflect on our critical assumptions as we attempt to understand Shakespeare's meaning; Katherine Armstrong's reading of *The Tempest* will serve as a concrete example of what happens when we bring a particular theory to bear on one of Shakespeare's plays. Like most students of Shakespeare, both of us favour a pluralist approach which allows us to profit from all kinds of theories and perspectives. The New Critics and the New Historicists, the postcolonialists and the Marxists, the humanists and the semioticians, the poststructuralists and the performance specialists: all offer special insights and advantages. But any individual act of interpretation is necessarily also one of selection. If we hope to produce a coherent reading of a text (whether in an essay or a performance) we will need consciously to define our critical approach so that the ideas we convey are neither confusing nor self-contradictory. As the following discussion of *The Tempest* illustrates, explicitly addressing the question of our own theoretical position at the outset can help to ensure that our critical reading is properly thought-out and logically presented.

## Feminism and Shakespeare: *The Tempest*

Feminism has proved one of the most productive and interesting approaches to Shakespeare of recent times, as other Shakespeare scholars have acknowledged. S. S. Hussey, for example, suggests that 'gender' is likely to be a more enlightening interpretative tool than New Historicism for Shakespeare studies in the long term.[11] Feminists, for their part, have been eager to engage with Shakespeare, first, in order to examine and sometimes contest the authority of one of Western culture's most canonical authors, and second, to participate in one of the most prestigious branches of literary criticism. As Lynda E. Boose explains, 'Shakespeare is a site of . . . competitive jostling [among professional critics] because Shakespeare is a site of enormous cultural power.'[12]

Since the subject areas of Shakespeare and feminist theory are well disposed towards one another, and are both at the forefront of literary and cultural studies, it is not surprising that they have intersected in significant and provocative ways since the the rise of second-wave feminism in the 1970s. At the same time, many feminist critics have argued that their interpretations of Shakespeare are as yet relatively unsophisticated and even simplistic; the focus is still, more often than not, on Shakespeare's portrayal of women, even if the emphasis has shifted from transparent readings of individual female characters to self-conscious analyses of constructions of gender in the plays.

This may be an unduly pessimistic view of feminist criticism, which has, as I have suggested, offered many illuminating and original perspectives on Shakespeare since the publication of ground-breaking work by Juliet Dusinberre, Lisa Jardine, Catherine Belsey and others in the 1970s and early 1980s.[13] Moreover, the feminist critique of Shakespeare continues to develop momentum, as is witnessed by the proliferation of books and articles in the field in the 1990s. The notion that feminist Shakespeare studies are in their infancy does, however, have some truth in it, and is borne out by the questioning tone of so many of the contributions to the recent essay collection, *Shakespeare and Gender*

(1995), edited by Deborah Barker and Ivo Kamps. A number end provisionally: Catherine Belsey's with a deferring 'I wonder . . . ' in answer to the question she has posed about Shakespeare's portrayal of love;[14] Leah Marcus's with an outline of the work future feminist scholarship must undertake in order 'to interrogate the canonical Shakespeare'.[15]

This sense of uncertainty and opportunity should be exciting to any feminist reader beginning to study Shakespeare; most of us, after all, are attracted to the idea of pioneering in our chosen field. On the other hand, some feminist critics have begun to question seriously the possibility of a positive reading of some of Shakespeare's plays – *The Taming of the Shrew* and *Othello*, for example. Given the extent to which Shakespeare, for all his supposed humanity and compassion, articulated the misogynistic prejudices of his day, it can seem almost hopeless to find any evidence that might make him an ally of feminism. The ending of Ann Thompson's essay on *The Tempest* is bleak:

> what kind of pleasure can a woman and a feminist take in this text beyond the rather grim one of mapping its various patterns of exploitation? Must a feminist reading necessarily be a negative one?[16]

These questions compel an answer, and in the rest of this chapter I shall respond to them by using *The Tempest* as a text which exemplifies the problems Shakespeare raises for his feminist readers. *The Tempest* will be used, that is to say, as a case-study. I hope to tread a path between the approach adopted by critics such as Dusinberre, who is confident that *The Tempest* portrays the 'reciprocal idolatry' of Miranda and Ferdinand (as opposed to the courtly idealization and objectification of Miranda),[17] and the pessimism of Thompson, for whom the play inscribes an oppressive ideology of femininity. Carol Thomas Neely has hinted at one way to read *The Tempest* which feminists might find more acceptable than either Dusinberre's uncomplicated valorization or Thompson's reluctant condemnation:

> But however qualified Prospero's transformation is, and however easy it is made for him to accomplish it, strikingly in this, the last of the romances, our attention is no longer focused on the destructive excesses of paternal power but on the cost of relinquishing it, on the pain of loosing a

daughter to marriage (II.i.121) and thereby confronting one's 'frail mortality': 'and so to Naples, / Where I have hope to see the nuptial / Of these our dear-beloved solemnized; / And thence retire me to my Milan, where / Every third thought shall be my grave' (V.i.308–12).[18]

For Neely, Prospero is a new kind of Shakespearean patriarch, but Prospero aside, in order to decide whether a more encompassing pro-feminist interpretation of *The Tempest* is possible, we need to weigh up the rest of the evidence for reading the play as an endorsement of patriarchy. Thompson mainly focuses on the marginality and passivity of the play's only female character, Miranda, but patriarchal assumptions are likely to have other consequences too for the text. Lawrence Stone offers a broad but concise definition of patriarchal power in Shakespeare's society:

[The] sixteenth-century aristocratic family was patrilinear, primogenitural, and patriarchal: patrilinear in that it was the male line whose ancestry was traced so diligently by the genealogists and heralds, and in almost all cases via the male line that titles were inherited; primogenitural in that most of the property went to the eldest son, the younger brothers being dispatched into the world with little more than a modest annuity or life interest in a small estate to keep them afloat; and patriarchal in that the husband and father lorded it over his wife and children with the quasi-absolute authority of a despot.[19]

Leaving aside the problematics of the relationship between society and literature, which Graham Atkin touched on earlier in this chapter (does the literary text reflect, mediate or constitute history, or all three?), how far can we apply Stone's account to the aristocratic society portrayed in *The Tempest*? The answer is unexpected, I think: Stone's familial and societal model has only limited relevance to the world of Shakespeare's play. I shall begin with Stone's first term, patrilinearity.

At first sight, admittedly, *The Tempest* confirms Stone's thesis that sixteenth-century society was ethnically and economically structured along patrilinear principles. The plot hinges on Prospero's anger at having been usurped by his brother, Antonio, and other moments in the play when patrilinear descent is threatened seem similarly foreboding. Alonso lent his support to Antonio; none the less, the plot by his own brother, Sebastian, to usurp Alonso in his turn is represented as evil and barbaric. When

Alonso believes he has lost his son he feels his entire family has disintegrated:

> Would I had never
> Married my daughter there! for, coming thence,
> My son is lost, and, in my rate, she too,
> Who is so far from Italy removed
> I ne'er again shall see her. O thou mine heir
> Of Naples and of Milan, . . .
>
> (II.i.103–8)

Ferdinand's reaction to his father's apparent death is similarly coloured as much by dynastic concerns as by a sense of personal loss: 'myself am Naples, / Who with mine eyes, never since at ebb, beheld / The King my father wrack'd' (I.ii.437–9). For all his grief, he is first and foremost conscious of having inherited his father's title, and within moments of learning of his father's supposed drowning he is offering to make Miranda 'The Queen of Naples' (I.ii.452). To both father and son their personal and political fortunes are inseparable.

Yet *The Tempest* never actually mitigates the threats to patrilinearity which are presented in the first half of the play. Prospero returns to Milan, but he has been effectively if benignly supplanted by his heir – and his heir is his daughter, not his son. And throughout the play Alonso's insistence on an exogamous marriage for his daughter, Claribel, is regarded as the cause and justification of much of his suffering: 'Sir, you may thank yourself for this great loss, / That would not bless our Europe with your daughter / But rather loose her to an African' (II.i.119–21). Though Sebastian is heartless to say this, and Gonzalo later right to declare the opposite – that Claribel's marriage was a hidden blessing ('in one voyage / Did Claribel her husband find at Tunis, / And Ferdinand, her brother, found a wife / Where he himself was lost' [V.i.208–11]) – it is undeniably the case that Alonso's loss of Ferdinand is poetic justice for his recklessness in marrying off Claribel, and that his treatment of his daughter is supposed to cast a favourable light on Prospero's assiduous efforts to protect Miranda. In other words, the play promotes a negative view of exogamy – marrying outside one's kinship network – and hence of patrilinearity, exogamy being one of the means by which aristocratic families in the early modern period were able to increase and consolidate their wealth. *The Tempest* much prefers the endogamous marriage of Ferdinand and Miranda, which adds no significant wealth or prestige to the Neapolitans and in material terms only benefits Miranda.

As regards primogeniture, the same points apply. Miranda is her father's only heir, and Alonso's treatment of his daughter is regarded as despicable, notwithstanding the fact that she is not his heir and might reasonably, according to patriarchal ideology, be regarded as his property to dispose of as he wished.

If *The Tempest* refuses to endorse patrilinearity and primogeniture, its opposition to patriarchy is arguably far more profound. Without exception the patriarchs in this play are intemperate, tyrannical and ruthless. They compete aggressively with one another: Alonso conspired with Antonio to usurp Prospero; Antonio with Sebastian against Alonso. Stephano, the drunken butler, is a ludicrous and gross parody of a patriarch, resting his foot on Caliban and demanding his complete subjugation.

But the most notable patriarch in the play is, of course, Prospero. The problematic nature of Prospero's government of his isle has exercised many recent critics, who are no longer content with a romantic equation of Prospero the semi-divine magician with Shakespeare the sublime artist. Prospero has emerged in recent years as at worst a colonial oppressor, at best a benevolent despot. In the past he was taken very much at his own estimation. Omnipotent and omniscient, he was seen to have restored order to Milan and undergone a personal journey, metaphorical as well as literal, from selfish introspection to righteous anger to acceptance and renunciation. Yet the play is extremely ambiguous as to the extent of Prospero's actual power, or the degree to which he has learned from his exile. In his last speeches he sounds chastened rather than uplifted, and in the rest of the play it is mainly Ariel's magic we see performed; moreover, the experiences of the new arrivals seem to owe as much to the remarkable properties of the isle as to its governor. Prospero is most proprietorial when it comes to Miranda, but even his sixteen-year-old daughter eludes his power when she names herself to Ferdinand. As Prospero himself acknowledges, 'They are both in either's pow'rs' (I.ii.453).

So far I have considered only those ways in which *The Tempest* explicitly addresses issues pertinent to a feminist reading, and have suggested that its portrayal of masculine power and authority is far from uncritical. Feminist criticism would be a rather predictable and straightforward affair if it confined itself to such obvious topics, however, and I now want to turn to the implicit ways in which the text deals with questions of gender.

According to Frank Kermode's influential interpretation of the play, its primary thematic opposition is between Art and Nature – the civilized, benevolent art of Prospero, and the brutish, malevolent nature of Caliban. As we have seen in Chapter 5, postcolonialist readings have challenged the assumptions underlying this interpretation: Caliban can be seen as a victim of Prospero's tyranny and of Miranda's misguided efforts to teach him language. Of course, Miranda's view of Caliban is fraught with racist implications. But a postcolonialist reading which ignores gender is as partial as one which ignores the racist and imperialist implications of the play. If we can destabilize Kermode's equation by applying the insights of postcolonialism to the relationship between Art and Nature, what happens when we apply the insights of feminism to the Art/Nature dichotomy?

Feminist theorists long ago identified the fundamental binary oppositions on which patriarchal ideology depends. Where men are equated with, for example, rationality, civilization, logic and knowledge, women are equated with feeling, nature, instinct and intuition. Prospero's language suggests that he shares the patriarchal view of art and civilization as a male prerogative; his paternal authority and his learning or art are closely identified with one another:

> Here in this island we arriv'd; and here
> Have I, thy schoolmaster, made thee more profit
> Than other princess' can, that have more time
> For vainer hours, and tutors not so careful.
>
> (I.ii.171–4)

Prospero also regards his art as both the inverse and the equivalent of his political power: 'my library / Was dukedom large enough' (I.ii.109–10); 'Prospero the prime duke, being so reputed / In dignity, and for the liberal Arts / Without a parallel' (I.ii.72–4). When, at the end of the play, he abjures his 'rough magic' (V.i.50), he also seems to defer to Ferdinand and Miranda. 'Every third thought shall be my grave' (V.i.311), he declares, and Gonzalo has already pre-empted him: 'Was Milan thrust from Milan, that his issue / Should become Kings of Naples?' (V.i.205–6).

Not surprisingly, Prospero's sense of self is grounded on a belief in the superiority of art to nature. Nature functions as his 'Other', just as feminists since Simone de Beauvoir have argued that woman functions as the Other who confirms man's image of himself.[20] For Prospero nature is variously supine, yielding, primitive and contemptible. He can dictate to it, dispose of it and exploit it:

> I have bedimm'd
> The noontide sun, call'd forth the mutinous winds,
> And 'twixt the green sea and the azur'd vault
> Set roaring war: to the dread rattling thunder
> Have I given fire, and rifted Jove's stout oak
> With his own bolt; the strong-bas'd promontory
> Have I made shake, and by the spurs pluck'd up
> The pine and cedar: graves at my command
> Have wak'd their sleepers, op'd, and let 'em forth
> By my so potent Art.
>                                        (V.i.1–50)

Again his language conflates political and artistic power (the winds are 'mutinous'; the sea is at 'war'; the cliffs and trees are his quaking enemies), and genders both as masculine ('my so potent Art'). Nature, by contrast, is disorderly and weak. Prospero explicitly identifies this rebellious yet submissive nature as female in his venomous attack on Caliban's mother. Sycorax's gender is continually invoked: she was a 'foul witch' (I.ii.258), a 'damn'd witch' (I.ii.263), a 'blue-ey'd hag' (I.ii.269), and Caliban's 'wicked dam' (I.ii.322). She is evil, not because she has supernatural powers – Prospero has similar powers himself, as he is quick to say – but because she has such powers while being female and 'Other'. Prospero's masculinity and power are coterminous: his 'elves' are his 'Weak masters' (V.i.41), his art is 'potent' (V.i.50), his position 'lord' (V.i.162) of the isle. Appropriately, when Ariel is commanded to 'Be subject to' (I.ii.302) his master, Prospero orders him to assume a female form: 'Go make thyself like a nymph o' th' sea' (I.ii.301), he says.

Nature as the opposite of Prospero's art is, however, most obviously suggested by the character of his daughter, Miranda.

Miranda has grown up 'ignorant' (I.ii.18) of the vices of 'civilized' society, and Prospero regards her as chaste, innocent, wondering and susceptible. That this suggests a respect for women in general is not the case: just as he either idealizes or demonizes nature as it suits his purposes, so he either idealizes women (Miranda; Miranda's mother), or demonizes them (Sycorax). And for all his humility in recollecting Miranda's unconscious fortitude and tranquillity during the tempest which brought her to the isle, he subjects her to his art more thoroughly than he does any other person in the play. Controlling Miranda – especially her instinctive sexuality – is more important to him than any act of revenge.

Given the infrequency with which Miranda speaks, and the absence of other female characters from the play, it might seem that Shakespeare was content to leave Prospero's assumptions about the hierarchical relationship between nature and art unchallenged. As Thompson has pointed out, we see Miranda entirely through Prospero's eyes, and there is certainly no explicit indication that her naturalness can overcome his art. Yet I have already discussed the ways in which the play might be said to question the ethics of Prospero's art and the ways in which the limitations of that art are made apparent. Prospero's authority as a father is absolute; he decides not only with whom Miranda shall fall in love, but even when she can wake or speak. None the less, he cannot help acknowledging her abilities to charm, nor that they equal his own: 'The Duke of Milan / And his more braver daughter could control thee, / If now 'twere fit to do't (I.ii.441–3), he murmurs of Ferdinand.

As a tiny child Miranda exerted a comparable influence on Prospero himself, who was awed by the vision of beatific calm she presented to him:

> O, a cherubin
> Thou wast that did preserve me. Thou didst smile,
> Infused with a fortitude from heaven,
> When I have deck'd the sea with drops full salt.
> (I.ii.152–5)

And when she does fall in love, right on cue, she arouses more anxieties than she can assuage. The point at which her father's power seems greatest – the encounter he engineers between Miranda and Ferdinand – is also the moment at which she begins to assert her own identity and to fall under the spell of someone else. Towards the end of the play, when Miranda and her lover are discovered playing at chess, they seem remote from the rest of the characters, not least from Prospero, who ostensibly presents them to his visitors:

> Welcome, sir;
> This cell's my court: here have I few attendants,
> And subjects none abroad: pray you, look in.
> My dukedom since you have given me again,
> I will requite you with as good a thing;
> At least bring forth a wonder, to content ye
> As much as me my dukedom.
>
> (V.i.165–71)

The word 'wonder' is partly responsible for this distancing effect, since it conveys not only that Prospero is able to perform miracles but also that his creations transcend him. The speech ostensibly argues that Ferdinand and Miranda are as marvellous as Prospero's dukedom; its effect is to make them seem far more so.

A similar transcendence is implied by the masque in Act IV, which begins as if directed by Prospero yet develops into a celebration of a nature whose superabundant fertility is so powerful that it overshadows the human agent who supposedly stage-manages it. Iris's apostrophe to Ceres evokes a landscape responsive to human needs, yet one in which the arts of cultivation are superfluous; nature chooses to provide, and is limitless:

> Ceres, most bounteous lady, thy rich leas
> Of wheat, rye, barley, vetches, oats, and pease;
> Thy turfy mountains, where live nibbling sheep,
> And flat meads thatched with stover, them to keep;
> Thy banks with pioned and twilled brims,
> Which spongy April at thy hest betrims,
> To make cold nymphs chaste crowns; and thy broom-groves,
> Whose shadow the dismissed bachelor loves,
> Being lass-lorn . . .
>
> (IV.i.60–78)

The masque which follows celebrates the power of a female deity, Juno, who sanctions and blesses the contract between Ferdinand

and Miranda and invites Ceres to bestow fertility on them, symbolized by the infinite bounty of nature: 'Earth's increase, foison plenty, / Barns and garners never empty' (IV.i.110–11).

At the end of the masque Prospero starts, as he suddenly realizes he has forgotten the 'foul conspiracy' (IV.i.139) of Caliban, Stephano and Trinculo: once again, the effect is to diminish his power and emphasize his age and 'infirmity' (IV.i.160). Throughout the play it is humanity, and not Prospero at all, which prompts the most wonderment from the characters: Ferdinand's 'Admir'd Miranda' (III.i.37) and 'O you wonder' (I.ii.429); Miranda's 'O brave new world, / That has such people in't! (V.i.183–4), and Gonzalo's

> O, rejoice
> Beyond a common joy! and set it down
> With gold on lasting pillars: in one voyage
> Did Claribel her husband find at Tunis,
> And Ferdinand, her brother, found a wife . . .
> (V.i.206–10)

Amazement is also expressed at the landscape and the elements, by comparison with whose splendour Prospero's magic seems no more than a series of special effects, an 'insubstantial pageant' (IV.i.155).

Ultimately, *The Tempest* inverts the traditional hierarchy of art and nature, privileging the latter over the former, and this, I would argue, enables us to defend a positive feminist reading of the play. It is true that Miranda is regarded by Prospero as a commodity, just as he regarded her mother as an object ('a piece of virtue' [I.ii.56]) and just as, conversely, he considers Sycorax as an object of contempt. Yet Miranda herself resists this commodification, and unobtrusively refuses to accept her father's misogynistic view of other women. 'Had I not / Four or five women once that tended me?' (I.ii.46–7) she asks, and her assumption that her servants were there to look after her contrasts tellingly with Prospero's assumption that they were status symbols: '[A]nd more, Miranda' (I.ii.48), he complacently replies.

For Prospero nature must be tamed by art, though he recognizes that some aspects of nature – Caliban, for instance – are resistant to cultivation or nurture. For Miranda the opposite seems manifest. 'Good wombs have borne bad sons' (I.ii.119) is her mild but pointed response to Prospero's implied slur on the mother who could have produced such a brother as Antonio. Miranda's line carries the implication that nature is the norm which human beings pervert, a lesson she presumably learned from teaching Caliban, unintentionally, to curse.

It is the female goddesses and the naiads who celebrate the union between Ferdinand and Miranda, and they enact a masque in which nature seems vaster than the human imagination – even Prospero's – can comprehend. And Miranda remains unchanged – immaculate – at the end of the play, whereas Prospero has had to learn from her example and develop the capacity for kindness, humility and patience. He is embraced by Alonso, and found to be flesh and blood after all. He discovers that the good will find love and the bad conspire without his art. In the end the people on his isle are as natural and impetuous as the very human gods and goddesses of Ovid's *Metamorphoses*, and they seem both smaller and larger than his fantasy of omnipotence. In the end Prospero is reduced from Faustian divinity to feeble old age.

This leaves the feminist critic with only one problem: Shakespeare would seem to be vindicating nature and woman through an essentialist equation of the two. The emphasis on procreation in relation to the union of Ferdinand and Miranda appears to support the idea that Miranda symbolizes a subservient nature whose fertility guarantees patrilinear descent. Yet the masque presented by Iris is an affirmation of Ferdinand and Miranda's joint and equal fertility. Juno invites Ceres to: 'Go with me / To bless this twain, that they may prosperous be, / And honour'd in their issue' (IV.i.103–5). And if the scholars are right who believe *The Tempest* was performed for the wedding of Robert Carr, Earl of Essex and Lady Frances Howard, the emphasis on mutuality is significant; Lady Frances had claimed that her first husband was impotent and therefore unable to give her children.

The charge of essentialism is also disarmed if we turn to the character of Gonzalo. For all Prospero's irascible references to his political power and importance, Gonzalo's vision of his ideal commonwealth (II.i.143–52) is arguably the most potent political moment in the play. It is, moreover, in some respects anti-patriarchal; there would be no magistrates, no 'succession' in this utopia.

Like Miranda, Gonzalo is Prospero's opposite. Kind and cheerful, and incapable of bitterness, he is repeatedly associated with

acts of charity and compassion. It was he who ensured that
Prospero had his books with him when he left Milan, and he who
constantly offers comfort to Alonso in his affliction. Prospero's
tribute suggests that Gonzalo is the closest *The Tempest* comes to
representing a mother:

> A noble Neapolitan, Gonzalo,
> Out of his charity, who being then appointed
> Master of this design, did give us, with
> Rich garments, linens, stuffs and necessaries,
> Which since have steaded much; so, of his gentleness,
> Knowing I lov'd my books, he furnish'd me
> From mine own library.
>
> (I.ii.161–7)

It is no coincidence that, in complete contrast to Prospero,
Gonzalo is (like Miranda) content with nature as he finds it,
whether it is the isle ('How lush and lusty the grass looks!'
[II.i.51]), the people in it ('Their manners are more gentle, kind,
than of / Our human generation' [III.iii.32–3]), or the events
unfolding before him ('Faith, sir, you need not fear' [III.iii.43]). By
comparison with his solicitude Prospero's treatment of others
seems like interference, not care. The two of them evoke gender
stereotypes: Gonzalo is the ideal mother, gentle and encouraging;
Prospero, the authoritarian father, is rough and proprietorial. Yet
gender stereotypes are also subverted, since Gonzalo is an old man
too, and the play ends with Prospero's acceptance of the loss of his
powers. For a few hours Prospero has been able to master time,
but his revels soon are ended and the harmony at the end of the
play is the harmony of youth, sexual love and procreation, an
assertion of the cyclical temporality of nature in contrast to the
laborious manipulations of Prospero's art which preceded it.

By reading *The Tempest* as I have done, with an eye to Prospero's
limitations as well as his aspirations, we are able to dismantle the
impressive but precarious illusion he constructs for us, and focus
instead on images whose simplicity is an effective reproach to his
art: above all, on his daughter. If *The Tempest* questions the ascendancy of art, as it surely does, then it must vindicate nature. And
though Caliban may be a pitiful object, he cannot be viewed as a
Noble Savage by any stretch of the imagination. It is Miranda who

represents benign nature in this play, but not a passive, yielding or unruly nature; rather she is dignified, gentle and passionate, her instinctive reactions more subtle and refined than any of the learned behaviour of which her father is capable.

None the less, one crucial issue remains unresolved, namely the implications of the play's emphasis on the chastity of its heroine. Even if Shakespeare refuses to endorse patrilinearity and primogeniture, even if he exposes the weaknesses of his various patriarchs, and even if he upholds kindness and gentleness whilst simultaneously unsettling their essentialist associations with the female, if he none the less makes chastity the most important attribute of his heroine *The Tempest* surely cannot be anything other than an objectification of Miranda which disguises a proprietorial concern for the disposition of her body as a proper, indeed pious regard for her moral purity.

The evidence for the objectification of Miranda is certainly compelling. Prospero's anxiety for her chastity is so acute that many modern critics have viewed it as a product of his sexual guilt about her. Strong paternal interest in a daughter rarely goes unchallenged in canonical texts nowadays; *King Lear* has been subject to similarly sharp-eyed reinterpretations. But even setting aside the question of Prospero's own sexuality, female chastity has undoubted symbolic importance in this play, Miranda's virtue being defined almost exclusively in terms of her virginity, at least by her father.

Yet I think it is possible to read the play 'against the grain', and discover in it an implied criticism of the patriarch's righteous insistence on a narrowly technical definition of female chastity. For Prospero chastity is equated simply with the intact female body: if Ferdinand 'dost break [Miranda's] virgin-knot' (IV.i.15) before the wedding, his marriage will be cursed with discord and sterility. The speech is grossly explicit, and contrasts with Ferdinand's earlier assumption that physical and emotional integrity are inseparable: 'O, if a virgin, / And your affection not gone forth, I'll make you / The Queen of Naples' (I.ii.450–2). Here virginity was prized less for itself than as an indicator of eligibility and unattached feelings.

Elsewhere in the play Miranda's chastity is presented not as Prospero regards it – as a treasure to be guarded – but as a symbol of a wider conception of virtue which encompasses purity, youth, beauty and love. And that Shakespeare could conceive of chastity as a sign of female moral autonomy is illustrated by the self-assertions of Isabella in *Measure for Measure* and Marina in *Pericles*. Miranda's chastity is a sign of her profound innocence, which has been preserved by her sequestered upbringing but which is innate. From infancy she has been impervious to sin or suffering, though interestingly this aspect of her is unvalued by Prospero. '"Tis new to thee' (V.i.184), he sourly remarks, when she exclaims with wonder at the prospect of the brave new world awaiting her. A more generous, inclusive notion of his daughter's virtue would have allowed Prospero to delight in her unspoiled pleasure at this moment; instead he regards it as the kind of naivety which will not survive exposure to the world beyond the island. Her goodness, in other words, matters to him purely in terms of her sexual continence; its broader dimensions go uncelebrated.

Ironically, however, the play does recognize that her chastity is a question of Miranda's personal will: she can choose, no less than Ferdinand, to delay consummation until marriage. 'I am your wife if you will marry me; / If not, I'll die your maid' (III.i.83–4), she tells Ferdinand. That Shakespeare admits other notions of chastity besides Prospero's is also indicated in his portrayal of Ferdinand. Just as the play emphasizes his fertility as well as Miranda's, so too it emphasizes his chastity as well as hers. No woman he has met before Miranda equalled her perfection (III.i.39–48), he tells her, implying that he has never been in love before. Iris explains that both 'man and maid' (IV.i.95) have taken vows to delay consummation, and Ferdinand's speech to Prospero is just as applicable to himself as to Miranda, despite the sexist glosses offered by most editors: 'I warrant you, sir; / The white cold virgin snow upon my heart / Abates the ardour of my liver' (IV.i.54–6).

Ferdinand's fertility and chastity lend him the same emblematic quality as Miranda, reminding us that we should not assume the play to be an objectification of the female before considering the extent to which it objectifies the male subject. Both Ferdinand and Miranda are objects of Prospero's supervisory gaze; both appear as a spectacle for the audience when they are found playing at chess. Indeed Miranda gazes at Ferdinand before he gazes at her, and her language literally objectifies him: 'What is't? a spirit? / Lord, how it looks about!' (I.ii.412–13). Feminist critics have regretted Miranda's monochromatic character, and the few lines she is given in the play, but Ferdinand is equally stylized and verbally confined;

it is as well to remember that this is not a naturalistic play, and none of its characters, even Prospero, has the depth we associate with, say, the heroes of Shakespeare's tragedies.

Historians of the early modern period have been increasingly concerned to challenge the assumption that it was as absolute in its imposition of patriarchal ideology as bourgeois Victorian society managed to be. Natalie Zemon Davis, for example, highlights the careers of three remarkably independent seventeenth-century French women in her latest work,[21] whilst Lawrence E. Klein argues that notions of the separate spheres of home and marketplace are inappropriate for understanding gender ideology before the nineteenth century.[22] Literary critics, for all their attachment to reading against the grain, have tended to accept that texts such as Shakespeare's embody the dominant ideology identified with the early modern period, so that even where the critical aim has been to reveal Prospero's feet of clay, he remains the focus of attention – as indeed the present essay to some extent illustrates.

Yet I have also tried to examine Miranda in her own right, and to suggest that she transcends the role her father envisages for her, as well, of course, as fulfilling that role impeccably. In addition I have tried to extend the feminist critique of Shakespeare to embrace more than simply his female (and male) characters, by exploring the gendered binary opposition which underpins – and eventually destabilizes – the patriarchal structures depicted in *The Tempest*. I have thus tried to show that, for all its paucity of female characters and the misogynistic rhetoric of its protagonist, a play such as *The Tempest* does offer hope to readers who would like to reconcile their admiration for Shakespeare with their commitment to feminist criticism. To be sure, *The Tempest* is a problematic text for feminist revisionism to tackle, being notoriously susceptible to exegesis. As Anne Barton puts it, '*The Tempest* is an extraordinarily obliging work of art. It will lend itself to almost any interpretation.'[23] Who is to say, then, that a feminist reading of the play is more valid than any other? All we can assert with confidence is that it is no more reasonable to assume that Shakespeare was wholly uncritical of patriarchy than to assume he regarded it with a degree of scepticism. If the Victorians were indeed wrong to encourage us to view the early modern period as monolithically patriarchal, we may well need to discard the assumption that authors such as Shakespeare reproduced patriarchal ideology unequivocally. We can begin, perhaps, to look in their texts for evidence of dissatisfaction with patriarchy's more brutal gestures. And just as some postcolonialist critics have found in *The Tempest* a subtle exposé of imperialist aggression disguised as an attack on the discourse of the Noble Savage, so feminist critics may find in the play a critical examination of paternal absolutism disguised as an attack on those who threaten that doctrine. We can never know for sure that Shakespeare hoped to show that the power of the state or the father rested on rhetoric and force rather than on ordained right. He may, after all, have been seeking to show that society depends on the maintenance of existing hierarchies, whatever their flaws and limitations. At the risk of repetition, the point is surely that neither interpretation can be proven, so that reading Shakespeare as a patriarch is no more – or less – justifiable than reading him as an observant critic of the methods by which patriarchs protect their interests. *The Tempest*, we should remember, is a play which dispels illusions, deposes dukes, and transfers power from the father to the daughter. Whatever Prospero was planning, Miranda chooses whom she marries for herself, and almost her last speech in the play is a joke in which she implicitly reduces male power struggles and manoeuvrings to a children's game. If Ferdinand cheated her openly at chess, she says, and if he won 'a score of kingdoms', she would indulge him and 'call it fair play' (V.i.174–5). This can be read as a fitting, and subversive, final comment on her father, whose wrangle with Antonio over Milan comes in the end to seem much more like a brotherly squabble than the conflict of tragic proportions described by Prospero at the beginning of the play.

## Conclusion

As well as an example of how to define one's theoretical position explicitly whilst using that theory to interpret a text, the above account of *The Tempest* should serve to demonstrate that every critical act forms part of an ongoing debate. It is easy to think that one's own studies are conducted in isolation, and that the real work of Shakespearean criticism is carried on elsewhere, perhaps by professional teachers, critics, and directors. Yet as we have argued earlier in this book, all students of Shakespeare contribute to the criticism engendered by his plays, and all of them, whether published or unpublished, are able to reflect on, develop and ultimately sometimes influence the critical and theoretical traditions to which they belong. The cultural materialist insistence on the interplay between text and context and between object and subject implies, as Graham Atkin asserted at the beginning of this chapter, that all who interpret Shakespeare are not just grounded in history but producers of history too, and that each of us plays a part, however small, in shaping the reception of his work.

## Notes

1. Howard Felperin, '"Tongue-tied our queen?": The deconstruction of presence in *The Winter's Tale*', in *Shakespeare: The question of theory*, ed. Patricia Parker and Geoffrey Hartman (London: Routledge, 1985), pp. 3–18, at p. 4.
2. A question famously posed, and mocked, by L. C. Knights in 'How many children had Lady Macbeth? An essay in the theory and practice of Shakespeare criticism', repr. in *Explorations: Essays in criticism mainly on literature of the seventeenth century* (1946; repr. Harmondsworth: Penguin, 1964), pp. 13–50.
3. John Donne, 'The Extasie' (pub. 1633), l. 68.
4. Harold Bloom, *The Western Canon* (1994; London and Basingstoke: Macmillan, 1995), p. 64.
5. Karl Marx, 'The Eighteenth Brumaire of Louis Bonaparte', in Karl Marx and Friedrich Engels, *Selected Works* (London: Lawrence and Wishart, 1968), p. 96.
6. *The Elizabethan Underworld*, ed. A. V. Judges (London: Routledge, 1930).
7. *Ibid.*, p. 189.
8. Louis Montrose, 'Renaissance literary studies and the subject of history', *English Literary Renaissance* 16 (1987), 5–12, at p. 6.
9. Andrew Bennett and Nicholas Royle, *An Introduction to Literature, Criticism and Theory* (Hemel Hempstead: Harvester Wheatsheaf, 1995), p. 93.
10. Stephen Greenblatt, *Learning to Curse: Essays in early modern culture* (London: Routledge, 1990), p. 24.
11. S. S. Hussey, *The Literary Language of Shakespeare*, 2nd edn (London: Longman, 1992), p. viii.
12. Lynda E. Boose, 'The family in Shakespeare studies; or – studies in the family of Shakespeareans; or – the politics of politics', *Renaissance*

*Quarterly* 40 (1987), 708, quoted in the editors' introduction to *Shakespeare and Gender*, ed. Deborah Barker and Ivo Kamps (London: Verso, 1995), p. 1.

13. See especially Juliet Dusinberre, *Shakespeare and the Nature of Women* (London: Macmillan, 1975); Lisa Jardine, *Still Harping on Daughters: Women and drama in the age of Shakespeare* (Brighton: Harvester Wheatsheaf, 1983); Catherine Belsey, *The Subject of Tragedy: Identity and difference in Renaissance drama* (London: Methuen, 1985).

14. Catherine Belsey, 'Love in Venice', in *Shakespeare and Gender*, p. 211.

15. Leah Marcus, 'The Shakespearean editor as Shrew-tamer', in *ibid.*, p. 231.

16. Ann Thompson, '"Miranda, where's your sister?": Reading Shakespeare's *The Tempest*', in *ibid.*, p. 177.

17. Dusinberre, *Shakespeare and the Nature of Women*, p. 157.

18. Carol Thomas Neely, *Broken Nuptials in Shakespeare's Plays* (New Haven, CT: Yale University Press, 1985), p. 190.

19. Lawrence Stone, *The Crisis of the Aristocracy, 1558–1641*, abr. edn (New York: Oxford University Press, 1967), p. 271, quoted in Coppélia Kahn, *Man's Estate: Masculine identity in Shakespeare* (Berkeley and Los Angeles: University of California Press, 1981), p. 13.

20. See Paul Brown, '"This thing of darkness I acknowledge mine": *The Tempest* and the discourse of colonialism', in *Political Shakespeare: New essays in cultural materialism*, ed. Jonathan Dollimore and Alan Sinfield (Manchester: Manchester University Press, 1985), pp. 48–71, for a fuller consideration of this idea. Brown focuses primarily on the play's representation of the colonial 'savage', but he also notes the gender implications of the colonialist discourse which influenced Shakespeare.

21. Natalie Zemon Davis, *Women on the Margins: Three seventeenth-century lives* (Cambridge, MA: Harvard University Press, 1996).

22. Lawrence E. Klein, 'Gender and the public/private distinction in the eighteenth century: Some questions about evidence and analytic procedure', *Eighteenth-Century Studies* 29 (1995), 97–109.

23. Anne Barton, 'Introduction', *The Tempest* (Harmondsworth: Penguin, 1968), p. 22.

# Conclusion

We hope this book has succeeded in providing students with a challenging and up-to-date guide to studying Shakespeare at degree level. In focusing on the practicalities – realistically how we can best approach the activities of reading, watching, discussing, writing about and researching Shakespeare – we have recognized the growing importance of what has been termed student-centred learning in higher education today. We have acknowledged that at times it raises unfamiliar problems for students, and we have aimed to propose solutions to some of them. However, we have also emphasized the exciting opportunities students enjoy when they take responsibility for their own learning. For example, they may find themselves being asked to choose their own topics or develop their own methodologies, whilst they are commonly expected to navigate their way through a wide range of information resources and to present their written work with a professionalism which few institutions used to demand of undergraduates before the advent of the personal computer. On-line databases and worldwide web-sites, almost unknown on most campuses just a few years ago, are now the first port of call for many students when beginning an assignment. In addition, through television, cinema and the educational programmes of subsidized touring theatre companies, most students nowadays have access to a range of productions of Shakespeare, recorded and live, mainstream and experimental, spectatorial and participative.

In Chapter 1 we explained the terms of what has been called the Shakespeare debate, and affirmed our own belief in the value of Shakespeare to present and future generations of students. In Chapter 2 we promoted discussion as a basic study technique which permits the fluid interchange of ideas and encourages originality and experimentation. In Chapter 3 we explored the variety of forms in which students can write about Shakespeare, from conventional essays to reviews to dissertations, and offered ideas for making all such work accurate, well structured and well researched.

Chapters 4 and 9 suggested that students can develop their understanding of Shakespeare by considering three aspects of the plays, text, media and reception. Under the heading of 'Text', Chapter 4, on language, stressed the need for the detailed and nuanced reading of the Shakespearean text, while Chapter 5 examined how far an awareness of Shakespeare's own society and of the contexts in which we now encounter him conditions our interpretations of that text.

Under the heading 'Media', Chapters 6 and 7 look at Shakespeare beyond the printed page, in performance and in electronic forms including multimedia and the Internet. Here we suggested how students can best exploit the resources of the theatre, video library and computer, and we also speculated as to the implications of global digital networks for Shakespeare studies in the future.

Under 'Reception', Chapters 8 and 9 dealt with more traditional approaches to studying Shakespeare, the reading and practice of criticism and theory. However, we once again assumed that such study will be partly if not largely self-directed, and we therefore described some of the methods by which students can systematically select from the vast secondary resources currently available. We also sought to demonstrate that students can and should develop the confidence to engage with, and contribute to, the interpretative and theoretical debates occupying professional critics. This parallels our belief, asserted in the Preface, that the distinction between tutor and student is a largely false one, given that all of us are involved in an ongoing and open-ended debate about the meaning of Shakespeare's plays.

It seems fair to assume that Shakespeare will retain his prominence in the curriculum in the future, but that he will be studied with increasing diversity. Courses are being developed and taught which focus on Shakespeare and film, Shakespeare and postmodernism, Shakespeare and postcolonialism, for example. Inside and outside the classroom there is enormous interest in Shakespeare in performance, especially in productions which use startlingly modern settings. Many students will have benefited in past years from the Cambridge Shakespeare and Schools summer projects, which have encouraged children to draw parallels between the world of the plays and contemporary society. Feminist appropriations of Shakespearean texts and plots have proliferated in the 1990s, so that we are now invited to consider, say, Goneril and Regan's perspective on Lear's behaviour, or Emilia, Desdemona and Bianca's views of Othello and Iago.

Study methods are changing just as quickly as the contents of courses: more and more students are using open-learning packages, for example, some of which are highly interactive. The latest CD-ROMs allow students to compare different productions of the same text, and to use virtual reality to design their own productions. In years to come there may be less communication between tutor and student in class than via e-mail. Already many students are devoting a significant proportion of their final year to the preparation of an extended essay or dissertation, researched and written independently or with relatively little supervision. And as we have have pointed out, such research has been transformed by the increasing availability of new resources, from online catalogues, to bibliographies, periodicals and newspapers on CD-ROM, to the Internet. Students are often more computer-literate than their tutors, and therefore have little choice but to find out for themselves when it comes to using electronic bulletin-boards, web-sites, on-line searches, and so on.

Though we have laboured the significance of the many technological innovations and critical-theoretical debates affecting literary and cultural studies as we approach the millenium, we hope that Shakespeare himself has remained our focus at all times. Whether they are performance-centred multimedia packages or radical departures in literary theory, new approaches to studying Shakespeare are inevitably more ephemeral than is his work itself. While it is vital to keep ourselves informed about new developments in our subject area, and while we should ensure we derive maximum benefits from the revolution in information technology, we should never lose sight of the original objective of our studies and the central concern of this book, to deepen our knowledge and understanding of Shakespeare's plays.

# Appendix

Most of the students quoted in this book belong to a group of 180 graduates and finalists from our own institution, University College Chester, to whom we sent this letter in October 1995:

**UNIVERSITY COLLEGE CHESTER**

A College of the
University of Liverpool

Dear Student

We have been contracted to write a textbook entitled 'Studying Shakespeare: A Practical Guide', and are keen for this book to include the voices of students, not just their tutors. We wondered, therefore, if you would mind taking a few minutes to reflect on your Shakespeare studies at school and college, and write us a few paragraphs expressing your views of those experiences.

We would prefer to have your individual response, so have not devised a questionnaire. However, you might want to consider the following questions:

- Which aspects of Shakespeare did you find most/least enjoyable?
- In what ways, if any, did studying Shakespeare differ from studying other authors?
- What gave you most problems in studying Shakespeare?
- Which of your tutors' teaching techniques did you find most/least helpful?
- How did you feel about compulsory Shakespeare at degree level – enthusiastic? indifferent? bored? aghast?
- Did you prefer to take a course on Shakespeare as a sole author or one where he featured with his contemporaries?
- Did you find discussing Shakespeare in class an effective way of developing your understanding, and if so, why?
- Can you think of any study tips which others studying Shakespeare might find useful?
- Can you remember any highlights from your Shakespeare studies (e.g. performances, lectures, reading experiences?).

Thank you very much for taking the time to help us with our research. We'll let you know when the book comes out.

Best wishes,

*Katherine Armstrong*

*Graham Atkin*

**Statistical breakdown of respondents**

> *Total*: 36
> *Post-A-level*: 18    *Post-Experience/Mature*: 18
> *1995 Graduate*: 24    *1996 Graduate*: 12
> *Male*: 10    *Female*: 26

# Index

221